Mooring Against the Tide

Mooring Against the Tide

Writing Fiction and Poetry

Jeff Knorr
Clackamas Community College

Tim Schell
Clackamas Community College

Prentice Hall
Upper Saddle River, NJ 07458

Library of Congress Cataloging-in-Publication Data
Knorr, Jeffrey.
    Mooring against the tide : writing fiction and poetry / Jeffrey Knorr.
        p.   cm.
    Includes index.
    ISBN 0-13-026011-8
    1. English language—Rhetoric.   2. Creative writing—Problems, exercises, etc.   3.
Fiction—Authorship—Problems, exercises, etc.   4. Poetry—Authorship—Problems,
exercises, etc.   I. Schell, Tim.   II. Title.

PE1408.K6886 2000
808'.042—dc21
                                                                99-089266

Editor-in-Chief: Leah Jewell
Senior Acquisitions Editor: Carrie Brandon
Editorial Assistant: Sandy Hrasdzira
VP, Director of Production and Manufacturing: Barbara Kittle
Managing Editor: Mary Rottino
Production Editor: Randy Pettit
Prepress and Manufacturing Manager: Nick Sklitsis
Prepress and Manufacturing Buyer: Mary Ann Gloriande
Marketing Director: Gina Sluss
Marketing Manager: Rachel Falk
Interior Design: Amy Rosen
Cover Design Director: Jayne Conte
Cover Design: Kiwi Design
Cover Art: Mark Andres

For permission to use copyrighted material, grateful
acknowledgment is made to the copyright holders listed
on pages 299–300, which is considered an extension of this
copyright page.

This book was set in 10/12 Palatino by NK Graphics,
and printed and bound by R.R. Donnelley & Sons Company.
The cover was printed by Phoenix Color Corp.

 © 2001 by Prentice-Hall, Inc.
A Division of Pearson Education
Upper Saddle River, New Jersey 07458

Printed in the United States of America
10 9 8 7 6 5 4 3 2 1

0-13-026011-8

Prentice-Hall International (UK) Limited, *London*
Prentice-Hall of Australia Pty. Limited, *Sydney*
Prentice-Hall Canada, Inc., *Toronto*
Prentice-Hall Hispanoamerica, S.A., *Mexico*
Prentice-Hall of India Private Limited, *New Delhi*
Prentice-Hall of Japan, Inc., *Tokyo*
Pearson Education Asia Pte. Ltd., *Singapore*
Editora Prentice-Hall do Brasil, Ltda., *Rio de Janeiro*

CONTENTS

PREFACE

When we first talked about writing a creative writing textbook comprised of the two genres of poetry and fiction, it occurred to us that most books on the market today use classic stories and poems as models of excellence for the aspiring writer to emulate. Certainly there is nothing wrong with this. In fact, both of us make allusions to such work in our respective sections of the book. However, we thought it might be more useful for the aspiring writer to have a book more closely modeled after the creative writing workshop wherein the students read and critique work of their peers in an effort to discover what is working in a story or in a poem and what is not working, and thereby apply these lessons to their own work.

The book is organized by genre with each respective genre organized by chapters defining the elements of fiction and poetry, followed by the workshop sections wherein student stories and poems are presented.

In the chapters covering the elements of fiction and poetry, we have presented utilitarian definitions for the reader followed by essays by guest writers. For example, in the chapter on Sound in Poetry, we present a definition of that element followed by an essay on sound by Alberto Rios who addresses the quality of sound in his own students' work. In the fiction section of this book, we define the various uses of setting in the chapter so-named. Following this definition is an essay by the novelist Valerie Miner who writes about the role of setting in her own student's story.

In the workshop sections of the book, we present first the student poem and student story without marginalia, followed by questions the reader is asked to consider. Following this is the same story and the same poem, this time with our marginalia and then our critiques of the student work. Finally, student revisions are presented with critiques.

It is our hope that the structure of this book will allow the readers to witness the creative evolution of poems and stories, and that they will see the process of writing as inherently dynamic as the writers go through draft after draft in the effort of crafting the finest fiction and poetry they are capable of. Whether used by a student-writer in a creative writing class or by a student-writer at home alone, this book will serve as a guide to steer through sometimes rough and unsure waters until the writer is safely moored against the tide.

Acknowledgements

I would like to thank my wife Sachiko, and my daughter, Maya, for their patience and support during the writing of this book. I would also like to thank my friend and colleague, Jeff Knorr, who, as ever, was a pleasure to work with.

—Tim Schell

Great thanks is due my wife Diane and my son, Gabriel for giving me time, support, and patience while writing this book. Also, thanks to Tim Schell, colleague and friend, who is great to work with and always an inspiration.

—Jeff Knorr

From both of us, special thanks is due our editor, Carrie Brandon for her belief in the project, unending patience, and energy. Also, thanks to Sandy Hrazdira and Stacy Prock at Prentice Hall for their support and dedication to the project. And to Joseph Lennon, University of Connecticut; Brenda A. Flanagan, Davidson College; Ron Carlson, Arizona State University; and Maria Fitzgerald, University of Minnesota, Twin Cities for their helpful comments.

—Jeff Knorr,
Tim Schell

Part One

Poetry

chapter one

GETTING STARTED

WHERE ARE THE POEMS HIDING?

There are poems hiding all around us—they are in corners of the room in spider webs, they are in the smooth handle of my grandfather's hammer in the garage, they are in the French toast for breakfast, and on the lawn of the old lady who lives across the street.

Finding subject matter we think is worthy enough for a poem can be one of the most difficult tasks we encounter. This very notion of finding worthy subjects is problematic because we tell ourselves that a poem deserves something better than we have come up with. This, unfortunately, is a losing battle. So, how do we win? We find subject matter which is accessible, human. People like to read about the world they live in, and as writers we ought to write about it.

James Wright was asked about his poem "Lying in a Hammock on William Duffy's Farm in Pine Island, Minnesota" and he said that he was not trying to do anything heroic in that poem, but rather he was trying to capture a moment in his life in which he felt a sense of delight. What he meant by not being heroic was

There is in one room in one day in one man's life, material for a lifetime.

John O'Hara

1

that the poem need not work on a grand level. A poem doesn't need to conquer us; it just needs to show us something and capture a moment. In doing so, this type of poem moves us. Sometimes a student-writer comes up with a "great idea" for a poem only to have missed what is really the great, moving moment at the middle of it. Why? These moments are often the smallest and most nonheroic moments, but for this reason they are also the most human. Over the years it has been put into our heads that poems must be larger than life, must have something great to say, and they do have great things to say. But poems are only great when they touch us. So I often say to students who are searching for subject matter, "Find a simple moment, a moment that is normal to you, or a part of your life, and figure out what is important at the center of that."

One of my students was on a road trip in Alaska with his long-time childhood friend when their truck broke down. So they slept in the back of the truck in a gas station parking lot in a very small town in Alaska. This is what came later.

North of Anchorage an Hour

Here, there is an amount of option;
Fashion stays on
the "Outside,"
where priority-mail
arrives sooner than   5
seven days.

Tonight, bars named after
guns and rabid animals
blink signs and
tomorrow, just as many   10
churches open at
eight and eleven.

JACKOB CURTIS

When Jake brought the poem to class, what struck me was that he had accomplished a great deal in the poem by keeping it simple. And he had created a poem that seemed to mirror the place. Moreover, this is not a poem that is larger than life; it is life. And note how much he says with the small details like "priority-mail" or "bars named after/guns and rabid animals/blink signs." And to close the poem, he contrasts the bar image against churches—giving them opening times like bars—and the idea of "options" that he begins with. Simplicity has given Jake some fine mileage.

On the first day in writing workshops, or even introduction to literature courses, we go around the class and each of us tells one thing we've noticed in the last two weeks that we didn't notice before. Of course the answers range from "The lady across the street uses a cane," or "I have a little spot of rust on my car door just below the lock," to "I noticed over the holiday that I really appreciate my family," and "I always go out with my dad to split wood. I never split it; I just go and talk with him." Once we have done this, we talk about these observations as topics for poems, and we usually agree that "appreciating my family" has the least strength of the four because it is abstract. For some reason we've missed these things previously, walked right by them. But now, simply because we've noticed them, they've touched us and held us tightly for a moment. And that makes them ready to be subjects for poems.

Seeing Your World as Poetic?

So now that we've figured out how to find the poems, to know their hiding places—at least sometimes—we need to figure out how to make this a regular event. Consider this the off-the-page writing process. This is where we begin to use the process of writing to interpret everyday events. In order to do this, we have to be open to redefining our world, to be ready to view it and define it at any moment. This should please anyone with "writer's block" because it means we are always writing.

Let's step back for a moment. When we went through the process of noticing something we hadn't noticed before, what happened was that for one instant we stopped or slowed down long enough to see it. And more, we slowed ourselves long enough to let that thing take hold of us. So, what's the key? First, slow down.

When I go out with my two-year-old, a walk around the block might take forty minutes because every few yards he says, "Look, Papa, a bug." Or "Look, Papa, a leaf." The list of things he notices is endless and most of them are rather exceptional findings, especially for him—he's two, and he's never seen some of these things. To define them in new ways, for example to watch the way a caterpillar moves, is to see them as fresh. And to couple these with feelings, to put the concrete with the abstract, is to begin to make poetry. So I have begun to note these things on our walks around the block, and my, how many poems live on our block.

After we've slowed ourselves enough to notice possible subject matter, the next step is to let it work on us. We may not do this at the moment, but then again we may. In this equation—slowing down and noticing things + feeling them = a good subject—the second part is not so separate from the first. In fact, they often happen simultaneously. But allowing ourselves to perceive a moment or thing as important, significant, tragic, delightful, harrowing, will let the moment blossom into some semblance of a poem later; these words themselves mean little because they are abstracts. Without

images to represent them, it is hard to relate to them or attach to them. And since we perceive a moment as concrete naturally when we create and notice subject matter, we need to re-create it for our readers when we write poems. Creating concrete images and allowing abstracts to remain below the surface is one of the most important tools in the craft of writing poetry. Take for instance this image, holding someone. The image itself is concrete, but the emotion and the desire for connection are left below the surface of the image.

> How I want to reach you;
> slip my hands past your canvas
> coat and hold you in the barn light as
> night folds its dark clench over us.

Look at the following poem. This student found that something that was in front of her all the time was actually poetic. It should be added that during the first week of class Jenelle said to all of us, "I don't even know why I'm taking this class." She had never written a poem before taking the workshop.

ODE TO FOOTBALL

Day after day
it entertains my father
so he won't speak
so harshly.

He watches young men   5
in suffocating white pants.

"Touchdown!"
father hollers,
he relives
high-school memories   10
when he was King.

Another family dinner
is delayed.
Another day at the beach
is postponed.   15
The king must be dethroned.

JENELLE EAGER

This was an important poem for Jenelle because it caught the deep emotion she felt about many days in her house. And she projected those feelings through the images she portrayed. The subject matter had been sitting in front of Jenelle, literally, for a long time. When she wrote the poem she also answered her own question about why she was taking the class. She found a new way to view her world and express it.

Keeping Notes: Mining for Poems

Once we have a handle on finding poems and subjects and seeing our world as a poetic place, the next step is writing things down. But this is hard. Students often say that it's hard to find the time to write, and we all understand this. Too often there are too many things to do in one day, so we find time to write when we can. We squeeze it in because it seems like a luxury, and the other things seem like necessities. But nobody is going to make time for us to write, so we need to find ways to make time for ourselves. And ultimately we must always be writing. I've written notes or pieces of poems in my head at the fair, on a napkin in a restaurant, on a piece of wood in the garage, on a leaf page of a cookbook in the kitchen. This is part of the process that comes before sitting down and writing the whole poem. This is the art of note-taking.

These moments of writing things down are extremely important. One object or occasion may not turn itself into a poem immediately. It may need some fermenting and aging like wine. But we need to get the initial note down—the same as putting young wine in the barrel before it can age—before we can ruminate on its possibilities. Later, when we sit down to work on a poem, to try and write the whole piece, we can pull out these notes and work them in step by step.

What is important is to take notes and to figure out how you'll manage them. Maybe you take notes on scraps; that's fine, but collect them somewhere—a shoebox, a shopping bag, a desk drawer, a bulletin board above your desk. Have them somewhere where you can find them when they're needed. This is your wine cellar of ideas. If you're not a scrap person or need a more disciplined approach, buy a notebook or journal book to keep notes in. Buy something you like, with paper that is friendly. I believe Garrison Keillor in his assertion that a blank eight-and-a-half-by-eleven sheet of paper looks as big as Montana when you don't have anything to write. So if Montana isn't your landscape, go with Rhode Island and get the pocket-sized notebook. If you want something a bit more classy and with some hospitality, go with Georgia and get the hardbound journal with fine pages. Whatever you decide, be comfortable with it and have it close by. And make yourself write notes.

Sometimes sitting down and forcing ourselves to write can be difficult, but sitting down to write notes can ease the pressure. Try some exercises. Write down five things from yesterday that you noticed that seemed poetic. Make a list of poems you want to write. Write an abstract word—sad, for example—and under it write a one-sentence image that illustrates that abstract. Write down five or ten one-sentence similes or metaphors. Later these things will find their ways into poems and in some cases may be the driving forces behind the poems.

These exercises and taking notes are the cornerstones of your poems. It is rare that a whole poem just comes, already formed, already packaged as a poem—it takes shaping and it takes crafting. When we have a reserve of images and ideas that we can work with, whole poems come more easily. A craftsperson in a woodshop, for example, needs to know what kind of wood to use for the frame, the sides and front, and the door of the cabinet he is building. And in the shop he has these different woods available—maybe some plywood, maybe clear-grain maple. Over time he collects more and more wood and more and more tools. Consider this as you build your note supply. Even if you don't put together whole poems each day, you will be collecting the substantive pieces that will make up your poems later.

IMAGERY

As writers, we strive to arrest the reader, to hold him in a moment. This is no easy task, but when we do it, and when we do it well, we achieve something powerful. But how do we do this? One of the ways we do this in poetry is through **imagery**. Put simply, an **image** is a picture created by our words. And through imagery we turn **abstracts**—feelings and ideas—into part of our physical, concrete world. Most often when we speak of images, we mean something that we can see. But don't forget that we use the term **image** when we discuss those words which touch our other senses too. When we use images in our poems, we give the reader a heightened perception of our world, we turn on his senses, and we allow our world to become part of his. We let the reader see a fountain of grasshoppers springing out of tall grass. And then he is there with us.

Often in poetry, there is more to an image than meets the eye. Under or behind the image is a feeling or an idea. This may simply be one feeling or idea attached to the image. Or the feeling may rise from the context of the poem. Images should stand in front of abstracts and veil them. When we make this happen, we create provocative images which show something rather than tell. This is when our language begins to take on power and become something much more than mere reporting. If we want reporting, we can subscribe to our local paper. But when we want to be

> *Poetry always endeavors to arrest you, and to make you continuously see a physical thing, to prevent you gliding through an abstract process.*
>
> T.E. Hulme

swept away in a poem, we need language that turns in on us, that steals our heart, or our ears, or our sight.

How Do We Create Them?

Images can be created in a number of different ways, but no matter how we create them or what types of images we create, images are the poets' best friends. I once had an instructor / mentor say two things that have hung around as two of the best basic pieces of advice I may have ever been given. First he told me, "It is too much to ask of readers to give them abstracts in the first sentence of a poem—give them images." And he told me (however harsh it was at the time, it held on as good advice), "I don't really care if you tell me how you feel in the poem—show me something and I'll figure out what I'm supposed to feel." As a reader and a writer of poems over the years, I've found both of these to be true. And there are ways to do this.

One of the ways we create vibrant images in a poem is to use **metaphors** and **similes**. These types of images are based on comparisons and allow us to relay abstract ideas to the reader in very concrete terms. What's more, we use these all the time in our daily speech without consciously thinking about it. A **metaphor** is a comparison which says one things *is* another. For example, I might turn to my friend and say "Luis *is* the moon." This is a very basic metaphor, but it serves the purpose for the moment. The thing to remember in this example is that now Luis is no longer Luis; rather, he has taken on the qualities of the moon. The effect is that the metaphor now causes the reader to think about the image, to think about Luis having the qualities of the moon ascribed to him, and ultimately the reader is pushed to a deeper level in the poem.

Metaphors can function at various levels in a poem. At times, they function within a line or a small number of lines. Maybe a metaphor serves to power a stanza and is the overriding image. There are two types of metaphors commonly used: the **implied metaphor** and the **extended** or **controlling metaphor**. The **implied metaphor** does not actually state in the comparison what the main object is being compared to; rather, it implies the comparison, usually through action or ascribing attributes. For example, we compare this man to a fish by saying *he finned his way across the room/ eyeing the bait*. In the following image, the implication applies to both people: *Mother squawked at me as I fluttered out the back door.* These metaphors work on a very subtle level but their impact should not be taken lightly. When we use them, they can offer great resonance and depth to our images.

The **extended** or **controlling metaphor** is another useful and powerful tool. It gets its name because this type of metaphor extends itself throughout an entire poem. In other words, it may control the entire poem, pushing it this way or that. One superb example of this is Alice Walker's poem "A Woman Is Not a Potted Plant" wherein the metaphor of a woman being potted, trimmed, watered or not watered, clipped back, et cetera, serves to illustrate her thoughts on how society treats women. At a more practical level, one student decided he would try a controlling metaphor poem after we discussed metaphor and looked at examples. Here's what Tom came up with.

Walking the Plank

One night we watched a silent pirate movie.
Douglas Fairbanks swashbuckled in all black,
shirt cut to show his chest.
Laughing in the face of death,
brandishing swords   5
fortune fell at his feet,
until, discovered,
blindfolded and hands behind his back
he walked with bravado into the sea.

He knew he was the star.   10
Celluloid heroes are always certain
and never feel pain
that can't be solved.
A living man is uncertain.
I fear falling when I walk the plank.   15
Even a wide road seems like a thread.

TOM HOGAN

Tom struggled at times with the use of the controlling metaphor, but he used it nonetheless and it was a fine exercise for him. In the end it got him thinking about how he could use metaphors—they could be extensive and create an entire context or they could be short and tight to create moments of depth for the reader.

A **simile** works in relatively the same way as a metaphor in that it is a comparison. But in the case of the simile, we use the words *like* or *as*. For example, "The brown winter river moved *like* molasses." Or, "The horse's flanks were strong *as* alder." In the first example we have details—brown and winter—to give us color and a sense of temperature, depth, season. But when the writer uses "*like* molasses" we know more about how the river is moving and what the color might be. In the case of the horse, we can draw some conclusions about how strong the horse is or what his flanks might feel like. Alder is a very hard and strong wood; hence, the author has chosen this detail carefully and appropriately. What's more, it's a natural detail that might also lend a hand in describing the horse's setting. Notice in the simile, unlike the metaphor, the horse remains a horse and the river remains the river, but the comparison still serves to add depth and information to the image.

As a younger writer, I worked hard to write images. How could I not? All of my professors, instructors, and mentors said to use images, or else. So I worked for the great image. But what I often found myself doing was trying to create strong images by using adjectives (those descriptive words that describe nouns), adverbs, and strong active verbs. And I actually did create some good images. These are certainly tools that help create strong images. So after class one day my writing instructor said, "Come by my office tomorrow so we can talk about the poems you've written this semester." Realizing he had finally noticed all my effort and the improvement in my images, I left class that day elated. When I arrived at his office the next day, ready for some solid praise, he said, "You know, your images have improved, but you haven't used a simile or metaphor all semester. How can you expect to write poems without similes or metaphors?" I was crushed.

The net effect, though, was positive. I adopted two strategies to help me create similes and metaphors in my poems. First, when I sat down to write, I always started by writing five similes or metaphors in my notebook. In a matter of weeks, I had collected pages of them. This was like stretching before running—it didn't take long, and when I was writing, I felt loose and ready to move around in the poem. The second thing I did was to revise for similes and metaphors. I would go through the poem and look for a place where I might use a simile or metaphor—maybe it was half created already with an image I was using in the poem—and when I found that place, I would create or insert a simile or metaphor. This worked well for me and still does today. And I often tell students in our workshops to do the same thing. Let's look at some workshop writing. The following stanza was from a poem by a beginning poetry student.

Today it rains.
The wind blows hard.
I feel the thunder
and know there is lightning.
You look at me with a rigid, gray face.   5

RHONDA ENOS

Now note Rhonda's changes in line 2 using metaphor, and she adds a simile at the end.

Today it rains.
The wind is furious.
I feel the thunder
and know there is lightning.
You look at me with a rigid, gray face,   5
eyes like coal.

While these changes were modest, they served to amplify Rhonda's stanza and add depth to the images. What's more, after she made the changes, she felt that she had captured an emotional sense of the stanza while keeping the poem concrete and image-driven. Her classmates in the workshop had urged a change to line two (*the wind blows hard*), suggesting that it certainly was concrete and active but a bit empty and dull. And they also liked the change at the end, saying that the "eyes like coal" suggested an even darker and colder feel to the relationship between these two people. They liked that the color of coal, as they saw it in their heads, went along with the gray coloring of a thunder storm.

Another element of metaphor that Rhonda employs in the above stanza is **personification**, which is giving a nonhuman object some human characteristic. For example, *the wind tiptoes through the trees.* Or in another case, *I swatted at air/ the wasp laughed and dove again.* The use of personification helps to bring alive those things outside our human world, and makes those other realms understandable to us. It also helps add to the zest of images by allowing the author to be original and fresh in her construction.

While we should always strive for fresh, original language use, at times we can bump up against some common pitfalls in constructing images, metaphors, and similes. When working to craft images, we might come up with **clichés**. These are phrases or images which are, and have been, so commonly used that they are not original at all. For example, *her eyes were blue pools* has probably been written in just about every adolescent schoolboy's notebook or first love poem. That doesn't discount the emotion behind it, but it's not crafted or original. Avoid clichés at all costs in literary writing unless you're using them for some satirical effect. And even then, triple check to see how effective they really are. Another pitfall is what Donald Hall has referred to as the "dead metaphor." This is tricky to find because a dead metaphor is a metaphor that seems original and crafted but in the end falls flat because it's too close to other metaphors and similes we've already encountered. Don't worry too much about this—even the best of the best writers struggle with this on a regular basis. So when it happens, just be able to identify the problem and revise it out of the poem. This takes time, practice, and most of all patience, but in time your sharp eye toward imagery will be well developed.

Imagery is one of the elements most needed by poets and most called upon in the writing process. Remember that images can awaken our senses, stir us, and move us deeply while staying relatively calm on the surface—like a stick that's used to stir what's on the bottom of a pond. And often the best images, those which are concrete and detailed, say more implicitly than they do explicitly. As Ernest Gaines said in a workshop I attended once, "'You know,' I tell students, 'just show me those things—I'm a pretty smart guy; I'll figure it out.'" And that's the way to proceed. As writers, if we worry about showing the world and crafting the details carefully, we can leave the wonder, the shortness of breath, the skip of the heart, to the reader. It's their heart and it's our duty to move it.

Essay by Diane Averill ————————————————

ON WRITING WITH IMAGERY

> The world is
> Not with us enough.
> O Taste and See . . .
>   *Denise Levertov*

In teaching students to write poetry, I've found that
their deepest thoughts and emotions are often complex,
but they don't yet have ways into that complexity. Focusing on inspirational exercises, with the intention of eliciting original images, helps them move from abstractions to specific details. Therefore, I've developed a series of in-class assignments involving about thirty minutes of guided writing, with a suggested assignment for the following week attached to each exercise. Although I require a certain number of poems and revisions each term, all of my assignments are only suggestions, as I wish to inspire people without limiting them to my ideas. Students bring to workshops any poems they wish critiqued.

I have presented many exercises designed to encourage experimentation with imagery over the years, but three in particular stand out in their ability to reach the greatest number of students. I will give you these exercises plus a student poem which came directly, or indirectly, from each.

The first exercise involves collecting reproductions of paintings and photographs. I have a drawer full of them from years of cutting up old calendars and used, or sale, art books. For each of the painters or photographers, I've written an individual exercise. After placing many images from the various artists around the room, I encourage students to pick up a copy of the exercise relating to the artist or photographer which most attracts them. Here is my Ansel Adams handout:

Exercise: Ansel Adams

1. Choose a photograph and bring it to your desk. Begin with silent contemplation of this place in nature. Close your eyes and see how clearly you can visualize it in your mind's eye. Allow the inner image to begin to change. Try not to control or judge what comes. Just notice the feelings your new image evokes. Now, write this down.

2. Imagine yourself alone in the scene. You may be anywhere you wish within it. Describe the shapes, the textures. Use images and the senses. Now allow another presence into the scene. This presence may be human or divine, an ancestor, a memory, a presenti-

ment, a lover, or an enemy. Ask it to describe itself and speak its wisdom.

3. Talk, in writing, to this natural beauty. If it could hear you, what would you want it to know? Address different elements, such as clouds, rocks, water, or trees, as if each were alive.

4. Using images, tell a story about this place. What has happened here before you were born? What might happen here after you die? What did this scene look like a moment before it was frozen in the form of this photograph? What do you think it looked like a moment after the picture was taken?

5. Now, describe the light side of your own spirit. Then describe the dark, or "shadow" side of yourself, in any way you wish.

SUGGESTED ASSIGNMENT: See if there's a poem somewhere within your writings about this photograph by Ansel Adams. Jot down the title of the piece you chose and take your thoughts about it home with you.

My student, Ron Rasch, brought the following poem to the next workshop:

CANYON OF MYSELF

FROM ANSEL ADAMS' "YOSEMITE"

I step into a canyon of myself,
who makes the song by seeing,
the sound by breathing,
the music by dancing.

Granite cliffs speak ocean rocks   5
caught in a flow of cedars,
held in the fingers of cloudwings
about to bless

a place existing before thought and time,
where I hear my mystical Minotaur,   10
conflict of beast and beauty—
stirring in a slow pavane.

RON RASCH

On this particular occasion I also played instrumental music while students were doing the in-class assignment. I've found that spare, quiet, music, such as Native-American flutes, encourages open-ended writings.

A second in-class exercise which often inspires students to use specific imagery involves setting up a still-life. I've arranged many of these. For example, pairing a hummingbird's nest with the bones of a raccoon's jaw produced interesting results; the juxtaposition of these objects created a tension between life-and-death imagery for many people. One of my intentions in this exercise is to encourage wildly associative imagery rather than linear poems. The following student poem, written by Regina Godfrey, came out of a freewrite in which I presented students with an overripe pear set in the center of a mirror which was decorated on the sides with stars, moons, and planets. This was the sheet I gave the students:

Exercise: Still-Life Description

The following questions are here to guide you, but don't feel limited in any way to these particular queries. Try wild leaping around the image of this still-life in your thoughts and details.

1. If this object were the only thing like it in the world, how would you describe it to someone who has never seen it?
2. Describe it from the inside out. Give it texture as well as visual qualities.
3. What profession, or activity, does it remind you of?
4. How does the world look to it?
5. What scents does it make you aware of? What memories do those scents evoke?
6. If it had a voice, what would that voice sound like?
7. What is the best of times and the worst of times for this object?
8. What will happen to it in the future?
9. Write a scene of two lovers, or sexually aware people, coming upon it.

SUGGESTED ASSIGNMENT: Write a poem about the still-life, or about any object, or objects, of importance or of interest to you.

Here's Regina's poem:

Still Life With Mirrors

A pear so beaten you cannot eat it
slumps on a mirror painted, fingerprinted,
by a solar system, in bright colors;
reminds me of Nona, who never threw fruit away.
The bottom smushed against the glass, it is defiant

but pliable, the chin of
an old woman hiding
three dark hairs
under the knot of a well-tied kerchief.
A mouth   10
wet and hungry opens on one side:
it is vaginal, rain-scented, heavy, darkened
at the edges and slick, like trees when they split
at the center.
Rounded and open, it learns to love   15
its reflection in the mirror, as women do
squatting over compacts in paid-for
self-love courses.
The pear, brown and yellow, swollen
and   20
scratched, oily to the touch,
wearing only a stem to wish on,
inspires us as it rots
over glass, the thumbprint of the Orion nebula
my lover keeps his dreams in.   25
It is the smell of the kitchen the day after
fruit salad,
so beaten you cannot eat it.
Adam and Eve reflect in the mirror's
dust, making me wonder—   30
was it an apple or a pear, rotted, that brought them
so close to earth?

At this point, I'd like to caution against the impulse to tidy up poems such as this one. If you resist the impulse to "fix" a wildly associative poem in a predetermined manner, and encourage yourself to critique such a poem based on its own desires, your suggestions will allow the poem to retain extraordinary qualities.

A third, and final, exercise designed to encourage imagery in student work, involves using colored pen sets to explore dreams. I distribute a colored pen set to each student, along with blank, white paper. The lack of lines frees up many students, allows them to go from the ordinary, linear thought processes they use most of the time in their lives to the mysterious, sometimes irrational, images and symbols of their dream worlds. The first step for this exercise is to circle the desks and allow students to share dreams, especially recurring ones, with the class. I begin by saying that we commonly speak of "dreaminess" as a vague state, and yet dreams often contain vivid images and transformations. We only believe they are vague because they are often difficult to remember. I encourage students to keep dream journals by their beds in the coming week. Some students already have dream journals, or have incorporated dreams into daily journals.

On Dreams

Use the colored pens, switching colors whenever you feel like it, to record a dream you've had. Use specific images and the senses. If it feels right or interesting to do so, you may want to combine dreams. If you can't remember any of your dreams, imagine one you might have had.

1. You usually dream in black and white, but this dream is in color. Record it that way.
2. Elements, such as fire or water, do not behave as they should. Indicate that through the use of color imagery as well as other details.
3. The dream seems to contain unlocked knowledge of a part of yourself, or of a future event.
4. There's a man or a woman performing a ritual. Elaborate on it, using a different color for each different object, or aspect, of the ritual.
5. You are in a place that seems familiar and yet unfamiliar at the same time. Use colors to bring out both qualities.
6. Something or someone is transforming into something or someone else.
7. Describe a dream that recurs in your life. Maybe you, or someone else, is doing something not ordinarily possible such as flying or experiencing sounds or scents as if they were colors.
8. Describe an abstraction such as "abundance" or some other idea you've felt in a dream using concrete images. Switching colors could bring these images into clear, sharp focus.

SUGGESTED ASSIGNMENT: Reread what you've written at home. Underline, or place a star next to, any phrases which bring out a wish to explore them further. Then write a poem from this material. You may add to, or embellish upon, what you've written. The idea is to be psychologically or spiritually accurate rather than to make each detail literally true. Now remove the colors from the images by typing it up, and bringing it to class.

An example of a poem using these techniques is the following one by beginning student Julie Henning.

Believing

She plants sacred shards
in her alluvial fields,
and buys her mandrakes
from strange traders.
Across her thighs she crosses 5
birch boughs and
green willow,
and between her breasts,
spices invoke
ancient blessing. 10

Kneeling before her hanging loom
she carefully knots and ties
each color in its place,
a cryptic spirit-offering.

When abundance arrives 15
she will gather pomegranates
and rich fig cakes,
anoint herself with fine oil,
and serve him wine
in cool olive groves. 20

JULIE HENNING

The exercises I've presented in this chapter are just a few ways to introduce original imagery into your poems. I find that the exercises usually work well, and at times even better, when coupled with reading. I insist that my students read both contemporary and classical poetry. I do this by bringing handouts of poems by accomplished poets relating to the exercise for that session, requiring a good anthology, and having each student choose a selection by his or her favorite poet from that anthology to read and to present to the class in the form of an oral report. Sometimes I ask them to underline any images from the anthology which seem striking to them, as a way of focusing them on this crucial aspect of poetry. Exercises, such as the ones I've presented on imagery, in combination with reading good poets, make for lively workshop critiques and fine work.

*   *   *

Exercise

Take an abstract word and write it on the top of a sheet of paper. Now write three to eight lines using an image to illustrate that abstract concept, but do not use that abstract word or any other abstract words in the image. You may only use concrete details. Use the following example as a guide.

Sad

The wind howls
and rain presses against the backs of clouds.
Leaves run and hide under bushes.
All this while the bagpipe screams
a funeral song.   5

chapter three

LINES AND STANZAS

One is often able to distinguish between poetry and prose simply by looking at the page. With the exception of the prose poem, we can look at a poem and identify it as such. While this is a very basic tool for identifying a poem, it is not insignificant. It works. The use of **lines** and **stanzas** is a major element in poetics. Hence, this is a very important tool for any poet to know how to use. A **line** is just that—it's a line of text in a poem. A stanza is a group of lines set together in a poem. A poem may be all one stanza or it may be divided into, say, six four-line stanzas.

Now that we know what they are, let's talk a bit about how and why we use lines and stanzas to effect our poems. Lines and stanzas often occur in a very natural, organic way. They happen because we've decided to break a line the way we think or feel the words dividing themselves. Or stanzas may occur because we feel a group of lines works well together conceptually. Let's look at lines first.

Lines do a number of things in a poem both spatially and conceptually. In relation to space on the page, the way words appear, lines provide a spatial context in which the words function. This is initially the way the words look on the page, the way we see them. But as we read the poem, it becomes not just how they look on the page but how they work with and against each other in the reading process. And ultimately, as writers, we

As you rub these words together they spark and whole new combinations happen.

Naomi Shihab Nye

need to be thinking about how our words are working with and against each other while we write. For example, note the difference in the following lines.

> The wind swept
> off the dunes and raced
> against the waves,
> pulling their white hair
> out away from shore.   5

Here, we have five lines broken ostensibly to show the images in each line. But note that the lines begin with an article, prepositions, and a present participle. These are not bad choices, but consider the possibilities in these lines. Think how many ways we might break them. Let's look at a revision of these lines.

> The wind swept off the dunes and
> raced against the waves, pulling
> their white hair out away from shore.

Notice that in this choice of line breaks we get longer lines. We might also notice a change in the rhythm we feel in the language. Having the words "and" and "pulling" at the ends of the lines doesn't seem natural, as does "out" in line five. But, it may create a sense of tension in the language or a sense that the wind is working against the natural rhythm of the waves. We might also note that this line structure seems to compliment the internal rhyme in lines two and three a bit more than the previous line scheme. No matter the changes, notice that the line acts as a frame of emphasis and causes us to focus on different emotions, thoughts, and/or parts of the poem with each change.

This brings us to another point about lines and their function. Lines provide for us a way to create or control the rhythm and musical sense of the poem. They provide for us the length of breath we might need, or the number of syllables working together in a unit of words. This is very subtle in poems but is the undercurrent to what we hear and feel in a rhythmic sense. One way to play with this, as you think about line breaks, is to simply count syllables in your lines. If you have three lines of roughly six syllables each, how is that different from two lines of nine syllables each? This is something to play and work with. And notice that as you change the rhythm of a line by making it longer or breaking it to be shorter, you also alter the meaning of the words.

When we begin to notice that the rhythm and meaning play off each other, and we realize that they're connected, we can see how **ambiguity** can form in poems. Ambiguity occurs when something is open to more than one meaning. This can be a positive effect. Remember that when we write poems, we want and need to get all the mileage we can out of each word—and that means we have to write with an expansive view of the way the words work rather than a narrow view. So as you begin to see how rhythm works in your lines, you'll notice that the rhythm changes based on the **syntax**, or word order, of your lines.

> leaning heavy on the dark sky
> the moon crested behind an oak

We can change these lines if we aren't satisfied with the syntax. And sometimes we ought to experiment just to see what is held in the change.

> heavy on the dark leaning sky
> the moon crested behind an oak

The change is slight. So try again and see what you think.

> behind an oak, the moon crested
> heavy on the dark leaning sky

Working with the syntax and seeing options in setting the words will not only open rhythmic possibilities, but will open more doors for meaning. One element of line breaks that affects rhythms is the caesura. A **caesura** is simply a pause *within* a line, and usually occurs because of punctuation—maybe a comma. But a caesura may also happen because of the way two words fall next to each other rhythmically. In this case, don't be fooled into thinking that using caesuras is a difficult technique. Just keep in mind that this is what pauses within lines are called and that they can make all the difference at times. Another element of line structure that is related to syntax, rhythm, and meaning is **enjambment**. This occurs when a line's grammatical sense and meaning carry over into the next. This, again, is not overly technical, but consider how we pause at the ends of lines in rhyming poetry whether there are periods or not. Enjambment is one of those tools to toss into the box and notice as you use it, so you become more and more aware of it as a force in your writing.

While all this can seem overwhelming, the benefit is that as you become more comfortable and proficient with the tools, your writing becomes sharper and more crafted. So while we recognize poetry on the page by its different look from prose—that ragged right margin—as writers, we come to know line breaks and structure as important tools. They often seem subtle, maybe even casual, to the reader. But we know differently. We know the power inherent in the crafting of lines and know that the writer works intently on breaking lines for reasons of meaning and sound and the music of language.

The Stanza

A **stanza** is a group of lines in a poem separated on the page by a space break from another group of lines. In free verse these groups of lines do not need to be the same in number, but a stanza usually signifies that there is some type of organizational structure to the poem. A writer often organizes lines into stanzas based on some conceptual coherence. No matter how many stanzas a poem has or how those stanzas occur in the poem (maybe some have three lines, maybe some have four, maybe all have two), the stanza serves to provide some sense of coherence to the lines. And the movements between stanzas help to guide us smoothly through the meaning of the poem.

In more formal poetry, or in fixed forms, stanzaic structure is guided by the type of poem (sonnet, sestina, villanelle, etc.), the dominant meter (for instance, iambic pentameter), and the rhyme scheme. For example, a four-line stanza with iambic pentameter, and a rhyme scheme of *abab* would be called a quatrain. The use of stanzas and their very fixed structures in fixed forms helps give a framework to the poem as well as a technical context wherein the content functions. But, let's go back to free verse since that's what most of us will probably be writing.

So in free verse, why use stanzas at all? That's a fair question and sometimes we use only one stanza. But that, too, has a history; it comes from the stichic tradition of poetry. This simply means that the lines fall into one unit and are arranged by their rhythmic quality rather than separated into stanzas based on either number or meaning. So why break parts of the poem with white space? One reason we might use stanzas is that they help us control what we want to say. In some ways it's not all that different from a conversation. And after all, in some ways, we, as writers, are having conversations with readers. In conversation, when we change the subject or even alter it by nuance, we note this in some way: a pause, a change in tone, a change in breath. These are all things that can be set off by stanza breaks. Hence we use the stanza form as a guide. If we want to look at it with a bit more severity, we might even say that we can control both the poem and the reader through stanzas.

What comes of this control, this movement of lines and subject matter, of rhythms and breath, is a control over the dynamics of the poem. With stanzas we take on the ability to bring the poem up to crescendo-like levels and then ease it back down again, to run the poem full-speed like a train, or slow it down. So ultimately we're back to a somewhat rhythmic control over the poem and guidance for the reader. We hope this use of stanzas, though, comes off naturally. When we take the poem up to a high point and bring it down again with the use of stanzas, we ought to do this because the subject matter calls for it. This way the stanzas fit; they're in the right place at the right time, and the readers hardly notice. But they notice how the poem feels. The stanzas, their structure and movement, ought to mirror or enhance either the subject matter or the emotional and intellectual context of the poem.

One of the things we do with lines and stanzas, as Robert Hass points out, is that we put our breathing, our rhythmic nature, into other people's bodies: "When one says somebody else's poem aloud, one speaks in that person's breath." So this is where our own physiology becomes part of the language. And this is where line and stanza structure meet and help create our poetic voice. Listen to the movement of the language, hear the rhythms around you and use them to fill the page, to move your lines and guide your poems.

Essay by Beckian Fritz Goldberg

HEY, GOOD LOOKIN', HAVEN'T WE MET SOMEWHERE BEFORE?

You're sitting in a bar contemplating your Jager-meister, and the person on the next barstool has just given you this line. What do you do? If you're a woman, you probably give him a withering glance and tell him to buzz off. O.K., let's say you turn to deliver your *buzz off* and you notice he happens to be gor-geous. So you hesitate, thinking, "He's gorgeous, but does he really think that kind of opening works?" So he's gorgeous and stupid. You have your standards. He strikes out. A cheesy line is a cheesy line.

In our parallel universe, you're sitting in a bar contemplating et cetera and you're a man. A woman comes up to you and delivers this line. What do you do? This situation is much more "iffy." If, for example, she's gorgeous *and* stupid, well . . . it pretty much makes your night. After all, guys are easy. If she's not so gorgeous, then you might pass and see if something better shows up.

Which brings up the first two points about the line. One, with the poem you can't always turn around and see the beguiling form of the speaker. You hear "Hey . . ." and you're on your own. And if you're try-ing to get the reader's attention, generate some interest, seduce a little, it doesn't matter how cute you are. You have to come up with something more likely to spark a little heat than, "Hey, good-lookin' . . ." In fact, *heys* should be avoided altogether until you really know how to follow up, as in: "Hey, Jude . . . na-na-nuh-na, hey, Jude." (See "The '60s" in an almanac or talk to your grandparents.)

The second point—there's a reason the Muse is traditionally thought of as female. Not only because a bunch of white male poets thought her up, but because she has standards for heaven's sake. (See first para-graph.) A poet who relies on a bad line is simply going to strike out. If you're going to approach someone—all those sensitive people at the bar reading Keats, for example—you need to know your audience. They've heard the "Hey . . ." until they simply don't look up anymore. And they've also heard, a hundred times, " Ah, thy beauty is to me as those Nicean barks of yore . . ." and all those other lines Poe used to try out on women. So it's important to use the right line for the right audience and remember that catchy lines that have been used before, even successfully, are clichés, like the guy in the bar in blue polyester who's still using, "Hi, I'm Virgo. What's your sign?" (See "The '70s.")

An opening line sets the tone and often determines the course of the evening—the course of the dusky and alluring poem. Yes, it's a lot of pressure. That's why poets end up in bars in the first place. If we take a look at some opening lines by students, we can see the effects of several different approaches. The first draft of one poem opens this way: "My grandfather used to shoot them." It's direct and it also makes us curious. We're likely to read on, at least for a bit. Of course, it's not a line that works well in bars. (See "Psycho," any decade, any century.) This line sets up an expectation, generally a nice thing for a line to do, but it also means the poet has obligated himself not only to let us in on what "them" means, but to follow through with something significant. If "them" turns out to be tin cans set up for recreational shooting, we're likely to think "so what?" The poet has let us down. If it turns out to be something we care about, then we are further drawn into the poem.

Another poem opens, "The smell of cut grass." Are you going to ask this one to dance or are you going to wait for something better to come along? It's a line that names a stock image, the smell of cut grass, the smell of rain, the smell of baking cookies, the whole long list of "Smells Of . . ." The second line of the poem is "of grease." O.K., I, for one, like the grease here because the expectation (if any) set up in the first line is that I was going to get some lovely springtime poem about grass and clouds and maybe even love. The grease is not a predictable move, so it helps. But why is it on its own line? As a *line,* is "and grease" one that works, that generates interest or moves the poem forward? Does it create a pace or rhythm that guides or seduces the reader? Here's the complete first stanza:

The smell of cut grass
and grease
takes me back
to grass piles in the bed of the Ford pick-up.
My dad standing over a lawn mower
ready for the yellowed stones of his palms
to push the blade over the victim of his hunger. Me
with riverock in hand, I aim at the rigid
back of my asthmatic brother.

5

The most noticeable thing about the form of the stanza is how different the first three lines are from the rest of the stanza. The opening pace or rhythm is deliberate, slow, broken into small phrases as if to feed the reader one small piece at a time. Then all of a sudden the fourth line rushes out, piles everything together: "to grass piles in the bed of the Ford pick-up." It's as if the poet got tired and just threw away the rest. The next lines, however, are a little more consistent in their rhythm which suggests that finally the poet has begun to find a more natural cadence, something closer to her own voice. In revising the poem, reading it aloud and listening to the way the lines break usually helps a poet hear where she hasn't helped the reader move through the poem. At the very least, that's what good use of the line *should* do.

Meanwhile, back to the shooting grandfather. Here are the first five lines of the poem, which runs twenty-seven lines and has no stanza breaks:

My grandfather used to shoot them.
I was about sixteen when he told me.
Ted was long gone, and he'd just come back from shooting Jeff.
Ted was mine, if a kid can ever call a hunting dog his.
"See the crooked-tailed one?" Granddaddy said.   5

Aside from scaring us a little with that third line, the poem's use of the line makes it sound stilted and static. There's no variation here, just a string of declarative sentences: "My grandfather used to," "I was," "Ted was," "Ted was." But clearly the poem wants to tell some sort of story about the speaker's past and his relationship with his grandfather and possibly with his hunting dog. The use of the line is getting in the way, probably because the poet, here, isn't sure what the difference is between a line and a sentence or statement. Each line ends with a period. Just like *Dragnet*. (See "The '60s" again.)

The poem continues:

"That'n's yours."
He turned out to be the best hunter of the litter.
I can still hear his, "Wraoooooo!"
Lady has lung cancer and
We're having a vet do it.   10
Even having him come to the house.
But it's just a useless old dog.
He used to dig a hole, then stand the dog beside it.

Wait a minute. That's the line we've been waiting for. Make that the first line and it will probably help with revising the whole poem. "He used to dig a hole, then . . ." One of the problems related to the serial-statement technique here is that all things get equal weight; there's no subordination, no emphasis, and no clear indication of time sequences, something a stanza break might help with, for example, between the eighth and ninth lines, where the speaker jumps from past to present.

There's nothing "wrong" or "right" about a particular kind of line:

short, long, broken with the breath, flowing with the rhythm of a story, or weaving in and out of one rhythm into another for effect. The challenge is to find the kind of line that works with the subject and mood of the poem, and to guide the reader through it, to make the kind of music a voice makes. The same poet who wrote about his grandfather in this poem, uses the same "brand" of line in a later poem, because he gravitates to narrative poems, but here he uses it much more successfully:

> Your '67 Nova taught you he was right about Chevys.
> This man could do anything.
> Built the lake house in Interlachen by himself,
> From the septic tank to the slab to the blocks to the shingles.
> You two slept there and caught and lost the biggest bass in the lake.   5
> Grass bass, boat bass, log bass—it all depended where you found them,
> But they were always near something. . . .

It's still a line that is direct, breaks with the natural movement of speech, but it has much more variety, different rhythms, and it moves the reader easily along.

In a poem that strives for a more lyric tone, another poet uses a line that moves carefully, attempting to emphasize a particular phrase and to slow down the poem which is usually what short lines do.

> My black rose thrives
> in the moist air
> under the tridge[1] at midnight
> in the shadows.
> I sit cross-legged   5
> on the wet
> picnic table
> watching the fog roll in.
>
> The match strike blows my silence
> as his Marlboro lights,   10
> across the river the alarm blasts out
> sending thousands
> flooding
> into the rain
> from the Ashman Court Hotel.   15

In these first two stanzas, the poem does benefit from the shorter line—certainly the poem moves slowly, quietly, emphasizing some sort of texture in most lines: the shadows, the fog, the rain, the moisture, the match flame. It is a poem of smaller gestures within a larger context, the rela-

[1]Note here that "tridge" seemed to be a regional slang term for a location in the local park.

tionship between the "he" and the "I" of the poem. What commonly happens with this use of the line is that we tend to break larger phrases into smaller parts, and too many of those parts are prepositional phrases. Just glance down at the first word in each line: *My, in, under, in, I, on, picnic, watching, The, as, across, sending, flooding, into, from.* The problem is first that prepositional phrases don't make very interesting lines: in the shadows/ into the rain/ in the moist air/ on the wet. Additionally, because of the line breaks, the first word of a line gets a little more emphasis than it would otherwise. Placing emphasis on "in" or "at" isn't usually productive. What happens is that these become the "leftovers," the empty phrases you don't know where to put. They are sacrificial lines, so that the poet can have another line such as "My black rose thrives" or "The match strike blows my silence..." Unfortunately, it often leads to a predictable pattern of *in the*'s and *of the*'s. A poem can't work up much energy this way. Try:

My black rose
Thrives in the moist air
Under the tridge, midnight,
I sit in the shadows,
Cross-legged on the picnic table,   5
Watching the fog
Roll in. The match strike

Blows my silence. . . .

There are, of course, many options here and they will depend, to some degree, on other changes the poet makes (dropping "at" before midnight, for example.) The most "radical" change in this version is the transition between stanzas. Putting "roll in" on the same last line as "The match strike," gives a little more energy to the moment, since the lines read almost as if the speaker is watching the fog roll in in the light of that match strike. In addition, the phrase "blows my silence" has more impact on its own because it's no longer a subordinate moment—it implies not only "blows" as in breeze but also as in "blows my cover." Since this poem does turn out to be about the break-up of a relationship from the speaker's point of view, the new line breaks and stanza break help the poem build to its moment. (See "Breaking Up Is Hard To Do," "The '60s"; "How Can You Mend a Broken Heart," "The '70s"; "You Give Love a Bad Name," "The '80s"; "My Heart Will Go On," "The '90s.")

A stanza break can do more than divide the poem into neat little "poem-paragraphs." It can signal a transition (in time or place), sharpen the impact of the poem's movement, or work as a poem's "cinematography," a change of camera angles. Note the effect in this student poem about a dream:

I am dressed in the delicate lace gown.
At the end of the aisle—an old boyfriend
who fucked me the way a tiger rends prey.
His sweat splashed against my face

In the church. I am shaking my head, backing away,   5
the congregation turns a firm stare,
he wants you, don't be a selfish girl.

Saving "in the church" until the next stanza suspends the reader a moment in time because the sweat splashed against her face seems solely connected with the sexual encounter in the past. Yet, that changes abruptly when the speaker reminds us that, at dream-present, they are in a church—and it's almost as if the present and past blur in that moment, an intentional effect here that matches the movement of dream. It's also an example that shows there are times when a prepositional phrase can be used effectively at the beginning of a line. There may even be times when "Hey, good-lookin'" works.

Nah. Let's not get carried away. You don't want to wake up the next morning in some roach motel with an ugly poem crumpled up next to you and your head pounding iambic pentameter. Next thing you know, you'd end up a fiction writer, and we don't want *that*.

*   *   *

Exercise

Write as you would when you sit down to write. But write in prose without using any line breaks. Then go back and break the prose into lines. Once the writing is broken into lines, break it into stanzas. Pay close attention to where, when, and why you're breaking the language where you are.

chapter four

SOUND AND THE POEM

Sound is everywhere. It is around us constantly and we are regularly moved or startled or taken by sound. Take, for example, the crashing together of two train cars coupling at the rail yard, the crunching of a can under a girl's foot, the fast panting of a dog in the shade of a tree, the screech of tires against asphalt, the plunk of a rock in a pond. These sounds we know, and maybe we hear them every day, depending on who we are and where we live. And often we don't think of them as poetic. But we have reactions to these sounds when we do hear them. Sound is something that moves us—it can frighten us, relax us, delight us. And because of this, we can capture the sounds around us in words, and add them to the sensory experience a reader encounters in our poems.

In our daily lives, we have learned to hear sounds and move right past them or through them. But the same magic that is held in imagery is held in sound. We need to slow down and listen momentarily to catch it. And, of course, this is what we're doing in a poem—temporarily slowing the reader in a moment in order to catch what is important. My young son regularly hears noises and looks at me with a furrowed brow and a cocked head and asks, "What's that?" He is hearing the world—in some cases for the very first time— and sound is a part of the magic in his world. The readers should get nothing less because often they are

> *You become a conduit for the spirit of language to flow through. At that point you become a musician or an actor. You almost become possessed in that the world flows through you, becomes through you.*
>
> Quincy Troupe

entering our world through the poem for the very first time. Should they be as captivated as a small child? Absolutely. Should they turn to ask us "What's that?" Probably not. In this case we should make sure the poem is clear.

So how do we create sound quality in a poem? The first element to consider is **diction**, which is word choice. The words we choose at any moment have much attached to them, and sound is one of the qualities to consider. One of the first results of diction is the **tone** of the words or poem. We know tones—kind, angry, sympathetic, jealous, ironic, sarcastic. The way in which word choice helps to create these tones is through the **denotation** or **connotation** of words. The **denotation** of a word is the standard, or dictionary, definition. The **connotation** of a word is the cultural and contextual definition. As poets, we have to be concerned with connotation—in fact, usually more than denotation—because these connotations give meaning to the world around us. When choosing words for your poems, it's important to consider how they will function in the poem and what meanings will emerge from them. Aside from using denotation and connotation to create a poem's tone, there are other conventions which affect the sound of our poetry within each line.

These conventions are largely technical, and they are also tools for creating sound. We need them and we need to know how they work and what they do for us. But when we write, they tend to show up a bit more naturally, or organically, than we might think. So if they show up naturally, why do we need to know them as tools? We need them because when we revise or when they don't just blossom onto the page, it's necessary to know when, where, and how to pick them up and use them.

Let's start by talking a bit about consonant and vowel sounds in words. Alliteration and assonance are two poetic elements which arise from the use of consonants and vowels. **Alliteration** is the repetition of consonant sounds usually occurring at the beginning of words, which produces an echo effect and links words through their sounds—for example, *the friends fought*. Or in another case, *the snake silently moved away*. Alliteration is a relatively easy tool to use and you should become conscious of it when you write. Next time you sit down to write, think about it and make a point to use it, and you will also begin to see it in the poems you read. **Assonance** is the repetition of vowel sounds in the final syllables of words and produces an effect similar to alliteration. For example, *pretend you're a tree and extend your arms*. In both cases, this repetition of sounds can cause the words to blend together closely, not only through sound, but in meaning as well. Let's look at a student poem in which alliteration and assonance both emerge.

Stalking

Extending their arms
towards ground
reaching for a frozen flower

Snow bends trees
The wind hisses against   5
snow covered trees
stressing bases
tugging their roots

Trees crack and snap
falling fast on those below   10
tremors through the forest

Startled deer take
escape routes
darting and dashing
away from fear   15

The passing deer
alerts sleeping cougar
who follows hungry
stalking

The white snow   20
now becomes red
the blood of deer
too slow to escape.

SUSAN MELLING

Notice how many times in this poem Susan has used alliteration, repeating consonant sounds both at the beginnings of words that stand next to each other and those on different lines. Moreover, she has employed assonance in the same manner. At times the repetition of the vowel sounds comes from words placed next to each other in the lines and at other times the assonance happens from one line to another. And in this serene setting of the poem— where the death at the end is somewhat ironic—so too does the sound become ironic.

Another element of sound to consider is **onomatopoeia**, when a word sounds like or resembles what it is. For instance, *a snake hisses* or *the wood fell with a thud onto the ground*. We can come up with a number of examples like *buzz, rattle, squeak* and more. And this is a very effective tool for sound because we can not only capture the sound an insect may make but we can couple words in very original ways too. Along with these aforementioned tools, it can be important to consider the number of syllables in words that come together in lines and stanzas, next to each other or on top of each other in different lines. Considering syllables alongside alliteration, assonance, and onomatopoeia can combine to produce **euphony** or **cacophony** in our poems. **Euphony** is the blending of sounds to produce a pleasurable effect on the ear while **cacophony** has the opposite effect and produces a noisy or unpleasant effect on us. This may happen from the true sound of the word, or the word's meaning, or it may happen based on line structure and grouping of words—for example, James Wright's lines "the cowbells follow one another/ into the distances of the afternoon." These cowbells are not breaking apart our afternoon with their clanging. They are actually producing some sense of relaxation.

While these technical conventions of sound need to be thought about consciously at first, the more you use them, the more they will show up in your writing naturally. And, while you use these tools, the way a carpenter uses a saw, remember this easy rule that can help you be successful with them—never force or impose a convention on a poem. The language should always be natural and fit what you write. For example, if you were crafting an image of Grand Central Station in New York City at rush hour, you would want to produce cacophony in the poem. Whatever the case, remember that these effects can help enhance an image as well as a whole poem.

NOTICING SOUND AND GETTING IT INTO POEMS

Sound is what makes us feel. The sounds of this world are great and abundant. Consider all the cultures, the languages, all the voice inflections, and all the cadences and tones we hear from people's mouths in the way they pronounce words based on their cultural or regional backgrounds. And if we're not familiar with some specific sound, we can find it easily. But we have to hear the sounds in our world and know them before we can use them in our poems.

Go to a place which is unfamiliar to you. If you live in a rural area, go to a place you don't normally frequent—maybe a nearby field, or a pond, or a farm, a meadow, or a logging road. Maybe go to the next town over, or your own town will do. Sit in front of the barber shop if you've never sat there before. And then listen. Hear those sounds that you haven't taken in before, those which are new or foreign to you. In a city? Go to an area that is outside your ethnic experience—a Chinatown, Little Italy, Little Tokyo, Northbeach, an Irish district, an area which is Hispanic or African American. First, just observe all that's going on—maybe markets are open and selling things you don't typically eat. Maybe people shop differently there. Maybe they have to call out to the man behind the meat counter. Maybe there is a small grocer on the sidewalk barking at people to come in and shop or buy from him—the sounds are abundant. Then begin to just listen to them, what they are, how they stir you, how they cause people to move and react and jump into action. This is when we see that sound can actually be the launching place for so much.

This exercise illustrates for us that sound can bridge many gaps, cause us to cross many boundaries and caverns and come upon some rather startling revelations—some we may understand quite well, maybe even logically. And others we simply feel because the wind sounded a certain way, or the man at the vegetable stand said something in Cantonese we didn't understand but made an old lady smile—and we understood her smile and that's what moved us. In that, we've watched a whole relationship form over sound. These sounds that we come to know and can ultimately place in our poems give richness to our writing and to the world in which we create.

It can be difficult to start a poem at times, and to have to concentrate on sound may seem to make starting even more difficult. But let's use sound as a tool to begin our work. When beginning a poem, there is no need to go in a straight line, to follow a specified path. We don't necessarily need to proceed logically from one place to another. Let connections happen. This can be part of your creative process. One way to allow yourself some room to create in your poems is to let the sound guide you and control the words a bit. You might be surprised how sound can become a driving force behind the language, pushing it forward, making people want to read the poem aloud. Listen to the words and let the syllables or letters connect and push you in a direction of choosing words. Take for instance the following lines.

> . . . As I took the stance I had seen my father use
> I saw the milkweed plant
> that grew beside the chopping block.
> Curled maple leaves scratched the ground like claws
> and trees rustled in the wind. . . .   5

JESSE WOODCOCK

While Jesse's lines are certainly image-filled, they are powered by sound. Notice the way the "s" sound runs throughout the lines, and inside the lines Jesse does a wonderful job with elements such as assonance—his repetition of "a" and "o" and "e" sounds. And we shouldn't forget the power behind the sound of the claws scratching the ground. These sounds propel the image and the poem forward. The sounds roll out of the mouth—these are words meant to be read aloud. We hear the scratching and rustling.

Sound can be one of the major forces behind a poem, the force which propels the language, which helps our sensory experience in the poem come alive. And more, when it's done well, the experience becomes real, the language becomes transparent, and we hear what is happening in the poem. Take note of how things sound and apply them to your use of language, your word choices. Capture the screech of birds, the clanging of crabs against the pot, the sizzle of rain on the pavement. And most important, weave the sounds into the emotional context of the poem so that the technical function of the words is woven tightly into the emotional or intellectual fabric of the poem. Push open the creaking gate of our minds and make us follow you into your world of sound.

Essay by Alberto Ríos

DEGAS IN VEGAS: SOME THOUGHTS ON SOUND IN POETRY

> I rhyme to see myself, to set the
> darkness echoing.
>
> —*Seamus Heaney*

Something that is "sound" is something that is well-made. Sound in poetry is a discussion not simply of what a poem's noises are. It also questions whether those noises are working—whether they help the poem to be well-made. This suggests that a poem's sound operates beyond coincidence, and that the poet is as aware of sound as a musician or composer. Sound, in this sense, is part of the poet's toolbox. It is one more choice that helps the poet to write a better poem.

Sound exists or does not exist in a poem—that is, as a reader you are very aware of it, or else it makes no *particular* difference. These two conditions may be thought of as sonic intensity and sonic distance. Sonic intensity refers to a condition in a poem in which the sound is everything. Sonic distance, on the other hand, occurs when sound is simply one more part of whatever makes the poem successful.

The poet may use sonic intensity for several reasons. First, a moment in a poem may be magnified or trumpeted by sound. This technique may serve to make the reader more aware of the importance of the moment, or it may suggest a complexity that the reader might otherwise have overlooked. Second, sound itself in the mouth of the reader may be the point of the poem. In either case, sonic intensity slows the reader down by making that reader pay attention. In doing this, the poem suggests a lateral, or sideways, movement, rather than simply straightforward movement. This kind of movement in a poem says to the reader, *I know you're in a hurry, but sit down for a moment and have a glass of cold lemonade—it'll make you feel better.*

Sonic distance, on the other hand, suggests forward or linear movement. This technique says to the reader, *Yes, I saw him, Sheriff. He ran that-away—you'll catch him if you hurry.* This approach may be equally important to the poet's intention and may also be used for a variety of reasons. The poet, for example, may not want the reader to linger. The point to be made may be farther down in the poem, or else there may be more to read before jumping to any conclusions. In this case, sound in the mouth of the reader is exactly what the poet does not want. The poet may purposefully use quiet or unpretentious wording in order to avoid drawing attention to the language, which may not be the point of that particular poem. Maybe the poet prefers the reader to consider the whole idea of a poem, or else the poem may be telling a kind of story.

Sonic intensity often leads to what are called lyric poems. These are poems of substantial, imaginative moment, where the beginning, middle, and/or end—the plot elements—are not as important as the moment experienced. Sonic distance, on the other hand, often suggests what are called narrative poems. In narrative poems, plot elements clearly come into play and have an importance equal to the single moment in a poem. What's happened and what's going to happen are as important to understanding the poem as what's happening in the moment.

These two approaches are not necessarily on opposite sides, and many, even most, poems blend both the moment and the story of a poem. In both sonic intensity and distance, however, sound helps to achieve the greater purpose of the poem. As a result, through the centuries sound has been especially associated with poetry.

But what kinds of sounds create this intensity or distance for the reader? Any single sound will do, but it is not the single sound that produces these results. It is, instead, a careful combination of sounds that creates one effect or the other. If a sequence of syllables, words, or whole lines makes the reader pay attention because of their collective sounds, then sonic intensity occurs. *Peter Piper picked a peck of pickled peppers, picked a peck of*—well, you know the rest. "Peter Piper" is a good, classic example of a group of sounds that make a reader pay attention. A tongue twister is purposefully difficult and challenging in the mouth, using alliteration to produce this effect. Alliteration is the repetition of the same sound at the beginning of a series of words. Much poetry, while more subtle than a tongue twister, exhibits the same attentive use of language, as in the following short examples of Anglo-Saxon prosody from student poems: "wept, awoke. I wandered and slept," "in her gravel garden, again," and "beside him icy saplings."

Rhyme, of course, is another way to make the reader pay attention. This is a time-honored device associated with poetry, and by extension, music. Rhyme is very effective. Like dynamite, it can absolutely do the job. So, the poet's first question when using rhyme should probably be: Is there a job to be done by the rhyme? That is, why is it being used? Rhyme may be pleasing to the ear, but upon entering the ear it reaches the brain, which may have a second opinion. If all it does is bring attention to itself without furthering the poem in any particular way, then things begin to fall apart. Children's poetry or silly poems written purely for fun are often the exception to this standard: *How now, brown cow.* But if the poem is meant to be successful on some greater level, then there has to be a point to the rhyme, in the same way choosing a certain word has a point.

Rhyme is certainly not a bad thing, however. At its best, rhyme's repetition offers to the reader a variety of pleasing sensibilities, including, for example, a sense of completion and recognition, both of which are comforts to the human spirit. Rhyme repeats a sound, which the reader recognizes as having heard earlier in the poem. This suggests a number of reasons for its usage—memory, for one. If a reader recognizes the sound, this means the reader remembers it, and therefore is actively engaged in memory, no matter how slight. But if a poet is writing about the future, then perhaps rhyme is not a congruent choice. Rhyme is certainly one tool in the poet's toolbox, but a good writer, like a good carpenter, does not use only a hammer to build a porch.

And rhyme is not simply one thing. There are many, many forms of rhyme. Too often the word "rhyme" is relegated only to its simplest and most overt association, true rhyme—as in *blue* and *glue*. Rhyme, however, can occur anywhere, and in any sequence, and is often much more elegant and surprising in something other than its true rhyme form. Rhyme may occur at the beginning of a line, for example, rather than at the end. And it may be more jazz-like than straightforward, as in the old wrestler's name, Gorgeous George. Rhyme is clearly there, but it's a little trickier to tame. Our impulse might be to think "Gorgeous Georgeous," but therein is the delight—it doesn't behave itself, and so as a listener you take notice. And therefore, what a brilliant name this becomes for a wrestler who himself would not behave.

Sometimes more than sounds or words get repeated. Whole lines or even whole sections of poems might repeat. In blues poems, for instance, the first two lines are usually the same, while the third is completely different. Repeating the first line focuses the reader, and builds up a dramatic foundation. It sets up the reader, who knows the third line is coming. This is reminiscent of watching Lucy hold Charlie Brown's football, and of the way she moves it every time he comes up to kick. Rhyme often plays a part in this repetition. A blues refrain line, then, is a cousin to the alliterated word. It's a mix of the familiar with the unfamiliar, and that juxtaposition creates energy. The first part is an introduction, a comfort, but the second part sweeps your legs out from under you. It's like: *shake hands*—which we know how to do, familiar and regular—*with the President of the United States!* Or, *with this grizzly bear!* Well, of course blues, and often much literature, is a little more interesting and funny than that. It's more like: *I love my girlfriend, I do I do with all my life / I love my girlfriend, I do I do with all my life / But oh but oh don't tell my wife!*

Many things, then, enhance sonic intensity. But finally, the best is the oldest technique of all, and one which combines all of these practices: reading aloud. You can only put one sound at a time in your mouth, while your mind on the other hand can race between ideas much more quickly, not being hampered by sounding anything out at all. This sounding out slows a poem down, and puts it to the lyric test. This shows, quite easily, how every word ultimately matters.

Sonic distance is the other side of sonic intensity. If in combination the sounds in a poem produce no particular effect, no jolting to the ear, the result is sonic distance. In a poem, this technique may lead to a greater narrative or story, to a consideration of ideas, or sometimes simply to quietude—but it absolutely has an effect as well, and is equally a part of the poet's toolbox. This is a poem without obvious rhyme, without a predictable refrain or structure, without the alliteration. It has no ready clues to offer the reader beyond the words themselves. It asks a small faith from the reader, and must offer something worthy in exchange.

Sonic distance cannot be described, therefore, by any particular characteristics. Rather, as readers, we must consider the whole poetic effect, the sense of genuine response we have in finishing a poem. In this way, *the reader* is the rhyme to the poem. The reader is the third line of a blues refrain, the one that is changed. This is a lot to ask of a reader, and sets the stakes high. "His eyes were his résumé," someone wrote. And I understood. Someone else wrote about "a compass on a lazy Susan," and the sudden science inherent in this image was beguiling, making the idea more forceful than even its carefully placed extra share of "s" sounds.

When thinking about all of this, when reading or writing a poem yourself, beware of instructions and rules and dissections. The best and first thing in trying to understand or write a poem is to listen and think for yourself. Taste the poem in your mouth. Listen to it as it comes out of there. The mouth is its ancient home. Understand too that no single rule or set of rules applies to all poems. The greatest gift a poem has to give is that it is new: Its subject matter and, at least to some extent, its own rules are new.

This does not mean to say that a great poem doesn't talk about old things, or that it ignores the rules that govern language use. A great poem knows, understands, and utilizes those very ideas, but in the same moment finds a way to go beyond them. The best poems, finally, may simply come down to good choices, which may not be consistent or constant at all—good choices, each step of the way, whether by rule or by invention or both. Regarding the words in a poem, have the patience to ask yourself, *Is this a good choice? A sound choice?*

Here is the final, great secret about poems and sound. A great poem is hard to read aloud, finally, because it takes your breath away. But this is a good problem. If by its sounds the poem has rendered you speechless, and if those sounds come to mean something important to you in that moment, then—no matter what rules ought to apply—the poem has done its job.

*   *   *

Exercise

1. Write three to five lines and pay close attention to using alliteration as many times as possible.
2. Write six lines and try to use assonance at the ends of the lines.
3. Create a few short images and try to use a word with onomatopoeia in each.
4. Create an image and in it use a new and original word for a sound. Rather than giving the mother in the image a human voice, apply the trait of some animal. Notice how the sound quality changes because of the power in your original use of language.

RHYME AND METER, THE MUSIC OF POEMS

I'm going to function under an assumption—that most writers (and especially young writers) don't like to use rhyme. And some who do like to use it don't use it well. Excuse me if that's offensive, but I'll clarify it in a minute. So functioning under that assumption, I'm going to take the role of the used car salesman and see if I can have you driving off the lot in the make and model of rhyme that suits you. That's important—I'm going to help you find the rhyme that suits you. Better yet, we don't have to deal with financing—you just drive away. But once you drive away, it's yours; you live with this one because there's a no-return policy. So let's start looking and I'll try to clarify some things about rhyme.

Some of the things I hear from students in my poetry workshops sound like this: "Rhyme seems too constricting"; "It's hokey—it sounds like a Hallmark card"; "Rhyme is way too conventional and conservative"; "Old poets use rhyme." And here's my favorite, "I don't know why, but I just don't like it." These are all fine things to say; I said them once too and most of my colleagues probably did, but somewhere along the line we drove off the rhyme lot with a winner. What I see as common among all these is that poets who say these things about their own work or others' work are not talking about the type of rhyme which works naturally, the kind of rhyme that just shows up and is unobtrusive. They're talking

The metric movement, the measure, is the direct expression of the movement of perception. And the sounds, acting together with the measure, are a kind of extended onomatopoeia—that is, they imitate not the sounds of an experience but the feeling of an experience, its emotional tone, its texture.

Denise Levertov

about the kind of rhyme that is imposed on poems. And that's the first rule of rhyme I want to state—don't impose it; rather, let rhyme happen naturally by having it raise itself in the poem. A quick example: I had a student once who loved rhyme. So one day she brought into class a very dark poem about a serial killer and it was a rhyming poem. Hence it had a sing-songy meter to it. None of us knew what to say. "Was she writing satire?" we asked. "No," she said, "I just like rhyme." O.K., fine, but that was the wrong time to rhyme. That was a poem that needed tension between the words.

Before we go any farther, let's lay down some definitions of rhyme and the types of rhyme we have. **Rhyme** is an echoing produced by close placement of two or more words with similarly sounding final syllables. There are a number of types of rhyme: there is **masculine rhyme,** in which two words end with the same vowel consonant combination (hand/band); **feminine rhyme,** in which two syllables rhyme (shiver/liver); **end-rhyme,** in which the rhyme comes at the end of the lines (this is probably the most commonly used rhyme); and **internal rhyme,** in which a word within a line rhymes with another word in that line or rhymes with a word of similar placement in the following line. There is also a type of rhyme called **slant rhyme,** in which the sounds nearly rhyme but do not form a "true rhyme" (land/ lend).

Knowing what types of rhyme we have available to us, let's just talk briefly about what rhyme does, why it's used at all. Rhyme can do a few things for a poet and her poems. One, rhyme can help a poet measure lengths of verse, either line by line or in larger chunks of language. It can do this by setting up recurrent points of rest in the language. Two, rhyme can help set a rhythm to the language we are using. And three, rhyme can help words become glued together in their sound and meaning so the poem gains a quality that is both pleasing to the ear and intellectually or emotionally stimulating. At its best, rhyme does not beat us over the head—in fact, we may read right past it or it may help us to read, guiding us musically through the poem, taking us up and setting us down in all the appropriate places. At its worst, rhyme can make a poem seem like a wrecking yard of greeting-card verse, and it can create a sense of predictability in lines and stanzas that makes us want to abandon the poem for something more fresh and alive—something that spurs our imagination.

Now that we have a bit of knowledge about the types of rhyme and why it's used, let's browse the lot a little and see what we like. Remember in this discussion that these are only types of rhyme and it's how and when they are used that make the rhyme effective or not. One poet we're nearly all familiar with, who used a great deal of rhyme, is Robert Frost. His poems are Cadillacs. Frost used end-rhyme frequently and he was great at it. Emily Dickinson used a great amount of rhyme, and her poems move so acutely through the rhyme (internal and end-rhyme) they're like fine-tuned sports cars. Of course, these are poets from the earlier part of the century. Consider James Wright's poem "Two Horses Playing in an Orchard." This poem is somewhat like a Frost poem. But here's a mid- to late-century poet who rarely wrote a poem with this much controlled rhyme and meter and it is a beautifully moving poem. We need not model these writers, but by examining their work, we can learn from them.

Now let's take a look at a poem by a past student. I use this example because this student, Amity, walked onto the poetry lot saying, "I hate rhyme, and I never use it." Well, from the first time she brought something in to workshop, what we all noticed was that her poems had rhyme in them. And, what's more, she didn't even know it. In one sense, that was good. Obviously, the down side was that she wasn't paying close attention to the sound when she went back to her poems. But what was good was that the rhyme was natural—it was coming out, and she didn't even notice. She wasn't imposing. And that's important, because during the writing of a poem, as Denise Levertov tells us, various parts of ourselves are working together and are heightened. Ear and eye, intellect and passion interrelate very subtly. And so, for the precision of language that must take place during writing, it is not a matter of one element supervising the others, but of intuitive interaction among all the elements involved. This is advice from a master. And it's good advice because what she's telling us is to use rhyme naturally and not let it overtake the poem—don't let it drive the poem. It's only one component. In the way that all the components of a car need to be working together to have the car drive smoothly, so do the components of a poem. So, Amity's poem:

March Day Kaleidoscope

Sunlight scalds neon yellow
scuffing feet up city streets.
Hawaiian flower in your hair,
and in the minds of kids wishing for paradise.
I sit and absorb colors
of the day and tie-dyed shirts.
Hues of the universe
mesh into marble and granite.
Hawaiian flowers paint the planet.

5

AMITY SKELTON

Now there are some things here we worked with for revision—images, lines, et cetera. But we're not going to go into that now. I want you to overlook the dents on the front of this car. Let's look at the rhyme. Notice the rhyme in just the first four lines of Amity's poem. While there is no end-rhyme until the end of lines three and four, notice how much internal rhyme we have (sun/scuff, scuff/up, feet/street, neon/street, light/Hawaiian,

Hawaiian/minds, kids/wish). For someone who asserted so adamantly in class that she "hated" rhyme, that amount of rhyme is remarkable. What is even better about it—and the reason I think Amity didn't even notice—is that the words which rhyme are not exact masculine and feminine rhymes. In other words, not all the vowel syllables rhyme, nor do all the consonants sound the same. So we get all the benefits of rhyme without it imposing itself on the poem or getting in our way—it's transparent to us. So the poem goes on like this until the last two lines, where we can feel the intentional nature of that end-rhyme (granite/planet).

So something to notice about Amity's poem and the one we're about to look at is the amount of internal rhyme. It seems to me that when most young writers think of rhyme, they immediately think of end-rhyme, "old" poems, greeting cards. Ah, but now you see it doesn't have to be that way at all. You can rhyme a great deal within the lines and get great mileage in your poems from doing so. This is the kind of technique that allows you to couple a technical use of poetic elements with an intuitive use of language and that plays upon the intellect and emotion of the readers without their consciously knowing it until they go back and look for rhyme.

All right, now here we are at the next example I want to show you. But this time, I want you to walk around it, take a look, kick the tires if you want—it's sturdy. Admire the paint job and some of the subtle exterior detail. Sit in it if you want. This is a nice compact one that gets good mileage.

At the corner of 38th and Division, my car stops

The meadowlark has returned again.
I watch a pair sing of winters spent
in warmer climates.
Watch as they play out their ballet
of clouds.   5
They fly past me.
My feet are cast in lead.
My arms bear no feathers.
My eyes sort out the twisting metal
made by man's hands,   10
see that I am not owned.

BEN RICKARD

I'm not going to say too much about this poem. But let's quickly look at a rhyme we haven't yet pointed out: the slant rhyme. Notice that in the first four lines, Ben ends the lines with words that almost rhyme (again/spent/ballet). Hence, we have a sense that there's a connectedness to the place through the birds and what they are doing. He does a nice job of subtly weaving those rhymes together with images and a sense of how the birds are moving. This one runs pretty well.

Let's talk for a moment about the end-rhyme that creates a greeting-card-type poem. I had a student ask me once (and not because he wrote this type of poetry—rather, because he was a retired social worker who loved to ask good and interesting questions), "What's wrong with writing greeting-card verse and using all that hokey rhyme? I mean, if that's what they're trying to do, why not?" Ahh. Tom had me. "O.K.," I said, "you're right. What's the big deal—if that's what they're trying to do, then great." But then I added, "Tom, I'm trying to teach people to write literary poems that deal with the complexity of the human experience. They can write greeting cards to make money later." In the end, what I was really trying to tell Tom was that greeting-card-type verse is fine if that's all you're after—that's not too hard to write. But when you're approaching poetry from a literary standpoint and weaving together elements of the craft to create a finely-tuned poem that moves us deeply, it's important that you not rely on one element, like rhyme, to make your language move. One other thing that happens in standard greeting-card verse is that strict repetitive meter is employed—usually iambic pentameter.

So let's talk a bit about meter, what it is, how it occurs, what types there are and what it does. First, **meter** is the arrangement of measured rhythm in poetry (*measured* is a key word here; you might think of how music is measured). This measurement is based on where the stressed and unstressed syllables are in words. On one hand, that makes it easy because the stressed syllables and the unstressed syllables in words don't change—they are what they are. But meter becomes a bit more complicated as we put a number of words together. Meter is measured in what are called **feet**. A **foot** is one measurement of stressed and unstressed syllables. Now, types of meter are based on these measurements.

Types of Feet in Poetic Meter

iamb	ă é
trochee	é ă
anapest	ă ă é
dactyl	é ă ă
spondee	é é

The above are examples of the types of feet in poetry. When we place these in lines and have a number of feet working together, we get a type of recurring meter (you may know the term iambic pentameter, for instance). Within these types of feet, we have what we refer to as rising and falling meter. **Rising meter** occurs when we go from unstressed syllables to stressed syllables. Therefore, the iamb and the anapest are rising meters. **Falling meter** is just the opposite—it occurs when we go from stressed to unstressed. The trochee and the dactyl are feet with falling meter.

When there is one foot in a single line of poetry it is called *monometer*; when there are two feet, it is called *dimeter*; when there are three feet, it is called *trimeter*; four feet: *tetrameter*; five feet: *pentameter*; six feet: *hexameter*; seven feet: *heptameter*; eight feet: *octameter*. These are the types of meter that we have, but it is rare to find poetry with more than six feet in a line. To illustrate, let's look at examples of two types of meter. The first is iambic (a rising meter) trimeter (three feet to a line) from Theodore Roethke's "My Papa's Waltz." This is a relatively common meter.

> The whiskey on your breath
> Could make a small boy dizzy;
> But I hung on like death:
> Such waltzing was not easy.

Something to note with this poem is that Mr. Roethke must have chosen this meter because it mimicked the beat of the waltz. Hence, the meter seems very natural in the poem and rises out of the poem—it is not imposed on the poem. Mr. Roethke couldn't have written this poem any other way.

And to illustrate a falling meter, here is a line of trochaic tetrameter, meaning the line has a stressed/ unstressed foot (the trochee) and it recurs four times (tetrameter).

> Fighting / was her / huge ob / session;
> she threw / pitchers / at her / husband.

Notice that the last foot of the first line breaks in the middle of a word. This is a reasonable thing to do when constructing meter and will provide you some latitude in your word choice and line structure.

This may all seem very technical, and to go back to our car metaphor, this is like the strokes of cylinders. In poetry, where we want a strict meter, and especially formal poetry, where we pay close attention to recurring metrical patterns, the beats in each foot of each line are like the spark plugs firing inside the engine. With a well-tuned line, the poem runs smoothly. When we feel the poem missing, we need to tune-up the lines and make sure the meter is in place. But let's remember that a poet might sometimes break the recurring meter for effect.

In the end, meter provides us with a sense of rhythm. At the least, say in nursery rhymes, meter provides for us a sense of beat and music and bodily pleasure. If we use it to mirror what is happening in images, we can re-create the natural rhythms that are taking place—say a horse galloping or people dancing. As we saw earlier, the meter in Theodore Roethke's poem, "My Papa's Waltz," mimics the waltz; it even mimics the father missing a step. At its best, skillfully used, as in Roethke's poem, meter is woven into the subtleties of the language. It is used according to the natural cadences of speech and the meanings of words.

Now that we've browsed the lot, looked at a number of things, sat in a few models, done some comparison shopping, sit back and think about which works best for you, what's going to get you through the long haul. Test drive a few models and figure out what you like. Choose what fits comfortably and what you can integrate into your poems without imposing too much on your craft. And be aware of your natural impulses and the rhythm of your language.

Essay By James Hoggard

METER AND RHYME

Although an organized use of rhyme and meter can enhance the elegance of a poetic passage, their major function is something other than decorative. Meters have particular effects, while the several types of rhyme organize passages by means of repeated, or echoic, sounds. Rhyme and meter both have their vocabularies, and it's important for poets to learn those terms so they can take advantage of the concepts behind them. Problems in poems often occur when rhythms or sounds are inappropriate to the experience being conveyed. Having access to terms of measure and rhyme, a poet can diagnose problematic passages more surely than one can without the terminology. Concepts of language, after all, are major tools a writer needs.

A. METER

There are five kinds of metrical feet commonly used in English, but before we define them, we should recognize that the custom of dividing sounds into two levels of stress—accented and unaccented—is more convention than hard reality. We commonly use four different levels of stress in ordinary conversation, but conventional marking identifies only two. This means, of course, that when we talk about meter, we are not dealing with metronomic purity, and for the sake of poetic pleasure that's fortunate. Jingles suggest triviality, not deeply moving speech.

The major patterns of metrical feet include the *iamb* (unaccented syllable followed by an accented syllable, or ˘ ¯, as it's often written), the *trochee* (¯ ˘), the *spondee* (¯ ¯), the *dactyl* (¯ ˘ ˘), and the *anapest* (˘ ˘ ¯). One should also be aware of the *amphibrach* (˘ ¯ ˘) and *monometer* (¯). Except for possibly the *spondee*, the odd appearance of one of the feet is not likely to be notable; but when used in a sustained way, the metrical patterns have particular effects.

The dominant rhythm of spoken English is *iambic*. That does not mean, of course, that in our conversations we speak in perfectly turned iambs, but it does mean that a sustained use of the iambic rhythm gives a conversational effect. A good example would be these opening lines of one of Shakespeare's sonnets:

That time of year thou mayst in me behold
When yellow leaves, or none, or few, do hang
Upon those boughs which shake against the cold

If one reads the passage out loud in a normal voice, one hears how conversational it sounds; and it should sound conversational because its rhythm is perfectly iambic.

The *trochaic* rhythm is much more rapid than the iambic one. Because of the quick, falling rhythm ($\bar{}\smile/\bar{}\smile/\bar{}\smile$), a series of trochees might call to mind someone moving the feet rapidly in front of each other to keep from falling. Lines three, four, and five of Robert Browning's "Meeting at Night" illustrate vividly the quickness of predominantly trochaic lines:

And the startled little waves that leap
In fiery ringlets from their sleep
As I gain the cove with pushing prow

One also notes that Browning sustains the trochaic pattern from line to line by enjambing the first line above so the rhythm continues without a pause into the next line, with *leap* being the first syllable of a trochee that is completed by *In* at the beginning of the next line, then followed by three trochees. The line closes with the monometrical *sleep*. The anapest and three iambs of the next line create a rhythm that is slower than the previous two lines that are dominated by trochees.

Although lengthy passages aren't ordinarily written in **spondees,** the spondaic rhythm does have a dramatic effect by slowing down the pace of a passage. The first two lines of the same poem by Browning illustrate this:

The gray sea and the long black land
And the yellow half-moon large and low

One might say that the first line begins with an iamb followed by a trochee then an iamb and finally a spondee, but that's not the way we hear it. We hear *gray sea* as a unit of sound just as we hear *long black land* as a unit. When we read the line, we realize that its relative slowness is created by the **spondaic** patterns in it. The second line begins rapidly with two trochees then is slowed down notably by the sudden appearance of three accented syllables together: *half-moon large.*

The next two metrical feet, the **dactyl** ($\bar{}\smile\smile$) and the **anapest** ($\smile\smile\bar{}$) create swinging rhythms C *tum da da* / *tum da da* then *da da tum* / *da da tum.* It's easy to forget the rhythm that identifies each term, but there's a (literally) handy mnemonic device that helps us remember which one is which.

The word **dactyl** comes from the Greek word *dactylos*, meaning *finger*. If one looks at one's index finger outward from palm to fingertip, one sees a long joint followed by two shorter ones, or ‾ ˘ ˘, and the **anapest** is just the opposite. In fact, the Greeks themselves used the same mnemonic device. *Dactyl* comes from the word for *finger*, and *anapest* comes from the word that means *reversed*—here, in effect, the opposite of dactyl.

The terms ordinarily used for the number of metrical feet per line also came to us from the Greeks. Sonnets are said to be written in iambic pentameter, which means five feet per line and most of the feet are iambic. **Penta** means *five* and **meter** means *measure*. Other terms to note include **hexameter** (six feet), **tetrameter** (four feet), **trimeter** (three feet), **dimeter** (two feet), and **monometer** (one foot). Another term one some-times sees for **dimeter** is *dipody*, or in its adjectival form *dipodic* (coming from *di* meaning *two* and *podos* meaning *foot*). One should keep in mind the relative effects of these measures—the longer the line, the lengthier, the more sustained the flow from line to line; and the shorter the line, the quicker the flow.

B. RHYME

In an essay titled "The Figure a Poem Makes," Robert Frost called poems "momentary stays against confusion." By that he meant that a work of art can have an order that is not present, or at least not apparent, in nature. The poet, then, is a maker, a shaper, or even an inventor of experiences; and rhyme is a common indicator of an order that has been either created or discovered in the portion of the world described or evoked. Rhyme has also been used as a device to help make a work memorable, both for the audience and for the person reciting or singing the piece.

In terms of placement and exactness of sound, there are several types of rhyme. *External* (or *end*) *rhyme* refers to the repetitions of sounds at the ends of lines, whereas **internal rhyme** refers to sounds that are repeated within lines. Although external rhymes are usually thought of as regular in their patterns of repetition (lines one and three rhyme, say, or lines two and four rhyme), internal rhymes are usually employed irregularly in a passage. In both cases, the sounds that are repeated, or used echoically, include both the closing vowels and consonants, as in *yellow, bellow*; *loon, rune*; *walk, talk*. If only one of the closing elements (a consonant but not a vowel, or a vowel but not a consonant) is repeated, one has *approximate rhyme*; other terms one might see that mean the same thing are *slant rhyme, half-rhyme*, and *pararhyme*. Since rhyme, whether full or half, involves echoic effects in words, the sonic repetition needs to be close enough to its mate for us to notice the similarities of sound. That's espe-cially true for internal rhyme. If, for instance, the sounds that get repeated internally are several lines apart, one is not likely to note the repetition.

Examples of both full rhyme and approximate end-rhyme are found in John Crowe Ransom's "Bells for John Whiteside's Daughter." The stanza that begins the poem sets the pattern for all but the middle stanza, with lines one and three closing with *approximate rhyme* and two and four closing with *full rhyme*:

There was such speed in her little body
And such lightness in her footfall,
It is no wonder her brown study
Astonishes us all.

Body and *study* give us half-rhymes, whereas *fall* and *all* rhyme exactly. Because this pattern is repeated throughout the poem, we find that a sense of tension in the speaker is expressed sonically; the poem alternates between fullness of order and incompleteness of order. This tension is also amplified in the speaker's phrasing: "her brown study / Astonishes us"; "we are sternly stopped"; "we are vexed." Sounds, we begin to learn, can affect the mood of a passage just as rhythms can. In the middle stanza of Ransom's poem, the rhyming pattern changes. Instead of the alternation between approximate rhyme in lines one and three and exact rhyme in two and four, found in the other stanzas, here both sets of lines rhyme exactly to indicate the Edenlike harmony of the child's world:

The lazy geese, like a snow cloud
Dripping their snow on the green grass,
Tricking and stopping, sleepy and proud,
Who cried in goose, Alas

When rhyming lines follow one another without intervening non-rhyming lines, the jingle-like repetition can create a perkily light mood, as we see in the wittily suggestive opening lines of "Sweet Lemon Iced Tea" by the undergraduate poet Nekesha Meals:

do you like what you see
when you look at me
this tall slender glass of sweet lemon iced tea

The enjambment between lines two and three softens the rhyme and prevents the effect of monotonous repetition that one often hears when end-stop lines rhyme.

Several other sonic devices that are related to rhyme need to be noted. These refer to the types of sounds, vowels, or consonants, that are repeated and to their positions in words. The three sonic devices noted here are **alliteration**, **assonance**, and **consonance**. It's also important to keep in mind that these sonic devices refer to sounds that are repeated, but not necessarily to letters.

Alliteration refers to the repetition of initial consonant sounds in words either within a line or close enough to each other to be registered by the listener. An example would be:

In the deep-blue **b**ay, **b**road sails
bellied in the wind

or:

The **b**ig waves **b**eat the hulls
of the **b**oats, all of them **b**lue

Assonance refers to the repetition of vowel sounds in a passage, with no distinction being made to placement, as in these two lines with their long *i*-sounds:

but the other n**i**ght just after dusk d**i**ed
I heard the first bullfrogs explaining spring

The other *i*'s are not included because the qualities of sound they evoke are different from the long *i*-sounds noted. Another example of asso-nance is also present in the first line, with the short *u*-sounds in *but, just,* and *dusk.* One might also note the internal rhyme in the last two syllables of line two: "explain**ing** spr**ing**."

The third sonic device noted here is *consonance,* the repetition of internal consonant sounds, or consonant sounds appearing at places other than the beginnings of words, as we hear in the *d*-sounds in this passage from a poem titled "Springsound":

They soun**d**e**d** as if they won**d**ere**d** which kin
woul**d** not anonymous escape the clay
but stay beneath a sun**d**rie**d** roof baked har**d**.

The *d* in *baked* in line three is not included because here the *d* is pro-nounced like a *t.* One also notices that assonance is prominent in the same passage, in the long *a*-sounds of the two *they*'s in line one which are echoed in *escape* and *clay* in line two, and *stay* and *baked* in line three. In effect, these sonic devices are musical in their effects as they organize phrases with clusters of sound.

Two other sonic devices that are especially important to know are *liq-uids* and sibilants. When used repeatedly, they give a soft, gracefully flowing, lyrical effect to phrases. Because they create particular effects, because they refer to particular sounds, and because their positions in words are not an issue, these two are considered separately from allliter-ation, assonance, and consonance. The liquids are the *l*'s and *r*'s, and the sibilants are the hissing sounds: *s*'s, *sh*'s, and aspirated *f*'s. Again, we're referring to sounds, not necessarily letters. The words *rough* and *tough,* for example, close with the *f*-sound, though the letter *f* does not occur in either word. On the other hand, the word *of* has the letter *f* in it, but no *f*-sound. A word like *nation*, for instance, contains a sibilant because the *ti* in the middle of the word is pronounced *sh*. Two other sounds ought to be mentioned as possible sibilants, though some readers do not include them in the group. They are the voiceless interdental fricative *th* (as in *pith* but not *the*) and the *z*-sounds (as in *blows*, *noses*, and *cries*). Two passages quoted below illustrate the smooth, whisperily graceful flow that occurs when numerous clusters of liquids and sibilants work together. The first includes the closing lines of "The Yachts" by William Carlos Williams:

they cry out, failing, failing! their cries rising
in waves still as the skillful yachts pass over.

The second example is the first stanza of Browning's "Meeting at Night," a poem referred to earlier in a different context. As we did above without distinguishing one from the other, we put the liquids and sibilants in boldface to emphasize their prominence in the stanza.

The gray sea and the long black land
And the yellow half-moon large and low
And the startled little waves that leap
In fiery ringlets from their sleep
As I gain the cove with pushing prow   5
And quench its speed i' the slushy sand.

Thinking in terms of sound and measure, one begins to realize the points of intimate involvement linking form and subject. In some cases, and they're often glorious when one discovers them, a sizable passage or even at times an entire poem may create or recreate simultaneously both the sensory and thematic dimensions of an experience; in fact, they might do that so intensely that the poem itself does not simply describe the experience but evokes the presence of the experience itself. When that happens, the passage—sometimes even the entire poem—becomes onomatopoetic, and the work truly sings.

*   *   *

Exercise

1. If you're a poet who doesn't care much for rhyme, write a rhyming poem. Or take a poem you wrote recently and comb through it to see how much rhyme there already is in it. Then revise it to add more rhyme.

    If you're a poet who likes to write rhymed poetry, then write a poem that has no end-rhyme. This may be hard. It may feel as though you are working against yourself, but trust that you are

still getting your rhyme in; it's probably happening more naturally.

2. The poet Robert Hass says "There's a sense in which poetry is not
   so much the writing of words as much as it is the movement of
   breath itself. To write it you must pay attention to the breathing of
   poetry, to *all* speech as breath, to the relationship of our thoughts
   and emotions and the actual way they fill our bodies. This is the
   emotional, physical centering of the activity of poetry." Take this
   quote and apply it to either a new poem you are writing or a poem
   you've already written. Notice how it might affect the rhythm or
   meter based on how the breath—your breath—is connected to the
   experience in the poem.

chapter six

VOICE AND HOW WE CREATE IT IN POEMS

Having talked about diction and tone a bit in the previous chapter on sound, this is a natural place to begin talking about **voice** in a poem. Voice is the expressive force and tone of the words spoken by the author and the **persona** in the poem. And, the persona is the person who is the speaker of the poem. When we read a story, we often know, very definitively, who is talking at any given time. Of course, we meet the narrator immediately, and we come to know the narrator's voice quickly and well. But in a poem, sometimes that identification of the character to whom we are actually listening, can be a bit more ambiguous. This is not a bad thing; remember, ambiguity is part of poetry. But, we also need to remember as we write poems that, it is important to create a very solid voice. This way the poem will avoid confusion.

So what makes voice and how do we control it? Voice in a poem rises from diction and syntax—put simply, the way we use language, the way in which we combine our words. The other thing that causes a voice to take shape is setting—the place from which the persona is speaking. Why setting? Setting is more than simply where and when a poem or story takes place; rather, the setting is the physical and cultural context for the way the world is viewed by the persona, the writer, and ultimately, the reader. So as we create a poem, we may begin by thinking of a very dis-

> *An author, that is to say, is a fashioner of words, stamps them with her own personality, and wears the raiment she has made, in her own way.*
>
> Marianne Moore

tinct persona (speaker) and we know that there is a distinct set of circumstances which has formed what he will say and how he will say it. Take, for example, Gary Snyder's poem "Axe Handles." This poem begins with a father speaking about teaching his young son how to throw a hatchet into a stump. During the poem, the father realizes that as a parent he is not only a teacher, but he is, and has been, a student of life. Throughout the poem the voice maintains a sense of consistency because of where the poem takes place (a rural setting, clearly the home of the father and son, and a place where he can teach his son to throw a hatchet) and the way in which the father perceives and expresses the experience. His connecting to his son in the natural world, in taking the time to help shape an experience for him with natural elements, causes the persona and the persona's voice to reach a level of clarity. The poem ends with the realization that generations shape each other and the realization comes in very clear and accessible language.

For another example, let's look at what a student from one of the past workshops put together. Kevin was from a farming and logging community and had grown up there. Notice how he uses the setting of the poem to spark the action and ultimately the sentiment of the experience—the missed connection between father and son, the want for love and togetherness, and the inability to escape the fact that they are tied by blood and generations. But what happens here is that while all of these things in the poem are tied to the setting and the actions there, it's Kevin's fresh use of language, his ability to keep this experience from sounding trite, saccharine, or even forcedly angry at key moments. He's been original and taken care to control the language throughout the poem.

By Barbed-Wire Fences

We stood silent and waiting
for a calf to cross
through a gate; its mother
waited. And in the truck, traveling
to town you were silent,   5
I kept talking, kept wanting
to find you. Unknowingly and
unwantingly those moments
lost themselves, soured
like milk into years, and a gate   10
between them I'm sure, no longer
reachable by foot.

In consistent light I thought was love,
through our barn, you and I,

but you turn away   15
the hay swirling glow—your back shining.
You look like memories;
my grandfather, your father, your
Irish hair dark as sorrow
shadows furrowed deep.   20

So that is why: your hands,
those hands of scars and strength,
those sawmill and logging town hands,
would slap my mother and choke her.
Those hands I longed to admire   25
to hate, a love like hard water.

How when we were rabbit hunting I wanted,
and turned the gun towards you.
Now, when you come home from work,
I am old enough. We walk silent to the barn   30
and I watch you load hay into the truck.
How I want to reach you;
slip my hands past your canvas
coat and hold you in the barn light as
night folds its dark clench over us. And winter,   35
winter we can bear because the numbness
is familiar. We will stand silent and knowing
that rain will be soon—it comes uneasy.
It arrives—sweet.
Together, in the only light we know,   40
the barn braces us against the cold east wind,
and I am no longer scared.

KEVIN SULLIVAN

In this poem, Kevin uses phrases such as "soured like milk into years," "you look like memories," and "hay swirling glow" to achieve some sense of freshness and originality in his language. But notice that they are directly tied to the setting and action of the poem. So what we have is the voice of the poet and persona directly tied to what happens and how it happens in the poem. This poem is actually long enough that toward the end we come to anticipate how Kevin might turn a phrase.

So once we've created a persona and a voice, we have to remember to control it in a way that makes it sound natural. How do we do this? First we write from experiences that we know. We hear this all the time—our writing instructors have always told us this. One of the reasons for writing what we know is that we need a voice that is authentic. When we hear a voice speak a poem or tell a story, we as readers should not have to concentrate on the words. As Louis Simpson said, "The words of poems should become transparent." But this will only happen if the language use and the setting and the perception of the character(s) all fit together naturally. As writers, we need to know the difference between the reaction of the mother who has just gone through labor and then holds her baby and the reaction of the obstetrician who has helped deliver the child. This only comes from real experience. And the sense of knowing this real experience will be delivered in our own unique and fresh voice.

The Writer's Voice

The writer's voice? Surely there is such a thing. It has been tracked like elusive, hunted lions and finally bagged after an exhaustive search with experienced guides. Maybe. We've all heard people talk about "when they came into their voice" and "I think I'm really developing a voice." But what does that all mean? Does it mean we should be able to sit down with passages in front of us and identify, without title or name, poets and their poems? Possibly. But let's not forget that the early work of a poet may sound awfully different from the middle and then the late work of a poet. The reason for this is that language use changes over time. On one hand, as individuals we have adopted very distinct ways of using language. But because our views of the world change as we age, grow, mature, develop, our language use also changes slightly. My best advice is this—don't try to sound any given way, just write things the way you might tell things to someone. Take to heart William Stafford's old maxim of *use the language you know*—maximize the gains and minimize the losses and you'll be all right.

This technique of writing the way we might tell someone something and using the language that we know, brings us back to that good old technical term, diction—word choice. I often find that students have an idea of their own language use which is something like this. There's the language you speak and the language you write. In the language you speak, there are all sorts of types—slang you speak with friends, a more standard polite language reserved for work or school or more conservative public occasions, and language with family. And in the written language, there is a formal type of writing for essays and research papers (this has short sentences, big words, sometimes many quotes, and never seems individually identifying) and a more informal type of writing for letters to friends or family, shopping lists, notes left on the kitchen table, and e-mail. I say, bring all of this closer together. Why have such a broad spectrum of language use? To me, it seems daunting to keep it all straight and pull out the appropriate one at the appropriate time. I say, elevate the level with which you speak to family and friends, abandon the myth of short sentences and big words in academic papers (that just breeds bad writing) and begin to create a way to express your views about the world which is largely the same whether you're writing or speaking. This way, you have one language you know well and are familiar with. Hence, when you write, you will not be searching a bed of language you don't know well or using a language based on the big-word myth.

Does this mean that if you do this you'll develop a voice and then someone might be able to identify your poems without name or title? Well maybe, but not necessarily. And, it's not that important that someone be able to identify your poems anyway. Some poets argue that if identification can take place, then the writer has stagnated and become stale. So it means that the voice you create as a writer comes from the way you express the world and fashion language. Voice is in the way we construct sentences and put word combinations together. It lies in original language use and it's as simple as the way two friends might choose to describe the same scene differently. When we create an image in a poem, we choose certain words because of who we are and where we're from and this combination helps create the force of our language.

The poet William Butler Yeats said that a poet's words have to be wedded to the natural figures of his or her native landscape. This is a concept that is not too difficult to understand on one level. Consider regions and their accents and their expressions—the way someone from Texas may say something versus someone from Columbus, Ohio. Certainly, the way in which we form expressions and phrases and our word choices are based on where we're from, what we've heard, and how we've heard language used. And because this helps create our perspective on the world, it also helps shape our voice in writing. It becomes the foundation for the way we express ourselves.

Essay by Kevin Stein

VOICE: WHAT YOU SAY AND HOW READERS HEAR IT

No aspect of poetry writing is more fundamental to the art—and yet more thorny to define—than *voice*. Critics give us a slew of technical terms meant to delineate subtle shades of difference in how poets use and readers respond to, voice. Poets, on the other hand, speak of it in hushed tones tending to beatify the mysterious process of "finding your voice." In truth, most poets own little idea of how they came to find the voice their readers recognize immediately as those poets' own, as distinctly James Wright's, or Anne Sexton's, or Frank O'Hara's. The usual bromides—read widely, write daily, risk daringly—seem just that: meaningless patter meant to keep the learner in the proverbial dark. Still, the good news, and the bad, is that finding one's voice really is a long trip in an ill-tuned Yugo, a journey that asks poets to read, write, revise, and to think about writing and think about thinking about writing.

What is voice? Well, I'll avoid hairsplitting technical terms in favor of simplicity: Voice is the way you, the poet, speak a poem. Of course, such a seemingly simple thing as how you speak a poem involves a gaggle of choices and decisions, some of them conscious and some of them not. Most folks will agree that voice involves two basic components: (1) *subject matter*, that is, what you choose to talk about in the poem, thus, what matters to you and just as importantly, how and why it's come to matter, and (2) *tone,* how you feel about the specific subject of the poem and your audience, as well as how you feel about yourself and the world in general. Big stuff, to be sure.

One helpful way to consider such an unwieldy subject is to appreciate the beautiful duality of the term *voice*. When we think of voice, we most often fall upon the literal sense of the word—the actual physical and auditory sense of spoken voice and language. Still, poets concern themselves equally, if not more, with the metaphorical sense of voice: what poets talk about in a poem, the language they use, their attitude toward the world and their place in it. When you've read enough poets, you'll find yourself able to identify a poem you've never heard simply by paying attention to these issues of subject matter and tone: "Oh," you'll say, "there's Dickinson again contemplating death in her short, tight line," or "There's another Sharon Olds poem openly grieving her father's death with strangely lush, almost sensual language." You'll *hear* a poem the way you *see* an unfamiliar painting, one so obviously cubist it must be Picasso's. In fact, most of you already do this with popular music. You know halfway to the chorus the song's by Mellencamp or Marley or Madonna. At first the sound of the voice may clue you, but after a while you notice the consistency of subject or attitude, the kinds of things the singer chooses to sing about and his or her feelings about those things. Maybe something similar has already happened to you. Say you've shown friends a new poem, and they've remarked, "Oh, that's just like you to write about your trip to Europe by gushing about Italian waiters and the erotics of foreign toiletry." If so, you've begun to develop and to exhibit a personalized sense of subject matter and tone.

Now, keep in mind this voice your poem presents needn't always be your personal voice, laden with your own opinions and concerns. It need only seem believably human and real, like that of a real person speaking about matters that concern him or her. You can always concoct a *persona* or mask and thus speak the poem as if you were Winston Churchill, Nelson Mandela, or your own mother. Why not, for that matter, violate the very rule I've set down above, and speak the poem as someone or something not human but surprisingly close to it—perhaps Mr. Ed, the talking horse of television sitcom fame?

Above all else, a poem's voice establishes a relationship among speaker, poem, and reader. Readers respond to speakers—and thus to poems—that convey an urgency in the way they talk. Readers want to believe speakers have something meaningful to say to them, and they respond most passionately to speakers who do so using memorable language, image, emotion, and thinking. More than anything else, a poem's voice—its subject and tone—determines how readers feel about the speaker and in turn how they feel about the poem. This accounts for advice such as Aristotle gives writers in his *Rhetoric*. There, Aristotle urges prospective writers to make readers care about them as humans, to display aspects of *ethos* and *character* in their work that will encourage readers to admire them as persons and thus to be more likely persuaded by their arguments. The poet W. B. Yeats, however, distrusts this notion of rhetoric applied to a poem. He suggests that while rhetoric is an argument with another person, true poetry is an argument with the self.

How then to make a poem's voice cause readers to feel they are witnessing, and perhaps partaking in themselves, a passionate argument with the self? How to make a voice so authentic readers believe the speaker bristles with humanity, the electric mix of flaws, foibles, and desires we recognize as human? How do you make readers succumb to an experience very much like falling in love with a voice on the telephone? You know, the person never seen or touched who exudes such vibrant energy readers easily imagine eyes, lips, hair, the curve of waist and thigh, laughter supple and intelligent.

One way to learn to do so is by trying on other poets' voices, as poet Theodore Roethke suggests in "How to Write Like Somebody Else." Roethke believes poets come to find their own peculiar voice by trying to learn to speak a poem in the manner of great poets. Read widely, the story goes, and finding a poet you like, try to mimic that poet's subjects, language, and form. One month W. H. Auden, the next Gwendolyn Brooks or John Donne. Try to discover what it is that makes that poet so unique, so distinguishable from others. None of these voices, of course, will fit you like your favorite pair of jeans. Your voice, like those jeans, is something unique fashioned by wearing it over time. With effort and faith, you'll gradually abandon or subsume those other voices as you shape your own.

Not everyone, however, agrees it's literally possible to "find" your voice. Philip Levine, for instance, thinks young poets spend altogether too much time worrying about this quest. "I never tell younger poets to find their own voice because I don't believe that's how voice comes to us. Once a poet discovers what his material is, his voice will come to him. The best thing is to practice good writing until you've got something to say so urgent it's got to be said. . . . I don't think anyone ever found his own voice; it found him." Find first what you *must* talk about, Levine argues, and your voice will come along in the bargain.

What makes the matter of voice so frustrating is the simple fact that it can't be taught. Your teacher might be able to give you exercises to sharpen your use of metaphor or image, for example, but no teacher I know can lead you to your voice by dint of classroom assignment. Voice isn't a technique, a trick, or even a skill. It's nothing less than the way you feel about yourself and your world, all that music plucked through the strings you choose to speak those feelings and ideas. Voice is individual and unique, a fingerprint in language. Voice speaks the world through your lips, and hearing it, readers understand it is yours and yours alone.

Here's a poem by a student of mine, Scott James. As you read it, look for spots where the poem springs alive, where a quirky and original voice is heard. Look for the human in the human words:

Exhale

I've got volumes of myself
stored back in my silences,
devoured by pyromoments
of misguided release.
I like the warm feeling   5
when I smile with my whole face,
skin that compresses into my eyes,
but the whole white picket grin
stands before a crude house,
and the distances that cower   10
are scars on skin.
I like stars behind clouds
that appear for blinks
then fade to aftertaste.
They say truth comes   15
through drunkenness,
our inhibitions demolished,
but I'm always sorry for something
when the sun returns.
I like clean socks.   20
They just feel good,
cotton and all, soft
and unaware
of the mouth they carry
or the mind it hides.   25
I guess I lie on greenish grass
six feet away

from "the other side."
My mouth
a six-pack away from honesty.   30

SCOTT JAMES

   The poem moves lithely through a series of revelations disguised as
friend-to-friend chatter, reader sitting on the grass sharing the moment
with the contemplative speaker. The speaker begins to talk about his shyness punctuated by "pyromoments" of things spoken that shouldn't
have been said. What follows, though, is a litany of some things the
speaker likes in this world he also pointedly distrusts: how his sweet
"white picket" fence smile hides a house of crude scars, for instance.
Then the speaker, probably drinking a beer and smoking a cigarette (see
the title, "Exhale"), swerves toward the apparent subject—how when
one is drunk such false fronts always collapse into the rubble of day-after
apologies.
   That's enough to make an interesting poem, but note how the
speaker allows his mind to follow its own path. The wonderful line about
liking "clean socks" comes seemingly out of nowhere, and its surprise
sweetens the pie. Sure, we've all thought something similar while
pulling on our socks in the morning, and thus we laugh and agree but
ask, "What does this have to do with lying?" Then the socks become
associated with the speaker's mouth and mind, and their apparent purity
is besmirched. Can nothing in this world be trusted? Is nothing innocent
really what it appears to be? Not even clean socks? The poem's subject
matter becomes expansive, far reaching, and troubling—this, suddenly is
no simple poem about the intersection of shyness and drunkenness.
When the poem concludes with a nod toward the grave, we readers get
the notion the speaker believes there's nothing trustworthy in this flawed
world. Take a breath, Dear Reader, and "exhale" at the news.

                                    *   *   *

Exercise

Often, after reading a poem we particularly enjoy we say to ourselves, "I wish I had written that poem." When we hear ourselves say
this, then we need to write the poem. What's happening is that we're
recognizing our idealized voice. So, capture it. For example, if you
read James Wright's "Lying in a Hammock . . ." and thought, "That's
the poem I want to write," then you need to sit down and write it.
Doing this will help you exercise your poetic skills in the voice you'd
most like to have.

POINT OF VIEW IN POEMS

One of our responsibilities as poets, writers of any sort, is to avoid beating up on people with language—they get that enough in the day-to-day world. We need to be honest in the way we come at things. Now that doesn't mean we can't alter our experiences or tell half-truths—as long as they represent our real experiences, we're all right. What I'm talking about is tricking the readers, deceiving them, making them believe something they shouldn't. Raymond Carver used to say, "At the first sign of a trick, I'm running for cover." So it's up to us to capture our experiences and relay the intellectual and emotional power behind them so that the readers feel they have experienced the world in a real and honest way. But how? By creating a speaker who can convey experience powerfully.

Now we've already talked about this speaker, the **persona**, and he is the one who takes on the point of view in a poem. The **point of view** is the stance taken by the persona, the attitude, and the view of the world he imparts to the reader. Along with this stance and attitude comes the **tone**—the emotional sense behind the voice of the persona. And without a clear and defined point of view in a poem we can lead the reader—and sometimes ourselves as writers—right into a murky swamp of problems. The readers may not understand who the speaker is. They may not understand why the persona happens to be the one narrating

And you've got to hear voices, from wherever they come. Sometimes I guess my own voice is coming in different kinds of ways, and I have to trust that there is something there.

Sekou Sundiata

the experience; this confusion usually comes from a problem in the relation-ship between persona and place or experience. This persona needs to fit into the context of the poem so that it seems real. Remember, no tricks. Let's take a situation. A white man and a Native-American woman walk into a restau-rant in, say, any rural area near where you live. They are hungry and want to have breakfast. They wait at the chrome-framed sign that says "Please Wait to Be Seated." No one comes to seat them. There are only two tables in the place being served. The rest are empty. Finally, the man says to the host, "Can we just go ahead and sit down?" The host glares a little and then comes up next to the white man and says—"We don't serve your type here." Thoughts race. What exactly does he mean? *Her* type or *our* type? O.K., he's a racist. Let's beat the hell out of him. What do we say? The couple leaves, and as they do, the waitress gives them a sympathetic and pleading look like "I'm so sorry; he's a horrible man."

All right, there's our situation. Now, we want to write a poem about it. First we have to decide how the story should be told. Should it be first per-son (I/me), second person (using "you" and addressing some other being seemingly reading the poem), or third person (he/she). Of course it could be third person limited, in which our narrator knows only limited details about what's happened or it could be omniscient, in which the persona/narrator knows all—maybe even knows that this man did the same thing only half an hour earlier. So let's say we decide on first person. Now, we have one more consideration, and this is an important one. Who should be the persona—the man, the Native-American woman, or the waitress? Examining this question will show us how the persona, the experience, and the context of place and time all help to build the evocative power of a poem. And remember, we have a different poem for each person in this situation. For years, the waitress has seen this man act this way. The white man is stunned and hasn't experienced either the man or the depth of racism and oppression the women have, espe-cially the Native-American woman. But he's empathic and in a relationship with her. The Native-American woman, on the other hand, has seen it before, can't stand it, wants to collar the white man, but has enough control from having endured it before to walk right out the door. All of these points of view bring up very different emotional and intellectual stances in the poem.

What comes of all this? We need to remember that our persona is the spokesperson for the psychological reality that plays out in the poem. And in this psychological reality, the kernel of the poem is delivered. This is the way the truth of the poem is handled and it needs to be handled well. Needless to say, in this example there is a different truth for each possible persona. As the poet we need to decide what truth it is we want to tell, what truth it is we know best, and what truth we can best show the reader. Outside of showing and telling the experiences, we need to remember that choosing the right point of view for the right experience lends itself to fresh insights and some surprise for the reader—provided we adhere to the Carver maxim and don't surprise the reader with tricks. For instance, we all probably expect the poem to be told from either the man or woman's point of view. The least expected point of view is the waitress's. But maybe that's the freshest poem. Provided we can evoke the depth of experience we want from her, then we have a fresh approach.

I had a student who wanted to write a whole series of poems about the Korean war. Well, he decided he'd write them from different points of view, mostly from the points of view of different soldiers he had encountered or read about. But then came a twist. He started writing poems from the mother's point of view back in Nebraska, and the point of view of the sister of one of the soldiers who lived in Winnemucca, Nevada. And it turned out that these were the most riveting poems. We had a sense of expectation—and it was achieved—in the poems from the soldiers. But the poems from the family members were unexpected and a little closer to many readers' realities because of their domestic quality. And there came a change in tone. And the change in tone and expressiveness in the stance of the persona became something we all attached to in the workshop.

When we decide who tells our poem, when we listen to the voices coming through to us, our inner voices and those of our characters, we need to pay close attention to them. We need to choose the voice that can express our moments in ways that are natural and honest—the voice that recreates the world so that what was once private to us becomes a shared and sensational moment for the reader. We need to pull the reader down the throats of our speakers and into their hearts.

Essay by James Hoggard

POINT OF VIEW IN POETRY

Understanding point of view is as important for writers and readers of poetry as it is for those concerned with prose fiction. In fact, the first thing a writer or reader of a poem should probably do is ask three simple questions: Who is the speaker of the piece? What physical or psychological situation is the speaker in when making the statement? Is there a notable connection between the situation the speaker is in and the subject he or she is talking about? If we begin with these questions, we can avoid some serious misreadings that come about when one mistakes the speaker for the poet; we can also see more clearly than we would otherwise the attitude and circumstances that guide the narration. A prominent example to illustrate this idea is Robert Browning's dramatic monologue "My Last Duchess," whose murderous, self-centered speaker represents the opposite of what Browning considered heroic and good. If we begin the poem assuming that the speaker is Browning himself, we seriously misread what the poet is doing. Poets, we should remind ourselves, have been storytellers at least as often as they have been direct singers of sentiment and opinion. Because of that, they are as inclined as short-story writers, novelists, and playwrights to use voices other than their own; and the range of voices available to all of us is as broad as the sweep of our imaginations.

In lyric poetry, that form of speech that most prominently filters the world through self—or *a* self—the first-person point of view is most common. The narrator refers to him- or herself as "I." Whether the speaker represents the poet or someone else, the narration's point of view is guided (and limited) by the speaker's perception. An interesting example of the first-person point of view is seen in Renée Klein's poem "Before Bed." An undergraduate student when she wrote the piece, the poet here is using the convention of direct quotation. In this work a child speaks to his (or her) parent, more than likely the mother, before going to sleep:

Does broccoli float in a glass of milk?
Is a tree a house for leaves?
How many stars in Infinity?
I love you five hundred and three.

Can I go down the bathtub drain?   5
Does Jesus make the crickets sing?
What do cats dream when they're asleep?
I love you five hundred and three.

The child says the entire poem and the poet says nothing directly. Certainly at times the child's speech resembles chattering as much as serious questioning, but that is appropriate because the poet here is conveying the personality of the narrator, in this case a child who, while delightfully expressing his love for the parent, cleverly uses delaying tactics to keep the parent around.

In poetry as well as in fiction, the second-person point of view is rare, most likely because it creates an odd effect in the narration. That also makes it intriguing. For example, instead of having the narrator say:

Running against the wind again
I keep thinking about you
and can't stop wondering why
you quit coming by

the poet would have the narrator say:

Running against the wind again
you keep thinking about her

and can't stop wondering why
she quit coming by.

In an interestingly illusory way, the reader becomes the narrator, and the effect this point of view has, when sustained, can be eerie. A curious tension is stirred in the reader. Perhaps the best-known work that uses the effect extensively is Carlos Fuentes' novella *Aura*. Being told that *you* are doing this and *you* are doing that, the reader of the work quickly feels disjointed, but that's appropriate and even useful because the reader has the same disconcertingly narrow range of understanding that the main character has. During a conversation I had with Señor Fuentes several years ago, I asked him why he had turned to the second-person point of view, and he said, "Poets have been using it a long time. I thought I'd try it in fiction."

The third-person point of view can take one of two forms, the limited or the objective. In the third-person *objective* point of view, the writer records surfaces without going into the mind of a character or narrator. Connotations of detail and phrase can, of course, suggest internal attitudes, but in this mode the writer maintains a distant stance, as we see in another poem by Renée Klein:

Mariya's Geese

KRYM, UKRAINE

Mariya Gerasimenko herds her geese,
guiding them to market
with her simple branch broom.
The goslings toddle with their heads down,
searching for grain and bugs,   5
while the large geese blare in protest
and Mariya urges them on,
"Tega, tega, tega."

RENÉE KLEIN

Keeping us at a distance from the character's internal concerns, the poet gives us a vivid image that suggests an ancient way of life; and even though the poem closes with a term from a language that is most likely foreign to the reader, the ending simultaneously emphasizes our closeness to the observed event and our cultural detachment from it.

The third-person *limited* point of view, however, allows a more direct presentation of internal concerns, as we see in another poem by Ms. Klein, "Behind the Screen Door," in which, while presenting the experience primarily from the outside, the poet's use of vocabulary—"She notes" (l. 4), "a merry cacophony" (l. 8), and "She . . . sleeps for tomorrow" (ll. 13-14) among others—takes us into the character's mind.

Her ancient hands rest
on the splintering divider
of the balding screen door.

She notes that the nests in the tree
have emptied and are tattered.   5
The trunk is adorned with cicada shells.

The crickets used to sing for her,
a merry cacophony of strings.
Then autumn arrived
and left her alone.   10

Sunrise
Sunset
She hangs up her cardigan
and sleeps for tomorrow.

RENÉE KLEIN

The omniscient point of view, which allows a narration to reveal internal responses of the various characters in a scene, is rarely used for several reasons. For more than a century, psychology has reminded us that we are all limited in our ranges of perception; none of us has direct access to the thoughts and feelings of others unless they reveal them to us. So a work told from an omniscient point of view might not be believable to readers or listeners. The omniscient point of view also tends to scatter a work's focus. If a narrative slips into the internal responses of various characters, the story's point of concern may blur and thus diminish a reader's involvement with the work. A version of the omniscient point of view, however, can be used effectively in relatively long works, or others made up of numerous sections. In novels or long poems, for instance, a writer might tell different sections from different points of view, as T.S. Eliot does in "The Waste Land." Usually, though, one would not mix different points of view within a single section.

    The speaker of a piece, then, is the reader's immediate guide through an experience, that personal voice that brings portions of the world before us. At the same time that we see those images and hear ideas associated with them, we need to remember that we are not seeing the world directly; we're seeing it through the filter of a character. It's important, then, to recognize the situation from which the narrator is speaking. In Dylan Thomas's great poem "Fern Hill," for example, the narrator is describing the magic of the farm where he spent time as a child, but the incantatory quality of the language he uses, as well as the conceptual organization of his phrases, indicates that he is speaking years after the fact; the images and situations he recalls are not seen directly when they occur but through memory. Thomas even lets us know that the act of writing itself is the method by which the narrator is recalling the past. We see this most directly in the last stanza, which begins:

Nothing I cared, in the lamb-white days, that time would take me
Up to the swallow-thronged loft by the shadow of my hand,
In the moon that is always rising

During the act of writing, as his phrases indicate, he notices the shadow under his hand, that shadow being a metonymic emblem of the act of writing itself. An idea like that is important because it reveals a context for the statements made by the narrator, and that context itself often reveals the terms of a drama. Keeping all of these matters in mind—speaker, dramatic situation, point of view—we become increasingly alert to the layers of a presentation, and we see the poem itself as a story whose narrative stance is both motivated and modified by the point of view from which the poem is told or said. Becoming more alert to that, we become more sensitive as well to the truth noted by the late Nobel laureate Octavio Paz in his book *The Bow and the Lyre:* "Every word implies two persons: the one who speaks and the one who hears" [35].

Exercise

Create a situation or take a past situation you were in. Analyze all the different possibilities for speakers in a poem: who ought to tell the poem. Then write the poem from that point of view. Then rewrite the same poem from a different point of view and notice how significantly changed the poem is.

chapter eight

FIXED FORMS: CREATING OUR POETIC WORLD

I am more and more fascinated by the idea of form as creation or fiction of a universe, as a way of "knowing" the real universe. Form as a mode of participation in the real. It is not only in order to participate in the universe but also to participate in the self.

Robert Duncan

Form in poetry is something that can be very difficult to work with. But at the same time, it is one of those things that once engaged in can bring a great amount of satisfaction and knowledge. It seems to me that the thing I hear most about form from students is that trying to write in a fixed form of poetry—say a sonnet or a villanelle—does nothing but inhibit their creativity. And generally I agree. But I agree not because I think form itself inhibits creativity, but because many people try formal writing at a time when they aren't yet comfortable with it. They try to adapt their work to the form rather than adapt the form to their work.

Take the process of cooking. I cook and I love it. It's important to me to eat well and since I can't afford to hire a cadre of chefs, I need to know how to cook well. But I'm an entrée and sauce guy and always have been. I've spent time learning how to clarify butter for sauces to accompany quail breast or chicken. So when a friend asked me to bring a pie to party, I shuddered nervously and said I'd be happy to. After ruining one crust and then throwing another whole pecan pie across my kitchen—I know that sometimes it would give writers great pleasure to be able to heave the weight of a poem across a room—I finally half succeeded. Funny, but that was five years ago and it is only now that I have really learned how to make pie. But it didn't just come five years later; I've been making pies all these years. I've had the occasional master-piece of a pie, I've burned some, I've ruined some. But now I can make a pie. I learned by following form and learning the necessary fundamentals of pas-try baking and desserts. Now, I can get to creating in the kitchen.

Take for instance someone like the French poet Rimbaud, who seems not at all a formalist. But in breaking conventions, he circled round and round to fixed forms of poems. Take Picasso and his painting. Most people think of Picasso as a very abstract artist who did not necessarily adhere to fixed forms or formal elements of painting. But I marveled at his sketch books—espe-cially his early sketch books—in one of the rooms of the Picasso museum in Barcelona, Spain. He had books and books of sketches that were almost clas-sical in nature. Finely detailed portraits. Landscapes with the most minute and real details. Why? Because by understanding those fundamental rules that formed over the course of history, both artists were able to smash them later in their lives.

Understanding poetic forms can be a part of the creative process; and it is an engaging intellectual exercise which involves some memory. So it is important to approach fixed forms in poetry with an open mind and an abil-ity to laugh while also taking them seriously. You're going to need to be able to look at some of the poems you create and laugh at them. But don't throw them away, as they give a yardstick of improvement and may in fact have something quite worthwhile in them. What will come of working through fixed forms of poetry is the ability to see practically and creatively how some elements we've already spoken of come together in a very structured way. And, most importantly, we will see that form is something requiring all of our poetic attentiveness.

Start with something that seems easy. I'd suggest a limerick or a haiku. While I say they're easy, I mean only in relation to such other forms as the sonnet or sestina. We can move up to these. The haiku, for instance, was and still is a highly-refined and conscious art form. It attempts to express much but suggest even more in the fewest possible words. Hence the *haiku* uses seventeen syllables in three lines of five, seven, and five syllables respectively. So begin with this. Write a number of them. Spend an hour a day for three days doing them in the morning and see how many you come up with. Some of the Japanese masters wrote thousands of them. And, while writing the haiku, you'll see something else happen, something that was part of their practice. As you form these three lines, often with three images, maybe linked explicitly, but often implicitly because of the need to suggest so much, you will find yourself becoming more alert to the world around you. This nota-tion of what's around us centers us—and this was part of their practice. So you can see that as our quote at the beginning of the chapter suggests, engag-ing in form is participating in the self and the universe.

Now that you've tried your hand at some form by working with haiku, you might try something a bit more difficult—say the *sonnet*, sestina or villanelle. What is important to remember here is that while we may work these forms with the understanding that they are from hundreds of years ago, we need to remember that our language has changed. Since it has changed, we need to try to avoid becoming archaic in our diction and syntax. Rather, try to use the language you know—use the regular poetic language that you would use if you were working in free verse. What comes of this poetry is the type of contemporary twentieth-century formalism that has been exemplified by such poets as Mark Jarman and Stephen Dobyns in their sonnets.

While we have three major forms of the sonnet, you may like one more than the other. In her essay that follows, Lynn Hoggard discusses the structure of these three and how each develops in its form and content. Try them all and see how you do. Maybe you find your niche in the *Petrarchan sonnet*. But after you've tried writing all three, maybe you find that you blend the *Petrarchan* and *Shakespearean sonnets*. When writing initial drafts with these forms, try to remember two things—give yourself some breathing room constructing meter and keep slant rhyme in mind. These two things will help you get through a draft without getting hung up on the end of a line not rhyming exactly with the previous line. You can come back and work with the rhyme and meter. And I think it is important to avoid letting rhyme push you around. Elements need to work together—we need sound quality, rhythmic quality (meter), image quality, rhyme. That's tough, but prioritize which of these is most important and then choose your words. What the sonnet can show us wonderfully, is how textured a poem can be if we skillfully blend such things as rhyme, meter, a stanzaic pattern, and the qualities of image and other elements. And that is being truly creative.

If you decide to have a go at the villanelle, remember that this is a very strict form too. People like Elizabeth Bishop, Theodore Roethke, and Dylan Thomas have used it so well in our recent memory that it seems all else pales in comparison. At its best the villanelle can set up chant-like qualities which can be haunting and remarkably musical. But at its worst, as I have experienced many times, it can be monotonous and remarkably boring. As Ms. Hoggard points out, the trick is to have the key lines grow in their force and "then give a final, concluding punch." I would add, too, that it seems necessary to come up with interesting and creative lines as well. Without them the poem may fall flat and seem not to carry the weight we'd like. But it can be very hard to master this form in its traditional sense and capture the sense of language that is so incantatory. What Elizabeth Bishop (in her poem "One Art") and Julia Alvarez (in her poem "Woman's Work") show us is that this poetry can become highly stylized and very interesting when we use our natural, contemporary language and patterns of speech with (or against, as the case may be) this very traditional and tightly-woven form.

In many ways, the same goes for the sestina. Give the sestina a try. It may turn out to be a brain-twisting exercise for you, but it will no doubt help you appreciate the artistry behind coupling form and content. The structure of a sestina is technically difficult—a complicated play of words. The **sestina** is a poem comprised of six stanzas, each with six lines. And the poem finishes with a three-line stanza called an envoy. Hence there are always thirty-nine lines in a sestina. The last words of the first six lines of the poem are repeated as the end words of the following five stanzas, and all the words must be included in the envoy. It is a traditional Italian form that was used as a form for love poetry in the thirteenth century. So if you wish to be somewhat true to form, here's your chance to write a love poem. What seems most taxing about the sestina is making our word choices work in each stanza. Hence, diction is at the center of this form. And we not only need the words to fit, but we hope that the words fall into the other stanzas and lines in a very natural and meaningful way.

While you may feel a bit beat up after working on some formal poems, don't despair. With all of this practicing of form, you hopefully will come out on the other side having learned some things about the tradition of poetics and how elements and structure can enhance your work, not hinder it. We don't have beautiful houses or plates of food without builders and chefs knowing the form and function of all their elements. And whether we believe in the Big Bang and evolution or some higher deity and creationism, we can all marvel at the order in the universe and the remarkable order in our bodies; and we also marvel at the universe's ability to create and adapt. While we function within forms as poets, we must not allow our language to be owned by the form; rather, we create and adapt. The use of form should not be imposed on our poems but rather chosen as an accompaniment to our content and used to illuminate what it is we have to express—the discovery of our world and of our selves.

Essay by Lynn Hoggard

FORM IN POETRY

Why not let the poem flow however it chooses from the poet's imagination? Why box it into an artificial structure that can hinder its freedom and movement? The answer to these and similar questions regarding poetic form carries us inevitably to the nature of human creativity. We know that our universe has form and structure at every level—from the cosmic to the subatomic. As *homo sapiens* we are ourselves a form, distinct from bees, bears, and bulldozers, who tend to follow particular patterns of design and behavior. Our nature consistently pushes us to understand the forms around and within us; our acts of creation, like small imitations of our world, also have formal boundaries.

So form is important to us. But why have we loaded certain types of poems with such exceptional burdens, such as the breathtakingly complicated *sestina?* Can there be any reason for such complex structures other than sheer pyrotechnical display?

The answer, quite simply, is yes. The vast body of lovely, noble poems created in amazing complexity tells us that not only does form seem not to hinder the poet, it seems, at least some of the time, to inspire poetry to greater heights. The Italian Renaissance poet Petrarch, for example, wrote 366 poems to and about his beloved Laura, most of them in a sonnet form that came to bear his name.

If poetic expression differs from prose in that it tends to be more condensed and highly charged, then this expression, within a congenial form, can become even more intense and perhaps truer to the form-conscious nature of human experience. For the poet (as well as for the appreciative reader), the successful marriage of poetic impulse to form reaches an artistic pinnacle that shows how imagination and craft can join self (poetic impulse) to world (the forms we live in). The very best poems may not always be the most formally complex, but they are poems in which form and content most consistently sustain and enhance each other.

The limerick, for example—one of the simplest and most playful of poetic forms (an impression created by its anapestic [˘ ˘ ´] beat that jogs between dimeter and trimeter feet)—works best with a simple, jaunty subject matter that sometimes ends with a smart-alecky kick:

There was a young man from Laredo
who ate nothing else but potato;
he swallowed one down
then remarked with a frown:
"I prefer my potato *alfredo!*"   5

Poetic scansion shows the five-line rhyme scheme to be *aabba;* lines one, two, and five (that is, all the *a*'s) are, with some variation, basically anapestic trimeter, and lines three and four (the *b*'s), dimeter. The ensemble rocks along with the insouciance appropriate to humor and satire but alien to serious or searching reflection. Most importantly, however, content and form are joined.

Whereas the lighthearted limerick is closely allied to Irish popular culture, the haiku, another technically simple form, comes from Japan and is often spiritual and reflective (requiring 17 syllables divided into three-, five-, and seven-syllable lines; the haiku in English translation sometimes varies this pattern). In fact, at its deepest levels, the haiku harks back to Zen Buddhism and the work of a seventeenth- and eighteenth-century monk named Bashō. Haiku has no jaunty meters or rhymes. Usually, it has an image of nature (a crow, for example, settling on a branch) followed by the superposition of another image (an autumn nightfall), leading us to see one image in terms of the other. This delicate, surprising, and understated perception of oneness in nature happens because the haiku form shapes and sustains the images:

On a withered branch
a crow alights, then settles:
now, autumn nightfall.

English and American poetry have tended to prefer the iambic (˘ ´)
stress or foot in a five-stress (pentameter) line, although the iambic
tetrameter (four-stress) line is also popular, perhaps because these two
meters approximate more closely than others the rhythms of ordinary
English speech. The four-line stanza (or quatrain) has also become the
most common division of a poem into segments; rhyming variations on
the quatrain abound, but the most common are *aabb, abab, abba, xaya,* and
axay (in which *x* and *y* indicate nonrhyming lines).

Among the more complex forms of poetry that incorporate the quatrain, the most well-known is the sonnet—a term from the Italian *sonetto*
meaning a little sound or song. In English, the classic sonnet form is fourteen rhyming iambic pentameter lines. Variations in rhyme pattern
divide the sonnet into three major types—the Petrarchan (or Italian), the
Spenserian, and the Shakespearean—with each type suggesting its own
formal structure. A brief look shows how each works.

The Petrarchan sonnet comprises an *octave* (or eight-line sequence)
usually rhyming *abbaabba* and a *sestet* (six-line sequence) usually
rhyming *cdccdc* or *cdcdcd*. As the form indicates, the rhyme divides
between the *octave* and *sestet*, suggesting a division in thought as
well. That division, in fact, is what Petrarch emphasized in the example cited below, in which the persona in the *octave* expresses sub-
lime and undying love for Laura (a love that continued even after her
death), then, in the *sestet*, falls back to earth to assess a less-than-sublime
reality:

Those eyes I raved about in ardent rhyme,
the arms, the hands, the feet, the loving face
that split my soul in two, and made me pass
my life apart from all the common throng,
the tumbled mane of uncut gold that shone,   5
that angel smile whose flash made me surmise
the very earth had turned to Paradise,
have come to dust: no life, no sense. Undone.

And I live on, in sorrow and self-scorn
here where the light I steered by gleams no more   10
for my dismasted ship, wracked by the storm.
Let there be no more love songs! The dear spring
of my accustomed art has been drained dry,
my lyre itself dissolved in so much weeping.

This two-part structure, then, dramatizes a dialogue between opposites. In the Romance languages (including French, Italian, and Spanish), where rhymes are plentiful, the four-rhyme Petrarchan sonnet is less difficult than it is in English, which is a relatively rhyme-poor language. The Spenserian and Shakespearean sonnets, therefore, enlarged the English rhyming possibilities while also modifying the way the poem develops. The Spenserian (named for Edmund Spenser, the sixteenth-century poet who wrote "The Faerie Queen" in honor of England's Elizabeth I) has three loosely-interlocking quatrains (rhyming *abab, bcbc, cdcd*) followed by a rhyming couplet (*ee*). If content parallels form, we can assume a series of three loosely-connected thoughts followed by a terse summation, perhaps delivered with flair and wit.

The Shakespearean sonnet relaxed the sonnet form even more by breaking the linking rhyme among stanzas (*abab, cdcd, efef*); one could therefore choose whether to interrelate the stanzaic ideas while still keeping, of course, the airy panache of the concluding couplet.

Let me not to the marriage of true minds
Admit impediments. Love is not love
Which alters when it alteration finds,
Or bends with the remover to remove:
Oh, no! It is an ever-fixéd mark,   5
That looks on tempests and is never shaken;
It is the star to every wandering bark,
Whose worth's unknown, although his height be taken.
Love's not Time's fool, though rosy lips and cheeks
Within his bending sickle's compass come;   10
Love alters not with his brief hours and weeks,
But bears it out even to the edge of doom.
If this be error and upon me proved,
I never writ, nor no man ever loved.

SHAKESPEAREAN SONNET #116, *NAP*

Even more daunting than the sonnet are the French *villanelle* and the Italian *sestina*, used nevertheless with success in English by some of the world's most renowned poets (including Dylan Thomas, T. S. Eliot, and W. H. Auden). The villanelle contains five three-line units (call *tercets*) rhyming *aba*, followed by a quatrain (*abaa*); however, instead of simply rhyming end-words, the villanelle repeats the entire line, as indicated by the following schema (whose numbers indicate lines): *a(1)ba(2), aba(1), aba(2), aba(1), aba(2), aba(1)a(2)*. Notice that line one of the poem is also the last line of the second and fourth tercets and that line three is the last line of the third and fifth. Lines one and three also form the last two lines of the poem. The trick, obviously, is to have these lines grow in the course of the poem to mean slightly different things each time they recur, then give a final, concluding punch. Dylan Thomas's poem at his father's death is perhaps the best-known villanelle in English:

Do Not Go Gentle into That Good Night

Do not go gentle into that good night,
Old age should burn and rave at close of day;
Rage, rage against the dying of the light.

Though wise men at their end know dark is right,
Because their words had forked no lightning they   5
Do not go gentle into that good night.

Good men, the last wave by, crying how bright
Their frail deeds might have danced in a green bay,
Rage, rage against the dying of the light.

Wild men who caught and sang the sun in flight,   10
And learn, too late, they grieved it on its way,
Do not go gentle into that good night.

Grave men, near death, who see with blinding sight
Blind eyes could blaze like meteors and be gay,
Rage, rage against the dying of the light.   15

And you, my father, there on the sad height,
Curse, bless, me now with your fierce tears, I pray.
Do not go gentle into that good night.
Rage, rage against the dying of the light.

New Directions Paperbacks

The *sestina*, the most complex of the many forms used by medieval troubadours, contains six stanzas of six lines each followed by a conclusion or *envoy* of three lines. Each stanza includes the same six end-words, but in a constantly shifting yet fixed pattern (for example, the schema of end-words might look like this: 1. *abcdef*, 2. *faebdc*, 3. *cfdabe*, 4. *ecbfad*, 5. *deacfb*, 6. *bdfeca*, and as envoy, *eca* or *ace*, possibly with the *bdf* rhymes recurring internally in the envoy).

Much less complex is the folk ballad, which is a short narrative song usually in quatrains (*xaya*) in which iambic tetrameter lines (one and three) alternate with iambic trimeter (two and four). Ballad meter, also called common meter, is used in hymns as well as folk ballads:

The wind doth blow today, my love,
   And a few small drops of rain;
I never had but one true-love,
   In cold grave she was lain.

    . . . .

"The Unquiet Grave," *NAP*

Finally, we come to free verse. What relationship exists between the set forms discussed above and the seemingly unstructured poetry often written in America today? Doesn't this contemporary style actually involve the absence of form and a rebellion against the patterns of the past? The poems themselves yield interesting answers. Yes, there does seem to be a desire to "free" poetry from rigid obedience to set forms, but this move to freedom does not, in its better moments, abandon form. Rather than being set previously and externally, free verse is more individualized, more impromptu, and more organically part of its context. Abandoning strict patterns of rhyme and rhythm, free verse searches (as did many forms of ancient poetry) for line divisions based on rhythmic phrases, breath units, or syntactical possibilities and for assonance, alliteration, and internal or approximate rhyme rather than end-rhyme. In free verse, words, rich with relationships to one another and full of connotative aftershocks are extraordinarily charged with formal responsibilities. Throwing off external restraints, free verse grows its own form from within:

Let the snake wait under
his weed
and the writing
be of words, slow and quick, sharp
to strike, quiet to wait,   5
sleepless.

    . . . .

William Carlos Williams, "A Sort of a Song," *NAP*

PUTTING IT ALL TOGETHER: THE WHOLE POEM

When I was a third-year college student, I spent a year studying abroad in London. To this day it remains one of the most pivotal and important experiences in my life. I gained a sense of independence, learned how to adapt in new places and cultures, broadened my view of the world, and created friendships with people from around the globe. I learned from some seasoned experts the value of traveling and how to do it well. And now when I travel I like to experience the whole of a place as much as I can. I like to eat as much as I can of many different kinds of food. I like to drink the local wines. I enjoy hearing music from the region, seeing folk dances, talking to people, and sitting to watch people in a plaza. Shopping can be great fun, too. I try not to miss the museums and places of religious worship and I soak in the architecture. If I can, I fish in the area. I know this sounds ideal, maybe even a bit extreme. And it takes more than a few days. But when I leave, I feel I've had a chance to see the whole of a place, and that's important to me. A bad day of fishing on a chalk stream in England can be counteracted by the charm of nice people and a few good pubs. Or reverse this last statement. A few bad pubs and rude people can be counteracted by good fishing. So, the beauty of traveling comes from having the whole of a place represented.

It isn't much different when it comes to writing poetry. We've already talked about many parts

A carpenter, a builder knows what Ponderosa pine can do, what Douglas fir can do, what Incense cedar can do and builds accordingly. You can build some very elegant houses without knowing that, but some of them aren't going to work, ultimately.

Gary Snyder

of the poem as separate entities. But as we write a poem, these parts come together to form a whole. They work with and against each other. They brace each other the way beams on a house hold up the roof and they give us room to move around inside. For instance a poem, say fifteen lines long, narrative in style and only portraying a few images while trying to make a point, may seem to almost work. But ultimately it's like a house that has only been framed. We know from the street that it's a house. We can even walk through and see where the kitchen goes, where we'd sleep if we moved in, even where the toilets go. But, it's not finished. Add some sound quality with careful diction, some rhyme (maybe internal, maybe end-rhyme), a close attention to the rhythm of lines, a bit of metaphor and/or simile in the images and soon the house becomes walled in and filled with character that speaks to us. Add the poem's core experience (the triggering and real experiences maybe) and now we have a place where we can live—now we (the reader and the writer) have a home. This is what a poem ought to be. And in all of this metaphor about the house, let us not forget Hemingway's advice that the elements are not mere decoration and adornment, but the structural and the architectural integrity of our writing.

When putting together a poem, it's important to remember that the poem doesn't just piece itself together nor does it just come all at once as a package. As Naomi Shihab Nye states in one of her poems, "You can't order a poem like you order a taco." Maybe not, but you can build a poem like you build a taco. And that takes work. It takes moving through the initial process of homing in on that triggering subject, then following that into the poem, letting the poem turn you in different directions and coming out the other side with a draft of something to work with. Along the way, count on it, we've included some things like rhyme and line breaks which have added some resonance or depth or artistic quality to the poem. But then again, we've missed some too. So, that's when we head back to work on other parts. But the only way we can do this effectively is to know where and when and how the pieces fit. Take the following lines, for example, in a poem about a boy growing up and living on an almond orchard.

> I climbed them and knocked
> the skirts of blossoms to the ground,
> the sweet smell of trees.
> If I got caught, my dad lashed us
> like an old school teacher.   5

Well, there are some good things here. But this was a first draft and in our workshop we all told the student to go back and work on it some more because this was one of his better outings. So he and I talked over the poem and I told him to revise for his images, sound quality (maybe some internal rhyme), and line breaks. As you can see, he was well on his way. The poem started when he came to class one day saying "I think there is a poem in the almond orchard I grew up on." Of course, there's a book of poems hiding in the orchard. Here's what he came back with.

I climbed them and
skirts of blossoms danced
to the ground around the tree,
the scent of young girls made of smiles.
To be caught, a dry switch sharp as fire   5
lashed my leg, quick as the wing of a bird.

We were impressed with the revision, as he changed some things significantly, added new elements (note the internal rhyme and the end-rhyme), and revised his images to include similes. And the piecing together that really showed some thought was taking the father out and only implying that he was the one to lash the boy. While this was a case in point about the quality of revision, it also illustrated how taking the time to add the elements together could help strengthen the whole of something. In this case, he derived more resonance from the lines and more power from the images. After getting his subject down, he took the time go back and work in the rhyme. He told us in class that he wanted to include as many parts of poetics as possible, so he made a list and checked them off as he went. Of course that may sound like a funny approach, and in class we all had a good laugh with him. But let's face it, it worked.

What he did was what the fiction writer Ron Carlson calls "taking inventory." While Mr. Carlson talks about taking inventory in the first paragraph of a story to see what's there, what will come up again, what won't, what might, what's there that's unexpected, we can do the same with a poem. While writing poems, it's important to take stock of what you have included and what you haven't. In the above example, the writer knew the orchard images were coming. He knew his father was coming, although he didn't intend him to come out so mean. But the girls? Where did they come from? For our writer, that was an unexpected twist that he liked—we all liked it. So he took stock of it. That specific image of girls didn't work itself into any greater image or thread in the poem, but it did come out later as another poem. But then an inventory happened on another level which was what really caused the writing to gain steam. He asked what poetic elements he had included and what he hadn't—and this led to building more and more inside the poem. Asking ourselves what we've included is important. Listening to where the poem wants to go and facing that is important too. If we do both of these things we'll wind up building a poem in which the reader can live and experience the world.

Nuts & Bolts Advice

What follows is some advice that I've picked up while writing. It's all been passed on to me by other people, and I wish it had been given to me a long while back. But then, that's not how we get advice. Some of it has come as rules or maxims I apply to my own writing and some has come in the form of quotes, but all of it is intended to be helpful in building poems.

- You can't write a good poem without having a subject to write about.
- Don't try to achieve greatness—you'll be disappointed. And often, as Marianne Moore points out, "a result which is sensational is implemented by what to the craftsman was private and unsensational."
- A poem should have the appearance of having meant something to you when you wrote it.
- William Archer said, "We have literature when we impart distinctiveness to ordinary talk and make it still seem ordinary."
- Let's face it, love and poetry are linked. When we fall in love, we write poems. But as we make mistakes in our relationships, so do we foul up poems. We can write bad poems about good relationships and good poems about bad relationships. And we can fix both.
- Write your dreams down; they tell us a lot.
- Don't throw things away because you'll never know when you might need them. A line that seems bad today may seem useful tomorrow.
- Read your poems aloud—to roommates, to your parents, to siblings, to your kids. Read them to anyone who will listen, and you too should listen. If something is wrong with the poem, you'll hear it.
- Don't be afraid to change the *truth* in order to help a poem. You own the poem.
- Listen to your parents and grandparents; they have stories to tell and they're our link to the past.
- Write about the tragedy in your life and make it ours.
- Each time you feel yourself getting better and reaching a new level of competence, find a few elements of poetry you haven't used or tried before and use them as much as you can, even if you use them badly.
- I had a teacher who said "Never use more than one abstract in the first sentence (not line, *sentence*) of a poem." Be concrete.
- Why avoid rhyme? That would be like a trumpet player avoiding slurs or sixteenth notes or holding notes. Rhyme helps create music and rhythm in the lines as well as other things.
- Write regularly and be receptive to what comes. Know that some days you'll be good and others you won't. But if you do this, you won't have to wait for impulses or subjects to come—they will be there waiting for you to open the door. And even on days when it seems as if you haven't written a poem, you will have written possibilities.

These nuts and bolts are intended to be helpful pieces of advice for the building of poems. When we sit down to write, there is much to put together and much we need to be attentive to. Write, rewrite. Write, rewrite. That's the building process. Within that process, be creative and put together an approach that works for you. Take note of your voice and how you begin to sound in poems. Notice what kind of stamp you put on your poems—maybe you use internal rhyme regularly. Maybe your favorite thing is metaphor or alliteration or ambiguity. No matter, these are the components, the materials which build that house we spoke of earlier, which frame it, wall it in, give us room to move inside, give it character. In the long and short of it, build us into your life, mortar us into your experience, and paint us into your flesh so we see your world as ours.

Essay by Virgil Suarez

LORCA'S *DUENDE*, THE ART OF ZINGERS IN POETRY WORKSHOPS, OR HOW TO TEACH STUDENTS TO ENERGIZE THEIR POEMS

Federico Garcia Lorca, while writing *Poet in New York*, listening to jazz and blues in New York's night scene, and while studying English at Columbia University, theorized about what he termed "*Duende.*" In Spanish, *duende* has several translations, and the particular one I remember from my childhood is that of the *duende* being a gentle guide, a sort of gypsy of the countryside, not entirely bad or evil, simply a force to be recognized and nurtured. It is a certain charm, recognition of darkness and light, a deep feeling, whether melancholia or joy that comes to the poet, the artist, anyone who believes in craft. When you work on a poem from invention, through revision, to its final form, the *duende* will be there. For *Star Wars* fans, the *duende* is like The Force the wise Yoda reveals to Young Luke Skywalker.

Lorca means for "*duende*" to be a positive force, not only in the *cante jondo* music he so loved, but in poetry. Having grown dissatisfied with early Romantic theories of *cante jondo* as a form of popular folksongs as "impersonal, vague, unconscious creation," he set out to define clearly what he meant by "*duende.*" In his lecture on deep song, he states that "the difference between a good *cantaor* and a bad *cantaor* is that the first has *duende*, and the second never, ever achieves it."

Without *duende*, the poet is left empty-handed, his or her poems will be flat, uneven; in many cases not even a strict form can help. Nothing will without it. Young poets in poetry workshops always mention that moment of pure inspiration when only then can they sit down to write. With *duende*, the moment is always there if you learn to summon *duende* through hard work and know-how. Craft comes to the poet through practice, through developing skills. The beauty of writing poetry is always that deep sense of discovery, the twist along the way that can surprise us, awaken in us a tremendous sense of awe. As a young poet myself, I had very good teachers who recognized early on not so much the talent, but my ability to be open for the *duende's* influence. Through the act of writing every day, you learn to stay in touch with the *duende*. By writing ideas, brainstorming for possibilities, contemplating the world around you, paying very close attention to the small details, through layering, through the dynamics of word choice, sentence (line) structure, grammar, you cause the *duende* to arrive. The trick of everyday writing is to stay close with your *duende*.

If you think of *"duende"* as the equivalent to what we call "mojo," then you are closer to understanding the force that makes poetry cry out with distinctive energy, and what I would call zinger.

A simple formula to remember as a student of poetry is *duende* = (unknown + known) = zinger. Zinger is a word for word energy, word combinations that will make your lines so distinctive and clear, nobody could ever mistake them for someone else's. I think here of three poets who come quickly to mind: Charles Simic, Charles Wright, and Billy Collins. If you look at each of these poets' poetry, word by word, line by line, stanza by stanza, impact for impact, you will see that their poetry breathes newness, originality of thought, pure zinger! I also have two good poet friends whom I consider masters of the zinger: Juan Felipe Herrera and Ray Gonzalez. You couldn't, having picked up a poem by either of these two poets, mistake their work. Every word is chosen carefully, combined with others that are fresh, thought-provoking, that constantly move the poem and the reader to a new level of meaning and observation about things that matter in the world.

Later in the same essay, Lorca approaches a more formal definition of *duende*: "The *duende* is a momentary burst of inspiration, the blush of all that is truly alive, all that the performer is creating at a certain moment. The *duende* resembles what Goethe called the 'demoniacal.' It manifests itself principally among musicians and poets of the spoken word, rather than among painters and architects, for it needs the trembling of the moment and then a long silence."

We are to believe, based on this definition, that the poet is possessed by both possibilities: the trembling of moment and then a long silence. I teach my students that they can train themselves to "know" how to recognize those moments when ideas will grip them, hold them, and that if they don't learn to summon the *"duende,"* learn to trust it almost as a sixth sense, then they can never write poetry that matters, that lasts. I'm intrigued, I confess to them, by the process of writing poetry, the mystery of the act itself, if you will, when suddenly an idea for a poem strikes you, and you better act, sit down and write, sit down and listen carefully. I've always written from having paid close attention to those voices that suddenly speak in my mind.

The *duende* is a helpful guide. When the right mood or inspiration doesn't arrive, the *duende* can see the poet through. Once the student has learned how to tap into this source for ideas, for what is known or not known, then the poetry will come easier. The job of writing poetry is never easy or to be taken lightly. It is work, like any other, and in order to achieve a mastery, one needs all the help one can get.

The *duende* can be coaxed through intense meditation upon the act of writing, the act of creation or invention, through revision, mostly during these long stages of revision, and during the completing stages of a poem. I know a lot of good poets who have learned to call their *duendes* forth through their rich, distinct voices. They have been able to unify content, poetic voice, and technique into one, which whether or not they recognize it as such, I would call *duende*. Among contemporary singers, *duende* is easy to recognize. Billie Holliday had it. So did Patsy Cline. So did Janis Joplin. So does Aretha Franklin. Frank Sinatra had it. Tony Bennett has it. It is always easier to recognize *duende* in performance. The poet works behind the scenes. In the lonely light of a room. In silence and solitude. All the poet can do is create the poem, then let it stand on its own. If it has *duende*, it travels far. If it doesn't, it dies instantly.

One more aspect of the *duende* is its insistence on perfection, follow-through of technique, its stubborn need to craft a better poem. It might take you a long time to finish a poem, but if it is possessed by *duende*, the payoff is tremendous. In my conversations with my good friend, colleague, and fellow poet David Kirby, who writes very long narrative poems, I've learned that his *duende* is with him at all times. I have been with David Kirby when he's reached into his pocket to bring forth a little scrap of paper and a pen to write something down. I've learned to recognize the flashes of ideas in his eyes, and he acts on them quickly. He is also one of the most voracious readers I know. David Kirby reads everything, from biographies to travel guides, magazines, newspapers, lots of contemporary poetry, essays on craft, interviews, and all the literary journals he can get his hands on. The poet learns not only through writing, but through intense reading and contemplation.

At the beginning of every semester, I tell my students in the poetry workshop to keep a living, breathing (I'll explain more in a moment) journal, to observe life in the world as though they were social scientists. I encourage them to read magazines like *National Geographic*, *Time*, *Double Take*, *Orion*, and many other wonderful magazines that mix photography with articles and essays about other people, other cultures. About nature. I encourage them to collect How-To books, field guides, dictionaries like *The Facts on File Visual Dictionary*, which I received as a gift from my roommate when I was in college. He had a form of dyslexia that prevented him from remembering simple names for objects, and I fell in love with his copy because in it you can find practically everything. For example, when you look up rifle, which I had to do recently while working on a poem, it names the parts, the all-too-important parts that make up the whole of the rifle—*hammer, firing pin, breech, firing chamber, trigger, lever, stock, butt*, et cetera. I urge my students to keep their junk mail catalogues, which list gadgets, things that clutter our daily lives, but which might make interesting ideas for poems.

The more the students read, the better. I encourage them to start their own poetry collection of works by other poets, a neat shelf by their worktable or computer, to begin with those poets they like, admire, whose own poetry inspires, reveals, enlightens. In my case, I keep Pablo Neruda, Stephen Mallarmé, Mary Oliver, Pat Mora, Leroy V. Quintana, and many others quickly at hand. When I sit down to write a poem and I get stuck, I reach over and page through someone else's poems. You take a little in, and a little goes a long way. It's good to know how other poets craft their poems. I read interviews like those found in so many literary journals and magazines. Both *Poets & Writers* and *The AWP Chronicle* are excellent sources.

By keeping a journal, the student keeps track of thoughts, ideas; you can cut and paste things into it from newspapers and magazines. What I believe most students like about keeping a journal, is the individual feel it brings to the act of writing, taking notes, remembering interesting moments. So much of my poetry comes from things I've written down in my journal: seeds for ideas, titles, even particular lines that come to me in the middle of the night or, more often than not, while I am driving.

If the *duende* is the method by which we allow ourselves to be open to and keep track of good ideas, then my idea of capturing the zinger is the daily tool. When we begin to workshop poems in the classroom, I tell my students to circle all the most striking words, images, lines in their classmates' poems. This is a good way of isolating the specific from the general bulkiness of a poem.

For example, last semester one of my students wrote this poem:

Spirit Warrior of Wisconsin

The story goes that Kenny just vanished in the woods
north of Menomonee Falls, WI, when he was fourteen,
that spirits of old Menomonee Indians crept from the furrows
of tree-shadows, their graves, to claim him, retribution
for a village with McDonald's, Wal-Mart, and Denny's   5
overrunning their ancient land. After two weeks,
the police stopped searching and it became local legend,
every missing softball at the park or MIA kitty was Kenny's
fault, now a junior Indian spirit warrior, indoctrinated

into a culture long-dead, his body tucked under mossy   10
logs and rotting like fruit left out too long in the sun, never
to be found again. When I was twenty-three, I saw Kenny
in Tampa, on a Carnival cruise ship heading to the Bahamas
on a three day turn-around. He dealt blackjack at the neon
glitz casino and served pina coladas during the midnight   15
variety show. The last night, he brought me a free whiskey
sour and asked how his parents were, and could I tell them
that he was okay, that he was just young and foolish
and didn't mean to hurt anyone? I said yes, but never breathed
a word to anyone. Some legends are meant to live, and I wanted   20
Kenny's soul awake on the mouths of children to come,
generations of kids who would fear the dark, the deep quarry
shadows, always wondering if Indian spirits stalked them,
war spears feathered and ready, longing again for bloodwork.

RYAN VAN CLEAVE

Obviously this is a poem from a more advanced student, but one that can get the workshop thinking in terms of zingers, those interesting words and lines that can be mined for energy and originality. A poem like this is always a good place to start, a poem that tells a story, not that they are the easiest, but they get a narrative started. It gives the poet (and reader) the sense that it has a beginning, middle, and end.

The analogy I use to introduce the idea of revision with a poem like this is the story of how I went out and bought a Sears lawn tractor, and how when asked by the salesperson what diameter blade I wanted I said the smallest, which baffled the salesperson because they are used to getting the right answer, which is bigger, and wider. The less time on the tractor to cut two acres, the better. With me, it is the other way. I opted for a smaller blade diameter because I enjoy mowing my lawn. I cut it every other Saturday. It's the rhythm of the cutting, the back and forth, the circling around each tree on my property, much like what happens when I write, then revise, my poems.

The student of poetry needs to realize that simply sitting down to write a first draft is not enough. As good as each word may be, as inventive as the idea, as energized as each line may sound, feel, a first draft is only a beginning. Like my riding a lawn tractor and cutting grass, the student needs to learn to ride through his or her poem time and time again. Slowly. Paying close attention to every word on every line.

I call this layering, this act of the back and forth. When I look at my lines or the lines of my students' poems, I like to isolate them. I often cut a rectangular window out of another piece of paper, wide enough for a single line to peek through, and I move the window down as I read. I isolate the lines, read them one at time, pointing out what my expectations as a reader and writer are for the previous and subsequent lines. It's a good method to help imagine what is likely to come before and after each line. I did this with the student poem I've chosen to discuss here.

"Spirit Warrior of Wisconsin" is a very strong beginning. I like the idea immediately that the poet is going to tell us a story, that there are very specific details, names of places, popular culture infused early on. There are also interesting word combinations like "furrows of tree-shadows," "blackjack at the neon glitz casino," and "awake in the mouths of children,". . . . And the poem turns unexpectedly for the better when the voice in the poem tells us that "I saw Kenny in Tampa, on a Carnival cruise ship heading to the Bahamas." This is a most welcome twist, one that I use to remind everyone in the class of the possibility of *duende.* One problem remains though. A problem with fact. Yes, poets are also responsible for verisimilitude and accuracy of fact. Carnival cruises don't leave for the Bahamas from Tampa. It's closer from Miami. I was able to bring this out simply because of personal experience. It sounds nit-picky but we want the poem to work at all the levels here. It is only when everything sounds and is right, that we breathe life into the poem. But the twist in the poem is extremely effective. This is precisely the kind of twist that knowing and trusting our individual *duende* can be illuminated in our poems.

There are times in the poem when the language gets a little tired, overused, like "fruit left out too long in the sun," "some legends are meant to live," and "local legend." They bring a chatty quality to the poem that's not necessary. I think the poem works best at the level of surprise and discovery. Things happen because they are possible in the world of this poem, and in our world as well. The fact that Kenny disappears, never to be heard from again is an interesting challenge to pull off, not only in the poem, but in real life. It is an interesting question. Can someone simply disappear one day and never be heard of or from again? Sure, it happens in America every day. When it happens in this poem, it awakens a sense of interest in us: the possibility that, like in real life, someone can walk away. Then the poem takes a leap into new territory. You could argue that the voice is as surprised as the reader by this "setup" of finding Kenny dealing blackjack on a cruise ship. Even the brief exchange between the persona of the poem and Kenny is an interesting turn because, why not? Kenny should come back; he should speak. That he asks the persona to tell his parents that he, Kenny, is okay, is good. The part about being young and foolish is not needed in the poem. I urged the student to cut that out.

Another important point is the connection between what happens to Kenny and the persona's recognition that "Some legends are meant to live, and I wanted Kenny's soul awake in the mouths of children to come...." This is what the poem is about, but it is written in an extremely flat and too-straightforward a fashion. The zinger needs to be discovered, a way by which the last three or four lines of the poem can be reenergized. Ending lines need to be as interesting as the beginning lines that beckon or hook the reader. I like "deep quarry shadows" and "war spears feathered and ready." These are interesting images, or image constructions, but the poem doesn't end correctly. "Longing again for blood-work" doesn't leap at us the way a strong zinger line ending should.

I almost wish the poem ended with a strong realization about the connection between the persona's desire for the universal and Kenny's sudden departure. This is what happens to people alive in the world—people who on a daily basis walk away because of a job in another state, because they go off to college, because they get married, because of madness, because of a crime—people can disappear. Vanish. This is a powerful idea for the poem. This can be a strong connection. Death makes us aware of what happens to people, though the debate still rages in terms of whether they go to a place called heaven or simply return as fertilizer to the earth. Regardless, the poem should end with a flash of recognition for these things.

The *duende* doesn't come fast, or cheap. The student must learn through daily discipline and work to coax it to come and stay. Many contemporary American poets are witness to the power of the *duende* in their poetry. Great readers know of the *duende* in poetry they like because they can recognize it on every line, every page. It's what brings them to the poetry of so many wonderful poets like Adrienne Rich, Sonia Sanchez, Alberto Ríos, Quincy Troupe, and countless others.

May the *duende* be with you, too.

chapter ten

REVISION

I grew up fishing with my grandfather. When I was very young and we fished together, I couldn't bait a hook, tie a leader, or put on a lure without him checking my work. And it's only now that I really recall how much he did check my work. This didn't bother me; I learned from it. He was an artist with a tackle box, and I considered him a master. He could rig lines, tie knots, bait hooks, weight lines, release fish, and clean fish with amazing grace and patience and elegance. He was better than anyone I knew. So when he checked my work, I watched and either got his approval or I got a lesson in doing it better and then did it again. This was revision at its finest. And it was my earliest lesson at how to go about revising.

Those of us who find life bewildering and who don't know what things mean, but love the sound of words enough to fight through draft after draft of a poem, can go on writing—try to stop us.

Richard Hugo

Since then I've learned a thing or two about revision in my life and specifically, how to revise my writing. Moreover, I realize that there's not a process we engage in that we don't revise. We are constantly revising. When we cook, we give the sauce a taste to see what it's missing before we serve our guests. When we mow the lawn, we go back and get the long spot in the middle that we missed on the first pass. When we raise children, we go back and assess how effective we were in praising or scolding. When we go out on a date, the next day we always say, "My god, did I sound like a total idiot when I asked her why she. . . ?" So there's no reason to avoid revision when we write.

The reasons we invent for avoiding revision when we write are many, though. As writers, we ought to love revision—it's our chance to make things better, to tighten our hold on something, to take out bad lines, to add something delicate or something powerful. And yet for many, revision is the scourge of the writing process. It's the moment in creating a poem that we like least, that we sometimes don't engage in. And then when we do, it's minimal. I see people regularly in our workshops who hand in "revised" poems with only one or two words changed. At the most, maybe a line is broken slightly differently than in the first draft. That line change is a step in the right direction, but one or two word changes don't really constitute revision. Why do we avoid it with such vigor? Maybe because we have spent so much time creating the poem, that we think we are finished with it. Or maybe we feel we would impose too much on what was "creative." Or, maybe we're simply overwhelmed by or uncomfortable with revision—we don't know exactly what to revise or how to go about it.

Before we talk about how to go about revision, it's important to briefly address the previous reason for avoiding revision. If you feel that you will take out the creative purity of a poem by revising it, just remember that you become creative when you revise. And that makes revision part of the creative process. Consider the fishing metaphor. When my grandfather was fishing and he wasn't catching fish, he'd change things. Maybe he'd change the bait or the lure. But maybe he'd just reel the lure a little faster or slower, maybe give it a little jig up and down occasionally. Sometimes he'd change the depth where he was fishing. But many of these little revisions to his presentation produced fish, and, of course, that was the exciting and fun result we were looking for. If, for instance, you're someone who is overwhelmed by the thought of revision, don't worry—taking it slowly will produce results. I often hear from beginning writers, "I can't even think of where to begin. It took so much to write the poem, I can't imagine how to find what to fix. I just wrote it—you're the poet; now help me." These are exceptionally valid and powerful feelings which can certainly inhibit the revision process. But, even the least experienced writer of poetry can go back and measure her work, check the reactions of her classmates, and see if she's hooking fish. If not, let's jig that lure a little. And so we learn to revise.

How Should I Begin Revising?

"What should I revise?" can be a daunting question sometimes. In fact, many beginning writers feel that they put so much into the initial draft that there's nothing left to put into subsequent drafts—that they've used all their knowledge and creative talent the first time around. But, going about revision by asking more manageable questions will push us into the process of revision. Approaching revision by asking questions is a helpful way to proceed because it gives us concrete points to focus on while we revise. What's more, we can take revision in a somewhat systematic way without getting over-whelmed by everything at once.

Ah, but where to begin? Consider the core of the poem. Ask yourself what the seed was. What was at the heart of the poem? What was I really try-ing to say? Then maybe look at the poem and make a list of what you see in it. Are the feelings or thoughts from the seed of the poem there? If so, note how they appear in the poem and when you think they are the strongest. These are creative points and places we will need to focus on and come back to. Some we will want to come back to as anchor points, as moorings, if you will, to keep us from floating too far from the heart of the poem. Others we will want to work on so they become stronger and more centrally connected or rooted in the heart of the poem. Once we've done some of this conceptu-ally creative revision we can begin asking some technical questions about our creative elements and tools.

We can proceed much the same way as we did with the creative con-cepts—by asking questions. Is there alliteration, assonance, internal rhyme, slant rhyme? Are there strong images? Are there metaphors and similes? After creating this list you can figure out a bit about what you have, and you can ask yourself what's missing. Once you know what you have, go through those things and check them for their quality, their relationship to the seed of what you wanted to say in the first place. Then you can begin to work with what is not there. I can remember when I first began to write poems, one thing that was regularly missing from my poems was similes. Once I noticed this missing link, I made a conscious effort to include them. But often this didn't happen until I revised. And maybe I had a great image of, say, a lemon tree, but when I added the metaphoric side of it, "the lemon tree stood like . . ." that's when the image took on some power.

Let's look at an example of some revision. In the following poem, our author sets up a number of images in the first stanza. We can see by the sec-ond stanza that the poem might focus on the father, the son, maybe, and their relationship, and some sense of Ireland or history or family history. By the end of the poem all of these things converge in some very moving lines with a focus on the father being central. Here's a draft of stanza one, two, and three.

The Smell of Summer Hay at Sunset

a ballet;
two tractors,
caked with Irish mud
fight to follow the red clouds
into the safe smell of peat   5

upon the fire
and brown
bread in the hand

my father watches
me drink hard cider,   10
he smiles the smile of a man
who lives his dreams,

tracking his ghosts
back into the island
that stole his father's heart   15
away from a family of eight;
hoping to find a memory of it
in the green grass.

DEVIN MCCARTHY

Following is the revision of the first stanza. Basically the first stanza is all that changes but the poet does this by removing lines. His reasoning, when we talked about the revision, was that he thought the images presented in lines 5-8 of stanza one leaned a bit toward the cliché. He felt that they presented too much abstraction and romanticizing, which detracted from what he wanted to focus on at the start of stanza two—his father. Devin went about this revision a bit more intuitively than systematically, but his feelings were perceptive and quite accurate. Note the difference in the stanzas and their relationship. Though subtle, his revision does help his father to be emphasized at the start of stanza two. Also, Devin does some minor revision in the third stanza which changes the emphasis of the language just a bit making the "hope" verb active (an important verb at this point in the poem) and making the article specific (going from "the" to "this").

The Smell of Summer Hay at Sunset

a ballet
two tractors
caked with Irish mud
fight to follow the red clouds

my father watches   5
me drink hard cider,
he smiles the smile of a man
who lives his dreams,

tracking his ghosts
back into the island   10
that stole his father's heart
away from a family of eight;
he hopes to find a memory of it
in this green grass.

The revision we've just looked at is something that has caused us to change our perspective of the poem—or at least the first and second stanzas and how they proceed. While this is not huge revision, Devin has achieved the goal. He has us focusing on the core of the poem now and without superfluous interruption. This should be a goal of most revision we make—to change the reader's perspective and maybe even to change our perspective in those lines and situations we revise. Consider those times when we say to ourselves "if only I had . . ." or "if I could do it over again. . . ." Well, consider revision our chance to do it over again and we can do it the way we feel it might have been best done the first or second time. And unlike in a real-life situation, with a poem we can go back and do it over as many times as we please—that dirty word, drafting.

Let me suggest a process that can be helpful in revising by drafting. Rather than spending a long time going through a poem and stopping in each line or couple of lines and asking what can be done here, set up a revision situation that will be successful. Set down for yourself what you will look for and revise for as you go through the poem. Say to yourself, "I will go through this draft and look now only at images. Then I'll come back and comb through the poem for sound quality, specifically, internal rhyme in my lines." If you proceed this way, it's likely you'll avoid that overwhelming feeling that can cause us all to abandon revision for the thirty other things we'd rather do.

Let's look at a poem that was revised significantly—in fact, so significantly that it looked like a different poem. But on close inspection we can see that, in fact, Jenelle has kept the core of the poem alive in both drafts. The situation here is that Jenelle has revised the poem so significantly that now she has to work through the revision process on the new draft. But she's hung tightly to the core. The poet Richard Hugo states that a poem has two subjects, the **triggering subject** that causes the poem to come up in the first place, and then there's the **real** or **generated subject,** what the poem comes to say. He also states that, in fact, we may not even consciously know what the real subject is, but just have some instinctive feeling about it. This idea of two subjects becomes clear in Jenelle's poem and her revision.

a long time ago

the hand shakes as it reaches out
to touch his pale lips
the mouth reaches down

to plant a goodbye kiss
gone is the lover   5
with golden hair
and bright blue eyes
why are angels always
blue eyes and fair hair?
I was an angel once   10
far away
but that was a long time ago
now I have black hair
and I suppose
I'm not an angel anymore.   15

This is definitely a first draft. She has started to do some things here that have merit and potential. There's some play with language, we have some ambiguity happening, there are certainly contrasting images creating some tension. Note that there are two subjects here. As the readers we can see what's going on. Jenelle may not have seen the "real" subject rising but she maintains it in the second draft.

Search for Pride

I was not made
in the image of God.
My ancestors did not live
in the Garden of Eden.

They tell me it's   5
Adam and Eve.
not Adam and Steve,
not "Brother Adam" and
"Sister Eve" from the hood,
or Eve, the slant-eyed   10
yellow-bellied gook.

Golden hair and
bright blue eyes
the epitome of "good"
the poster-child for "princess."   15

No, I was made in the image
of my mother
my father and
my ancestors,
who were made in   20
the image of beauty.

Such revision is dramatic. But note what she's done. The sense of the poem is actually made stronger by her having collected ideas and placed them in stanzas—this allows for her tone to be a bit more provocative. And stanza two—entirely new to the poem—allows Jenelle to connect the speaker of the poem to a broader set of lives and members of society who she also feels are outcast, who are being moved against. While there is much good here, now Jenelle is ready to go back and revise this draft again, this virtually new and different poem. But, in calling it "different" let's also note that she has remained attached to the triggering subject and actually heightened the real subject by using it in the title, by creating stanzas and circling back to the first stanza at the end of the poem. Our writer here has hung tightly to another Richard Hugo maxim of revision: "When rewriting, write the entire poem again. If something has gone wrong deep in the poem, you may have taken a wrong turn earlier." We can see, based on Hugo's advice and our writer's example, that this type of revision can pay off with a little sweat and hard work.

But once we engage in this type of rewriting it's necessary to be able to gain momentum, to shift things, to change things as we see fit. While we need to write from our own experiences, we need to be able to think about them in a frame of reality/fiction that allows us the elbow room to create. Memory is an important element here and we all remember things slightly differently. A student wrote the following lines about his grandmother's death despite his not having been there when it happened.

> She lay on the ground
> the beating stopped
> her face gray as the cement
> on Christmas day.
>
> and later my brother   5
> threw her fruit basket out the window
> screaming down the 405

He came to class and said "I want to change them." "Why?" I asked. I was thinking, *why in the hell would he want to change these lines?* And he said "because my mother flipped when she read this. I wasn't there and she said this isn't the way it happened." And I was thinking, *to hell with his mother*, but I told him, "Look, you may not have been there, but it's part of your experience and how you remember and want to express how your grandmother died. Tell it the way you want." My point was not to create an irreconcilable rift in his family, but rather to get him to keep his sense of how something had happened. This was his poem. I later found that in fact his brother didn't throw the basket out of the car window—he tossed it in the garbage at home. But the student thought that was a more poignant and compelling detail. He was right. What I found compelling too, as a teacher and a writer, was that he had the nerve and sense enough to change a detail from how it did happen to how he thought we'd want it to happen so we'd feel more in the experience. Now, that's getting to the core of revision. Because he saw that in the end, the reader wasn't going to say "Nice writing," no, the reader was going to say "Wow, I feel that deeply."

When revising poems, remember that no matter how you go about it, whether you've adapted rules or mantras from this chapter or made your own, the importance of allowing yourself to create and re-create is paramount to success. And remember in revision, too, that nothing is permanent—if you don't like it, go back and change it. Try new things, reshape the experience, change the memory and take us deeply into the heart of the matter.

Essay by Gary Thompson ——————————

MOONSHEEN AND PORCHLIGHT: REVISION AS ILLUMINATION

A very good poem might matter to the poet who wrote it for much of a lifetime. The poem brings pleasure and insight each time the poet reads it, especially when reading it aloud. Not surprisingly, that same good poem will very often provide pleasure and insight to others. Galway Kinnell has probably read or recited "The Bear" a thousand times in the thirty-some years since he wrote it, yet each time I hear him read the poem, I notice the great joy he takes in saying it aloud, and how that pleasure has shifted from one section to another over the years. Needless to say, "The Bear" is a very good poem and it has provided both pleasure and insight through these decades. But in the midst of writing a new poem—in struggle or frenzy, pain or joy—how do we poets make the decisions that might turn this emerging poem into a good poem, and hence a poem that matters to us, and perhaps to others, for a lifetime?

For most poets I know well enough to be privy to their working methods, initial revising is a basic part of writing that first draft. My first drafts, for example, always have words erased, or lines scratched out, stanzas eliminated or moved, titles changed, linebreaks shifted. These decisions or hunches are an integral part of the discovery, and they come within the rush and flow and excitement of a first-glimpsed poem. Most poets have experienced some version of this simultaneous writing/revising, although it is true that some prefer to jot down a very rough, yet whole, draft before making even small changes. It is also true that it becomes more difficult, and probably less thrilling, to make productive revisions after a few hours, or days, or weeks, or months have passed since the initial excitement of creation. However, these later revisions, made under the full light of conscious scrutiny, are often the most important ones we can make because they help us illuminate the deepest and often the most difficult parts of our poems. Simply, we can come to see our poems, and perhaps ourselves, better. Revision, then, is a way for the poet to learn what is important. Like all worthwhile knowledge, revision is an art we must teach ourselves, but we can learn this art more quickly if we are honestly open to the comments and observations of other poets, readers, and editors. We must make ourselves vulnerable.

There are many ways to think about poetry, many models and metaphors that attempt to explain how poems actually affect the reader or how poems are written. There are so many models, of course, because poems are, at best, mysteries. It's unlikely that any one explanation will satisfy a poet or reader for any length of time, let alone a lifetime. Our understandings change, broaden with each poem we read or write; therefore, our personal model (and we all have one, consciously or not) of poetry subtly shifts and evolves over time, and obviously then, our sense of what makes a good poem will change too. So it is remarkable when a poem of ours continues to provide pleasure and insight after any length of time at all. Most fail this test, but when one succeeds, it succeeds mysteriously. In a talk about revision given at the Foothill Writers Conference, George Keithley suggests why the very good poem continues to resonate: "Remember that the mystery which moves us in a poem is not the meaning of the poem, but how the poem achieves that meaning. Its existence is the essential meaning of the poem."

"Writing is seen as a splurge of emotion rather than a combination of inspiration and craft."

Matt Barnard

This observation, cited from *The London Times*, suggests two ways (from a myriad of ways) of looking at the process of writing poems, and each contains its truth. Also, and perhaps more significantly, each implies a completely different approach to revising poems, and again, each has its validity. If we look on writing as a "splurge of emotion," then how do we revise the words, phrases, lines that were created by this emotional outpouring? Certainly it would be helpful to listen to what others have to say about our draft, but do we really want to change anything, since to change the poem in a different, perhaps cooler and less expressive, mood would diminish the splurge effect that we so value? The poem is what it is: words caught in the moment of emotional excess. The way to revise, it appears, is simply to write the next poem, hoping that each poem teaches us something that will be useful in the next. Eventually, the poet hopes to find a burst of words that produces the very good poem. In this, it resembles learning to surf where the novice, after perhaps a few words of wisdom from a teacher and a couple of lessons on the beach, paddles out and tries to catch waves. Each teetering ride teaches something, but the wave can't be caught again. It's the next wave, the next poem, which is important. Eventually, given luck, that great wave and the skills required to ride it will come together at the same time, and that ride will be remembered and celebrated for years.

However, if we look on writing as a combination of inspiration and craft, then we have ways to set about revising the first draft of a poem. Certainly, this model brings the craft of poetry, the various skills a poet learns and uses, to the forefront and more likely into our consciousness. The poet might find it useful to analyze the sounds and rhythms of the poem, for example, and ask questions about the findings. Linebreaks, images, and all issues of craft could be isolated, scrutinized, and nudged toward perfection. After all this precise work, however, will we have written our very good poem? Not necessarily. We've all read poems that are soundly crafted; yet they have no life, no magic, no surprise, no mystery. This is where inspiration plays its important role in our model. *Inspire:* the word has many meanings and contexts, and several apply to the writing and revising of poems—to fill, to arouse, to impel, to animate, to give rise to, to infuse by breathing, to inhale. In other words, the poem begins to breathe, to be filled with life. At some point, the very good poem mysteriously takes on a life of its own, and this is both because of, and in spite of, the poet's craft. It's important to remember that this inspired moment can occur at almost any stage of the creative process. It might happen just as the poet is penning the first word, or at any stage of that initial draft, or later when the poet is concentrating on issues of craft, or during the later stages of revising. Eventually, something *must* inspire the poem or it will remain simply a construction of words. So the first stage in later revision for me, whether looking at a poem of mine or a student's, is to ask: What is inspired in these lines? Where does the poem come to life?

Let's turn to a specific example of the revision process. This poem is by Karen Seipert, a bright, talented, and serious student in my recent summer workshop. I think this poem may be especially instructive because it was discussed in an earlier workshop taught by another instructor, and Karen kept the various drafts, worksheets, and notes about her observations. So the poet had been thinking about this poem for some time before she brought it to my class, and we can follow her thinking pretty clearly as she revises over a number of months and with various sources of feedback. The first draft was written on a computer, so she doesn't have a record of the earliest revisions made during the initial writing. She does remember that the changes were minimal. Draft one:

Jealousy

The sill creaks
while the window
groans upwards.
Faded paint,
the peeling culprit,   5
telltales pained ascent.
My cousin Jeffrey,
halfway in
mostway out
escapes   10
onto the roof.

Moonsheen
on his Chevy
illuminates the plan.
I tiptoe   15
across cold wood
a willing conspirator—
but the Chevy's rolling
lights extinguished
down the gravel   20
drive towards emancipation.

KAREN SEIPERT

What's inspired here? For me, it's the first view of cousin Jeffrey being "halfway in/ mostway out" of the window. That "mostway" certainly catches a visual image of the teenager sneaking out the second-story window. It also mimics the slangy quality of teenage talk, as well as implying the fact of his age, since he is mostly grown and mostly gone. The second inspired moment in the poem is the description of light on the Chevy. "Moonsheen" is a fascinating coinage here. It suggests the romance of sneaking off into the night world, as well as the illicit quality of the action (perhaps by its proximity in sound to moonshine). Finally, the third inspired moment in the poem is the image of the Chevy's "rolling/ lights extinguished/ down the gravel/ drive . . ." This clear image of the car also suggests the way some teenagers speed off, blindly and dangerously, into the world. So there's much to admire here, even in this very early draft.

What might the poet consider in her next version of the poem? Certainly, there are some craft issues, such as linebreaks (why does the next-to-last line break differently from all the rest?) and why does the strategy change from detailed punctuation to almost no punctuation? Also, most of the poem is so concrete and visual that three phrases stand out as being quite different, quite abstract: "telltales pained ascent," "a willing conspirator," and "towards emancipation." The question might be put this way: Can the simple, playful, almost-childlike language of this poem carry the extra weight of these abstractions? All of them? And finally, why is the poem titled "Jealousy"? Jealousy connotes a certain bitterness and anguish, but who is jealous of whom or what? These are some of the questions Karen might mull over before revising her poem, and it appears that most of these questions were brought up during that first workshop, because her next draft responds in part to these issues.

Draft two, revised a month or so later, is called "Envy," a title that better prepares the reader for the wistful and yearning tone of the speaker, without forcing us to ask questions that lead outside the emotional territory of the poem. Other notable changes: the window is now an *aged* window; the paint now telltales *painful rising;* and the Chevy's *already* rolling—a small but brilliant change that reinforces the unfolding action in the present tense and adds to the drama. She also changes the inconsistent linebreak, and attacks the punctuation issue by placing periods after each short phrase, a strategy that seems at odds with the relatively smooth flow of the speaker's thoughts and words. Karen's notes about the class discussion of this draft indicate that she is still uncomfortable with the "telltales" line and the overall punctuation scheme; she also recognizes that "Faded paint. / the peeling culprit" simply explains that the window is old, which has already been stated by adding "aged." A student in the workshop has evidently questioned whether "moonsheen" might be too romantic, and Karen notes this observation with two poignant question marks.

Draft three is the end-of-the-semester version to be turned in to her instructor for comments. Three significant changes occur in this draft. First, Karen begins to solve the problem of inconsistent and ineffective punctuation by eliminating all punctuation (except parentheses that enclose lines 3-6) and allowing the natural linebreaks to control pacing and meaning. In conjunction with this strategy, she also eliminates all capitalization (except for proper nouns and the first person pronoun), and this emphasizes the lines as lines, rather than as parts of a sentence. In her notes, she surmises that writing in lower case is more "dreamlike," and I suppose it is. The third significant change is not so productive, at least in my opinion. Apparently swayed by her fellow student's argument, she replaces the splendid "moonsheen" with the ordinary "porchlight," perhaps feeling that the first draws too much attention to itself for this little poem. Adroitly, her instructor responds: "I somewhat prefer 'moonsheen' because it adds to the furtiveness and romantic excitement/longing that the young girl must feel." This advice is sensitive and clear, and it helps steer the poet back towards the strengths of her poem.

Draft four, the draft submitted to our summer workshop, reflects the many small decisions the poet has made over the months since that first draft called "Jealousy."

Envy

the sill creaks
while the window
groans upward
(faded paint
the peeling culprit   5
telltales pained ascent)
my cousin Jeffrey
halfway in
mostway out
escapes   10
onto the roof

moonsheen
on his Chevy
illuminates the plan
I tiptoe   15
across cold wood
a willing conspirator
but the Chevy's already rolling
lights extinguished
down the gravel drive   20
towards emancipation

KAREN SEIPERT

   The discussion that followed Karen's reading the poem aloud (a
practice that helps the class, as well as the poet, hear each poem's distinctive music) was lively and productive, and I think it allowed her to
think about the poem in ways that hadn't come up in her previous workshop. Our discussion, as I recall, began with praise for the clear, fresh,
unpretentious imagery that conveys so much about the people and the
situation. We also took delight in the music, especially the sounds and
rhythms of the second stanza. One student even traced the sound patterns in that stanza, and then explained why he liked them and what they
contributed to the poem. It could be implied, I suppose, that the music in
the first stanza isn't quite as interesting or as integral, and that may be
something the poet wants to attend to, should she decide to write yet
another draft. The third major area of our discussion focused on diction,
the word choices the poet makes as the poem unfolds, and this conversation opened up our primary suggestions for revision.

1) "Emancipation" is an odd word choice in the last line. It is quite abstract, and if it is meant to convey a general sense of freedom, then
   that is already implied in the previous lines. We know cousin Jeffrey

is stealing away from the authority and rules of the house. If emancipation is meant to be a legal term (as in cousin Jeffrey driving off to attain his legal civil rights), then there is much that is unexplained in the poem. Also, the young speaker is envious of the older cousin's freedom, though she isn't particularly angry about his betrayal at not taking her with him. Would she be likely to think about legalities at this point? Most agreed with the suggestion, as I recall, to omit the last line which allows the final powerful image to speak for itself.

2) There also was a good deal of discussion about the sixth line: "telltales pained ascent," and rightfully so. Her notes indicate that both poet and reader have been uncomfortable with this line since that first draft. Let's look at it more closely. "Telltales" seems like an interesting coinage, changing the noun/adjective to a verb form. It hints at the fact that the speaker didn't tattle, although the old house tried to, albeit unsuccessfully. "Pained" is playful, a pun on windowpane. This explains why the poet has chosen one form or another of the word in various drafts. However, clever as it is, the resultant personification of the window blurs the image and we tend to lose sight of the main point of this stanza, which is cousin Jeffrey's escape. The class offered a number of suggestions, but the more I consider this line, the more I've come to believe that the solution is not so easily confined to that single phrase. The first six lines describe the window and sill, and there are three qualities that must be made clear for the reader to fully appreciate the rest of the poem. First, the window and sill must be old because the house symbolizes the adult world of authority that the cousins wish to escape. Second, the window must open or rise so that we are catching the cousins as their scheme unfolds; in effect we share their secret and become conspirators. Third, the window must make some sort of noise, a groan or creak, to indicate that this escape scheme could be discovered and thwarted. My suggestion to Karen, after these days of following her poem from draft to draft, is to rethink the opening and rewrite the lines. In so doing, she will likely rewrite these lines with the same insight, zest, and inspiration that already define the best of "Envy."

This shouldn't have to be said, but experience tells me it does: any suggestion for revision—whether offered by a friend, classmate, teacher, or editor—is just that, a suggestion. The poem is the poet's to tinker with as she sees fit. The poet is not just learning to use the tools of her craft, she is also developing and refining a sensibility, her own way of shaping and understanding the world. When she studies her poem, when she turns the tensor lamp up high, the poet may illuminate a self she has only glimpsed in the past, and this vision could be the essential insight she needs to write new poems. That is why revision is an art.

* * *

Exercise

Take a poem you wrote a while back. If you're new at poetry, even just a month ago will do. Read through the poem aloud. Then read through the poem for analysis and make some lists. Note what elements it contains. Note what you like about the poem and why. Note what you think the poem is really saying—and along with this note the triggering subject and the real subject. Then revise the poem one element at a time. Go through it just for imagery, then just for tone, just for rhyme, etc. Make a number of passes at the poem. You will have a number of drafts by the end of this process, but ultimately a draft that ought to look significantly revised.

chapter eleven

THE POETRY WORKSHOP

The cornerstone of a workshop's success is participation. That sounds simple enough, but it's really not as easy as it seems. First, not everyone is comfortable speaking up in a group setting. Add to this that it's even more nerve-racking to talk about something (in this case poems) which may cause us to feel a bit like a novice. So it's no surprise that the first day of workshopping poems can be utterly silent. When I teach a poetry class, we don't workshop a poem until the third—sometimes the fourth—week of class. This is for good reason. We go over elements and writing strategies, do exercises, get comfortable with the process of producing work. But still, that first day of workshopping is a doozy. Inevitably, I have students who come up and say, "I didn't know what to say, how to comment—this is so much better than anything I could write." If I'm lucky, they show up at my office door before class asking for help, but they still say the same thing to me.

And this is a reasonable thing to say. But I like to draw the analogy that there are plenty of coaches out there who coach athletes who are better players than they are. Take Michael Jordan for example. People say he's the best basketball player ever. Does that mean he shouldn't have a coach? Of course not, and Mr. Jordan (humble as he is about his talent) would probably be the first to tell us that he appreciates what his coach can

. . . a poetry workshop / an epicenter of originality, companionship, / pain and openness . . .

Jimmy Santiago Buca

do for him. Once we've settled into the coaching role, the peer, the colleague—all the terms that calm the nerves—we can start talking about workshopping. The first thing I always tell students who are uncomfortable
commenting on someone else's work is, "Start with something positive. Then
you can get to the not-so-good."

I have a theory about emerging as a writer that can be summed up in one
word—accident. There are times when we do very good work and it happens
by accident. There are also times when we do very bad work and that, too,
can happen by accident. But, I'm more inclined to think that bad work happens by a lack of intellectual or creative effort. So the way in which this affects
the workshop is that when something good happens, maybe an image in the
poem everyone is taken by, the writer needs to know why it is good. They
may not have even thought that the image was a main concern. But by accident it becomes a pulse in the poem. And they need to know why it's good
so they can see how they created it and then they can do it again in another
poem. This is one of the main goals of the workshop—to learn to figure out
how and why we've done things and then repeat them or stay far away from
them. And figuring this out in others' poems helps us find it in our own. A
second goal in the workshop process is to learn to be able to go through one's
own work with the clarity with which we view others' work.

I usually set up a few simple rules in my workshops:

1. No meaningless answers (e.g., I really like this poem, that's a great
   image, it's nice, etc.).
2. Don't get personal (Boy, Randy, that poem is really horrible. The
   whole subject is stupid—why are you even in here writing poems?).
   I know, you're thinking that nobody would ever say this, but I've
   seen some rude people in creative writing sessions who think they
   have a license to say whatever is on their mind. Stick to the work at
   hand and to the text in that work.
3. Find positive things to say and give reasons why the work you're
   noting is good.
4. Be gentle with negatives and again give reasons. Help by showing
   someone how they might fix it. If something isn't quite right but you
   don't know why, you can bring it up and defer to someone else for
   technique on fixing.
5. The writer who has her work on the table for review doesn't get to
   talk unless we need an answer to a question regarding why she did
   something. The author ought to be taking notes.
6. For your own sanity, don't idolize anyone else in the class because
   you think they write better than you'll ever write. We all do good
   work and we all do bad work.

I know, it may sound pretty rigid, but these rules simply provide the
highway we drive on all quarter. And it gives a framework within which we

function, a road map of sorts, so we're all headed in the same direction. When someone brings in a poem to be workshopped, he needs to bring the poem to us on Tuesday if we're going to look at it as a class on a Thursday. We all take it home, and on Thursday everyone is to bring back the poem with hand-written remarks on it and a paragraph or more of typed comments, all of which gets returned to the writer. The hope then is that there's plenty of solid feedback for the writer to go out and work on revising his poem. Then he can bring it back to us if he wants, or simply turn in at least two drafts of it in a portfolio at the end of the quarter. In the end, we hope that the writers get solid feedback. And while providing solid feedback, the classmates learn more about creating constructive feedback for their own work and hone their editing skills. Finally, it's applying all the technical and elemental sides of poetics to the practical side of creative writing.

chapter twelve

WORKSHOPPING A FREE VERSE POEM

WORKSHOPPING A POEM

Let's take a look at one of the poems that came in and was discussed in one of our beginning poetry sessions. Jake hadn't been writing poetry long, but had always had an interest in reading both novels and poetry. He is from a rural community and went to high school in Estacada, Oregon—a traditional logging town. But he is far from being traditional, has traveled widely, has a passion for learning Spanish, and is a relatively avid conservationist. So here's a poem he brought in at the start of the quarter.

For the New People

There is a dead dog buried in the ground.
Actually, there are three dead dogs
down a ways from the house,
by the creek. Other places have more.
It's the road you live on.   5
Claims about a dog per summer,

At least it used to, when
twenty or thirty log trucks

barreled by in one day.
Your dogs will be fine.   10
Besides, don't you raise
really smart dogs?

Not too many cats have died here.
They live much longer than dogs. But
you won't believe the birds. It is beautiful,   15
the view from three windows six feet by
six feet. But you won't believe how many birds
try to fly right through.

Sipping whatever you drink will
sometimes be made less pleasant   20
when a hollow thud jerks your eyebrows.
You do love them, animals, and
often times a bird can be nursed back
to fine shape. Still,

You have purchased   25
an extraordinarily large space of land,
with so many birds
and such a generous amount of air
in which birds gain tremendous speed.

Jakob Curtis

Now that we've read the poem, in order to comfortably form a solid response to the piece, we can ask some questions and think about the techniques and elements of writing poetry we already know. This poem lends itself to asking a multitude of questions from the basic to the complex. But let's focus on a few that will allow you entry into Jake's poem and almost any poem you come across.

1. Is the language accessible and why? In other words, do you understand what he's saying?
2. Are there images in the poem and if so, how well has he used imagery? And why do you think the images work or don't work in Jake's poem?
3. In what places does line structure help the dynamics of the poem and in what places is the poem hurt by its line structure?
4. What types of sound elements does Jake employ in the poem and how do they function—what do they do for the poem?
5. Is there a triggering subject and is there a real subject and how do these work in the poem?

Answering these questions will give us a handle on what kind of comments we might want to give Jake. What's more, these questions get at elements that ought to be present in most poems. But, specifically, they get at the heart of what elements ought to be working in the poem Jake brought to the workshop.

Now that you've had a chance to think about what kind of conclusions you'd draw about the poem, let's look at the poem with margin comments, talk about why the comments were made, and then see what Jake decides to do with the poem in the long run.

For the New People

Great title and good subject matter

There is a dead dog buried in the ground.

Nice use of the element of surprise.

Actually, there are three dead dogs
down a ways from the house,
by the creek. Other places have more.
It's the road you live on.   5
Claims about a dog per summer,

Good momentum

At least it used to, when
twenty or thirty log trucks
barreled by in one day.
Your dogs will be fine.   10
Besides, don't you raise
really smart dogs?

Where is this going?
This is almost cliché
and has some troubling
line structure. Consider what it
is you really want to say and do
here. Then consider how the lines
might work.
A great shift into
the "real" subject.

Not too many cats have died here.
They live much longer than dogs. But
you won't believe the birds. It is beautiful,   15
the view from three windows six feet by
six feet. But you won't believe how many birds
try to fly right through.

Sipping whatever you drink will
sometimes be made less pleasant   20
when a hollow thud jerks your eyebrows.
You do love them, animals, and
often times a bird can be nursed back
to fine shape. Still,

This ending has resonance
because you've used original
concepts and images
to represent them

You have purchased   25
an extraordinarily large space of land,
with so many birds
and such a generous amount of air
in which birds gain tremendous speed.

Jackob Curtis

Jake,

Well, there are some fine things in this poem. It's obviously an early draft, but you're doing some good work and following some varied and deep currents in the poem. What's more, you follow some good basic tenets about writing. Jake, you're writing about what you know and using a language that is natural and accessible for the readers. After stating these foundation points, we can head into the poem and look at what there is that you've done well and what it is you could revise, take out, reshape in some way.

So, let's start with some of the good you have going in the poem. First, there's a great title working here and it is because it is not a title that gives away the poem or predisposes us to view it one way or another. If anything, it's relatively obscure until we read the poem. Then we realize it is tied to both the triggering subject and the real subject, and that in fact the poem is not about birds and dogs at all, but about the new people moving into rural areas and ostensibly folks from the suburbs. Then you move into the poem with a wonderful beginning. Not only does the first line work well but the first stanza does a fine job setting the tone of the poem, establishing both the voice of the poet and the voice of the persona. Largely this is accomplished through the use of short and emphatic statements. What's more, they're statements that surprise us—dead dogs? we might ask—and at the same time intrigue us, pulling us into the poem. Here you're following the old rule of beginning in the middle of things, after things have happened. In these emphatic statements, Jake, you do well for yourself and the poem by establishing some very concrete imagery and a sense of where the poem is and what is in the poem. You are not pelting us with a spray of abstracts.

In the second stanza you continue with this very strong sense of the images and action in the poem. And the action and tension mount with log trucks. As well, the tone is heightened a bit by using the direct "you" of the second-person point of view—as well as a question pointed at them—to address these "new people" and the way they perceive the intelligence of their dogs. So, the momentum of the poem is moving ahead, and some dynamics begin with the rhythmic quality of the lines and the sound quality of your word choices. Notice that there are some rough spots in the line breaks and grammatical structure in stanza one, but in stanza two you're really moving along with some tight lines that are broken at similar lengths. I say "tight" because of your use of elements of sound (the "s" in line 1, the rhymes when/twenty and log/dog, the alliteration in "barreled by") as well as a line structure that moves quickly. And, it almost feels like the lines are barreling by like the log trucks.

Now, in stanza three there is some good imagery but this is a problematic stanza for its syntax, its line structure, and subject matter. Jake, where are you going with the cats? It seems this is an interruption to the poem that potentially throws us off the track. I'll address this just a bit later.

Now, in stanza four, notice the consistency in voice and the persona's tone. You have remained consistent in point of view, and opened this stanza with a wonderfully fresh image of the "new people" sipping their drinks. And then, not entirely surprising, but somewhat, you have the birds mentioned above slamming into the "wonderful" plate glass windows, which is a fine twist to throw at us in the poem. Here is where you have left the trig-gering subject behind—the dogs—and gone on to the real subject, that of people moving to the country and living their entire lives (from their animals to their houses) in a way that isn't suited to rural living, and maybe it's not suited for anyone. What's more, Jake, you continue your very fine use of sound quality throughout the stanza.

And moving into the final stanza, we're right on target with the real sub-ject and things are still fresh and interesting for us. Here are the birds being purchased with the land, a sensible image since birds live in trees, but then another slight twist. Who thinks of buying air? And you have made some wonderful word choices, images, and line breaks in "and such a generous amount of air/ in which birds gain tremendous speed." There is a very sub-tle and implicit quality to what the persona is trying to tell us and since it is done with images, rather than abstracts, the power is not lost on us at the end.

So largely we have a reasonably strong poem here. It's a poem that is really ready to be worked on hard in the revision process and turned into an even better poem. While there are many things here which work well, there are some rough spots to the poem too. For instance, let's look at some of the grammatical structures (syntax, punctuation, etc.) as well as line breaks. In two stanzas in particular you have trouble around these and it harms the dynamics of the language that might occur if they were smoothed out.

In stanza one, the first line and sentence is great. But then we move on to another longer sentence where you employ some enjambment. This works fine. But starting a new sentence in line four ("Other places . . .") and then stopping and then starting again creates a jerky motion in the language. In lines five and six, seemingly these two thoughts are related and would normally go together, but you've separated them and have actually tied line six in stanza one to line one in stanza two. That seems grammatically odd and it seems to affect the rhythm of the language as well as the meaning. I'll be interested to see later what revision takes place.

In stanza three, we get in to the bit about the cats. Here is where the turn to the real subject begins, but cats are superfluous to the real subject. It's almost as if the cats were just a way to get to the birds. And let's look again at what has happened with line structure.

Not too many cats have died here.
They live much longer than dogs. But
you won't believe the birds. It is beautiful,
the view from three windows six feet by
six feet. But you won't believe how many birds   5
try to fly right through.

As the line breaks occur, I wonder why you've broken the sentences into lines the way you have—leaving "But" at the end of line two, starting line five with "six feet," the last two words of the sentence. And the syntax of the sentence "It is beautiful . . ." is a bit odd. Why start with a pronoun reference using "It"? Why not start with the words "the view"? After all, this is more concrete and tighter given word economy. Well, this is an awkward stanza, and given the cat and bird relationship, almost too "cute" for the poem.

    Jake, there's some real fine work here. I look forward to seeing the revision.

—*JEFF*

Jake got quite a lot of great feedback from the class when he brought this poem in. People genuinely liked it, felt they could relate to it, and thought it embodied enough poetic elements to make very natural language seem poetic. When we asked Jake how much of this was conscious, he said only part was—the rest just fell in. That's fine, because at some level he was thinking about it and it made it on to the page. In fact, one of the biggest compliments to Jake the day he brought this in, was that one young woman in the class said, "You know, what's great about this is that you just say it, but it really is a poem." And isn't that the goal?

Revised Version

For the New People

There is a dead dog buried in the ground.
Actually, there are three dead dogs
down a ways from the house,
by the creek; other places have more.
It's the road you live on—   5
claims about a dog per summer.

At least it used to, when
twenty or thirty log trucks
barreled by in one day.
Your dogs will be fine.   10
Besides, don't you raise
smart dogs?

The view is beautiful,
from three windows
six feet by six feet.   15
But you won't believe the birds, how many
try to fly right through.

Sipping whatever you drink will
sometimes suffer interruption
when a hollow thud jerks your eyes.   20
You do love them, and

often times a bird can be nursed back
to fine shape. Still,

You have purchased
an extraordinarily large space of land,   25
with so many birds
and such a generous amount of air
in which birds gain tremendous speed.

JAKOB CURTIS

Jake,
Good work here in the revision. You have done some things, largely with the
language at the sentence and line level, which help tighten the poem. Your
only large-scale revision, which was a necessary one, was getting rid of the
cat lines in stanza three. And that also meant that the revision to the dominant image of that stanza had to be somewhat significant. So stanza three
becomes relatively big, but that's an important stanza because this is where
the poem makes its run into the real subject.

If we take the poem stanza by stanza, some of the subtle changes
smooth the poem's nuances of sound. And while some of the changes may
not seem altogether large, the changing of nuances between the drafts makes
all the difference. Remember Jake, in crafting poetry, sometimes a subtle
change in where a word falls, or how a line ends, or how enjambment is used
may stir the reader in just the right direction. You've done well cleaning up
your grammatical structure in lines four, five, and six of stanza one. Adding
a semicolon, which seems to work rather well for those two thoughts, was a
good idea. But more, you've connected the last two lines of the stanza and
kept them from running into stanza two. So you've solved a line problem, a
stanza problem, and a meaning problem all at the same time. Good work.

Almost entirely you've left stanza two alone with the exception of delet-
ing "really" which is one of those vague words which did nothing for the
line or images. This is fine as that stanza was doing well already. So in stanza
three, I'm glad to see you've made some significant revision, and it's here
where the poem turns. And rather than trying to grab the wheel and jerk the
poem in the right direction, you subtly let us move with the language and
take us to the real subject through setting. Following the comments from the
workshop on this stanza—which indicated there were unrelated subject
matter and awkward lines and an inconsistent voice—was a fine idea for
revision. I think you hit the mark. Hence you've revised to a shorter line free
of grammatical or syntactical problems. As well, you set up the lines to
heighten the effect of the internal rhyme as well as the alliteration. What's
more is that this stanza now cleanly takes us into the final two stanzas.

Fine work revising, Jake. And a good job noting what ought to have
been left from your previous draft.

—JEFF

Ultimately, Jake came away from this poem feeling as though he had done something pretty well. That's good, and I would hope he'd feel that way. And he felt as though working through this poem with the feedback he received in the workshop gave him a better idea of how to implement elements of poetics at a conscious level during revision. As for the things that just showed up during the first draft, Jake's comment was that he'd just let the chips fall. But I attribute the chips falling to Jake's thinking very consciously at some point about all the elements (rhyme, alliteration, imagery) that showed up in the poem. Outside of Jake, many in the class felt that they got even closer to their work by workshopping his poem. Part of this was because many related to it because it was local in its setting—they knew where it was set. But really, the setting and tension in the poem could happen anywhere, which is good because that's part of what allows for any audience to read it. And it seems the class found the poem an example of using real, ordinary, accessible language to get at the heart of something.

chapter thirteen

WORKSHOPPING A FIXED FORM POEM

Writing a fixed form poem can be tough. But most of us, no matter the torturous nature of it, could sit down and at least do it as an exercise. It may not come out very well, but we've tried. On the other hand, it might just come out fine, and then we try again. Maybe we begin to write much fixed form poetry. Whatever the outcome, writing it is different from workshopping it. So, even if we've given it a try—and most of us have—it can still be disconcerting when a classmate, colleague, or friend walks into our workshop or writing group and says, "Hey, I brought my sonnets for you to look at today." Inside, we groan and think, why? Oh, but come on, is it really that bad to have to workshop fixed form poems? I don't think so, and I'd venture to say that after a workshop session, at worst, most people are a little enthused about what fixed forms can accomplish and at best, someone runs right out and tries it. But somewhere in the middle—the average response—is that we come away having learned something about form and writing. And that's both rewarding and enlightening.

But why this groaning reaction? Because deep down, as contemporary writers, most of us resist form for one reason or another. But to be able to workshop it, we need to know something about it. All of the questions that students have and the discomfort with workshopping someone else's poem is only heightened with a fixed form poem. And when we spend the time to learn a bit about the form, and we give some knowledgeable, grounded feedback, we become better poets too. Whether we write one or not isn't the issue. The issue is that we've given some fine advice and we've learned a little something about the tradition in which we're working.

WORKSHOPPING A SESTINA

Most poets today say the sestina is a form for frustration, a brain-twisting exercise, a breathtakingly complicated poem, and the list goes on. So why then would someone try to write one. Because, in fact, it can be a very good exercise. But more important, it allows us to take part in the tradition in which we're working and to learn something about how language works within structured forms. "But why not write a sonnet?" you might ask. After all, it's shorter, and if we're going to complicate things with form, let's get in and get out. That is the response of many students I have in workshops. But when they realize that the sestina doesn't have to rhyme and there is no exceptionally strict meter to the poem, they may think about approaching it. Yet, while it doesn't have to rhyme and meter can be a bit loose (*blank verse* was the traditional meter but in contemporary poetry this seems to have been replaced by a *free-verse* approach), there is a very determined line sequence. And what's more, we have to run this sequence based on the words we choose at the beginning of the poem. So when we think we're out of one trapping, we're actually into another. There's no hiding—that's part of fixed form poetry.

The sestina runs like this. It has six stanzas of six lines and concludes with a final stanza of three lines called an envoy. Each stanza must use the same six words to end the lines but they shift in their order: 1. *abcdef* 2. *faebdc* 3. *cfdabe* 4. *ecbfad* 5. *deacfb* 6. *bdfeca*. And the envoy has possibilities of finishing *eca* or *ace*. The envoy traditionally repeated the six words within the stanza as well as having one of the above end-word schemes and the envoy either summarized the poem or dedicated it to someone. Well, that's reasonably complicated, and is slightly more complicated when we think about the words ending the lines. This can be a sticking point for any type of form because we might get hung up on what words to use at the end of lines. And well we should think about this since these words will be repeated over and over and ultimately produce a given effect of sound and meaning within the poem. One way to go about this is to think about your subject and poem, make a list of words you see as key to the subject of the poem and how they might work as end words. The other is to begin drafting the poem and at the end of the first stanza decide how your line breaks should fall, and what words ought to appear at the ends of the lines, and proceed from there. Either way it is not easy.

So when it's finished and we read it, what should happen? Why have the form? Well, the sestina's technique of repeating the words ought to provide a very close weaving together of meaning in the poem with the sound of words. As well, if we've carefully chosen the words, they may have some sense of rhyme to them which may also help to glue the words together in both sound and meaning. In creating line breaks so the words are placed appropriately in the form, we set up recurrent points of rest as well as a rhythmic structure to the poem. And the rhythm then becomes tied directly to what the poem means because we can't get away from using the words based on their meaning. So while we're trying to write a line that has some meaning relevant to the subject, we're also trying to end it with the right word. That's what makes it hard. But when the sestina is finished, one measure of its success is that the language seems natural, unforced. We would hope that those words we've chosen are words that call attention to themselves. But they should do so in a subtle way or the way in which the elements of poetics they embody (rhyme, imagery, etc.) enhance the poem. We want to notice them the way someone attractive and well dressed, across the room at a party, catches our eye. So, let's look at a sestina and go through workshopping it.

Reflections at Dawn

We arrived in Aurora just after dawn,
Which, all in all, seemed a most appropriate time.
On our drive up the Willamette, the morning had broken
With shots of rose and mauve, reflecting
Off the river, and in the farmhouse windows,   5
Still newly washed by autumn rain.

Although overcast and threatening rain,
The day began dry at dawn.
We walked around town peering in the windows
Of the antique shops, knowing there was plenty of time   10
Before they opened. We saw ourselves reflecting
Among the displays inside. Most held old and broken

Tools and implements and we looked broken
In the old glass of the old buildings in the new rain
Just starting to sprinkle. The droplets on the panes reflecting 15
The night lights in the stores and the dawn
Colors underlined what time
It was. So we walked around not looking in at the windows

Of the old houses in the old streets. Light from those windows
Was broken   20

By breeze driven shrubbery and the folks inside checking the time,
And checking the weather channel to see the rain
Was going to start again after dawn.
We commented of the state of the old houses, reflecting

Our own interests in historic buildings, while reflecting   25
On the paradox that was Aurora. All the old stuff in the windows
Left over from the dawn
Of Aurora, much of it repaired after being broken
Or left out in the rain
Like the rusted and veneer-sprung sewing machines from a time   30

When utility had beauty. For there was a time
When Aurora was a forward-looking community, whose windows
Revealed the enlightenment of a new century, their views were reflecting
Innovative and edifying ideas. So we stood there in the fitful, spitting rain
Discussing the new economy built on the antique trade, a broken   35
Trend from Aurora's 19th Century modern dawn.

You looked in at the windows of the railroad station reflecting
How over time it had been moved and turned away from the tracks, a broken
Link from a useful past. Now, in the rain, just an antique shop to open
     sometime after dawn.

ELISABETH MILES

When looking at this poem and creating some responses to it that might
be helpful to the writer, we can ask ourselves some questions based on the
above discussion of the sestina.

1. Does it follow the form? Map out the lines and take a look.
2. This one breaks a little, you'll notice, but only slightly. So what effect
   on the poem does breaking from the tradition have? Does it matter?
   Do you like the way the lines and words fall?
3. Has the author chosen powerful end words (think in relation to
   sound and meaning together) and does she use them to their
   potential?
4. Does the envoy do what it should in relation to the tradition of the
   sestina?
5. Does the language seem natural? Has the poet adhered not only
   to form but also the standard elements of poetics (imagery, line
   breaks, point of view, voice, etc.) which help to make a poem
   "good"?

Reflections at Dawn

Good word choices to
end lines!

We arrived in Aurora just after dawn,
Which all in all, seemed a most appropriate time.

Is this too wordy?

On our drive up the Willamette, the morning had
  broken

You might make this active.

With shots of rose and mauve, reflecting
Off the river, and in farmhouse windows,
Still newly washed by autumn rain.

There's a nice sense of
movement and action here
and it's naturally working
with your line-ending words.

Although overcast and threatening rain,
The day began dry at dawn.
We walked around town peering in the windows
Of the antique shops, knowing there was plenty of
  time
Before they opened. We saw ourselves reflecting
Among the displays inside. Most held old and broken

Could we include more
internal and slant rhyme
in these stanzas (1-3)?
It might help the
rhythm of the lines.

Tools and implements and we looked broken
In the old glass of the old buildings in the new rain
Just starting to sprinkle. The droplets on the panes
  reflecting
The night lights in the stores and the dawn
Colors underlined what time
It was. So we walked around carefully not looking in
  at the windows

Of the old houses in the old streets. Light from those
  windows
Was broken

This seems a
wordy and awkward line.

By breeze driven shrubbery and the folks inside
  checking the time,
And checking the weather channel to see the rain
Was going to start again after dawn.
We commented of the state of the old houses, reflect-
  ing

Our own interest in historic buildings, while reflecting

Too abstract.

On the paradox that was Aurora. All the old stuff in
  the windows
Left over from the dawn
Of Aurora, much of it repaired after being broken
Or left out in the rain

Nice image!

Like the rusted and veneer-sprung sewing machines
  from a time

When utility had beauty. For there was a time
When Aurora was a forward-looking community, whose windows
Revealed the enlightenment of a new century; their views were reflecting
Innovative and edifying ideas. So we stood there in the fitful, spitting rain
Discussing the new economy built on the antique trade, a broken
Trend from Aurora's 19th Century modern dawn.

You looked in at the windows of the railroad station reflecting
How over time it had turned away from the tracks, a broken
Link from its useful past. Now, in the rain, just an antique shop to open
sometime after dawn.

ELISABETH MILES

Break in form.

Might ask yourself
why and if it matters?

Nice image.

Rather wordy.
The language in the
envoy becomes prosaic.
Consider trimming and/or
inclusion of more
poetic language.
Not really a
dedication here
in the envoy.

Beth,

This poem is doing some good work. One thing that we might note quickly is that you've followed the William Stafford maxim of "use language you know and capitalize on it." This is an accessible poem. And that's a good start because the form doesn't get in the way of our reading of it. I want to touch on five main points central to the poem's success and we'll take a look at a few other things too. First, we should ask whether the poem in fact follows the form. We can see that it doesn't quite follow, but it's pretty close. We go for five stanzas following the traditional word/line scheme but without the traditional meter of blank verse, and then in the sixth stanza and the envoy you break the traditional scheme. Is this a problem? For a traditionalist yes, and even someone not prone to traditionalism might say, "Why have the form if you're going to break it?" This is a valid point, but it's only in the line order that you have veered. In fact, Beth, you've kept your ending words and their effect as well as the appropriate number of lines. If we had had a more severe break from the form, I'd say it was problematic, but here it's relatively benign.

Now let's take a look at word choices, line breaks, and how those words work in the poem. This poem is about going somewhere, about showing someone around a town that you know. So we are taking a trip with the persona in this poem and it's set up in a first-person narrative sense. The line-ending words are *dawn, time, broken, reflected, windows, rain*. Let's look for just a moment at how these words relate to the sense of going to a new place. We have five of the six words (*dawn, time, broken, windows, rain*) talking about a sense of place and the time we're there. This is good. And one which specifically gets at some action—*reflected*. But that's a double action by the second stanza in the poem because we realize that we're talking about how the persona and her friend see themselves in this place. Well, in that regard, then so, too, do *windows* and *broken* become double-edged words. Beth, you're getting some mileage out of these and for a sestina to work well, we need these line-ending words to be this way. In terms of line breaks, abandoning a sense of blank verse and opting for free verse instead seems to work fine and help you in the process. O.K., so this is working for you—and probably the readers too; as I've said, the poem is accessible—and at times this helps to create a nice sense of rhythm or lack of it in the poem (notice line two of stanza four).

Now, let's comment generally on the elements of poetry and how they affect the sense of the form. This is something to remember when writing fixed form poems—using elements of the craft is not separate from the form itself. So in stanza one I made a comment about changing line three, that it was a bit wordy and awkward. But that means another change to line five because if we take out the river in line three, we can't have the sun reflecting off of it in line five. One quick comment on your choice of the word *reflecting*. I'd suggest using *reflected* to make the verb active—we're following the persona here and we ought to have as much action as possible. There are some fine details throughout the poem, and of course this is good because we're being shown around this town.

One of the comments I made early in the poem is that it might be nice to have a bit more rhyme within the lines—maybe some internal rhyme and slant rhyme which would add to the musical quality of the language as well as helping some of the images blend together through how the words sound. Farther on in the poem, line three of stanza four "by breeze driven shrubbery . . ." seems an awkward line in its diction and this awkwardness affects the image. And in line two of stanza five, the word "paradox" is just too abstract and doesn't do anything to create an image. This is a place to show us something. In the next line, though, you shift to a double use of *dawn* taking us from the time of day to the birth of the town. And that's nice.

The envoy, despite the line-scheme shift, functions reasonably well. It summarizes some of the actions in the poem while continuing others. And, while it doesn't follow the traditional pattern of dedicating the poem to a person, it does in some way dedicate it to a town despite an almost elegiac quality. However, in the envoy, line two seems a bit wordy with the "had been moved and turned" phrase in it. The language here, as in a few other places, becomes a bit prosaic and too straightforward.

Nice work, Beth. I look forward to seeing your revision.

—*JEFF*

Reflections at Dawn

We arrived in Aurora just after dawn,
Which seemed, after all, a most appropriate time.
The morning had broken
With shots of rose, cerise and mauve, reflected
Off the puddles, and in farmhouse windows,   5
Still newly washed by the overnight rain.

Although overcast and threatening rain,
The day began dry at dawn.
We walked around town peering in the windows
Of the antique shops, knowing there was plenty of time   10
Before they opened. We saw ourselves reflected
Amongst the displays inside. Most held old and broken

Tools and implements. We looked old and broken
In the old glass of the old buildings in the new rain
Just starting to sprinkle. The droplets on the panes reflected 15
The night lights in the stores and the dawn
Colors outside underlined what time
It was. So we walked around carefully not looking in at the windows

Of the old houses in the old streets. Light from those windows
Was broken   20
By the shadows of folks inside checking the time,
And checking the weather channel to see if the rain
Was going to start again after dawn.
We commented on the state of the old houses, reflected

Our own interest in historic buildings, while we reflected   25
On the paradox that was Aurora. All the old stuff in the windows
Left over from the dawn
Of Aurora, much of it repaired after being broken
or left out in the rain
Like those sewing machines we saw, rusted and veneer-sprung, from a time 30

When utility had beauty. For there was a time
When Aurora was a forward-looking community, whose windows
revealed the enlightenment of the new century; whose views reflected
Innovative ideals. So we stood there in the fitful, spitting rain
Discussing the new economy built on the antique trade, a broken 35
Trend from Aurora's 19th Century modern dawn.

We looked in the windows of the railroad station and reflected
How it turned away from the tracks, a broken

link from its useful past. Now, in the rain, just an antique shop to open
sometime after dawn.

ELISABETH MILES

Beth,
Good effort. You have done some fine revising work in this poem already
and have set the stage for another draft to be worked through. Your revision
to lines three and five in stanza one work well. Despite having to take out the
river (which is a nice thing to have) the stanza is a bit tighter. Although a
minor revision, let it serve to illustrate how one revision can often spark
another. Also, Beth, you've tightened the lines just a bit here. In stanza one,
interesting revision of the last words of line six, "autumn rain" to
"overnight" rain. On one hand, this might be considered an overrevision.
"Autumn rain" certainly was not a bad choice, but then again, "overnight
rain" is a bit more specific and maybe a fresher use of language. Here's a
revision there's no right answer for; rather, you, as the writer, need to know
what you like best and why. Also, as mentioned in the earlier notes, the revision of *reflecting* to *reflected* is made which subtly changes the sense of the
word. Just as important, changing the grammatical structure of the word
means changing the grammatical structure—however slight—of the lines in
which the word shows up. And for the most part this will tighten the syntax
of your lines. Good work.

Farther on in the poem, I noticed that the awkward line three in stanza
four "by breeze driven shrubbery" was changed to "shadows." What a fine
choice. Not only is it one word for many, but it focuses on the important
image—the people inside—and raises a sense of ambiguity about them. And
it becomes a fine figurative word to use here. Beth, you've squeezed more
out of this line with that revision than appeared to be in it in the first draft.
If you look at what you've done here, applying this to line two in stanza five
for the word "paradox" might add some mileage too. And again you might
apply this rule to stanza six in line two by making the phrase active and
saying "Aurora looked forward" as opposed to the passive phrase of "was a
forward-looking community." But in the envoy, the rule applied, tightens the
second line considerably, removing the prosaic quality and creating a more
resonant language for the end of the poem—especially given the elegiac
quality we spoke of earlier.

Good work, Beth. You've managed a fine balance between form and
your own very natural language use. Keep working on this one.

—JEFF

Overall, Beth has done a fine job of working through such a complicated
form and has kept a language which is clean and available. One main rule of
writing fixed form poems, to which Beth has adhered, is to avoid letting the
form push you around. She hasn't allowed the form to alter her language use,

make it archaic, or change the syntax from natural speech patterns and rhythms. Rather, she has allowed herself the flexibility to alter the form slightly to fit her language and her sense of the poem while still maintaining a clean use of the sestina form. So in the end, she hasn't traded her creativity for mere adornment of her language.

chapter fourteen

SURROUNDED BY STORIES: WHERE OUR STORIES COME FROM

It seems that if someone wanted to be a writer but could not think of anything to write about, he would have the proverbial cart before the horse. Why would you want to write if you didn't have something you wanted to write about? Why speak if there is nothing to say?

With that said, it is apparent that you, the reader, are interested in the creative arts, and specifically in the craft of writing fiction. Each of us has a unique world view and it is through our stories that our view will be given the light of day. But where do our stories come from? The short answer to this is that the stories come from our own lives and from the lives of others. Remember this: *We are surrounded by stories.* Anyone suffering from the psychosomatic syndrome known as Writer's Block might do well to repeat this over and over again as a mantra to unleash the mind: *We are surrounded by stories. We are surrounded by stories. We are surrounded by stories.*

Certainly, the more experiences we have, the more stories we have to tell. It seems to me that one of the more beneficial things you could do for yourself as both a person and a writer is to travel as widely as you can afford. The reason for that is twofold. First, by traveling away from home, you

> *I write about my personal experiences whether I've had them or not.*
>
> Ron Carlson

will see home with new eyes, and in that sense you will be seeing your home for the first time. If you have never left your hometown of Portland, Oregon, for example, what do you have to compare it with? But if you have been to Prescott, Arizona, then you will see Portland with new eyes and you may recall detail that you would not have brought to your level of conscious thought (and to your writing) unless you had gone somewhere else. I believe the only way you can truly see your surroundings is to leave them in your wake.

The second benefit for the writer who travels is the more obvious of the two: travel is almost always adventure—unless you dilute the experience by staying in five-star hotels—and from adventure come stories. Whether you drive from Seattle to Boise or take a train from Shanghai to Beijing, you will see places and people worthy of writing about. The key, of course, is to keep your eyes open. When I have finished a writing project, especially a long project, I like to go somewhere I have never been before, for it invigorates me, and from these new settings new stories always come. The destination need not be exotic, however; it could be a part of the city where I live but have never been. It could be just around the corner.

In 1987, my wife and I took a ship from Kobe, Japan, to Shanghai, China. It was a small ship, more of a ferry than a cruise ship, really, and nothing terribly exciting occurred on the two-day voyage. In 1994, something reminded me of that trip of seven years before, and I thought that a small ship cutting west through the East China Sea to Shanghai would make a compelling setting for a story, and I wrote "Slow Boat to China." Travel to new places offers new settings which can always provoke me to use them as foundations for stories to stand upon.

But even if we never left our hometowns, there would be enough stories to write for the rest of our lives. I believe eavesdropping to be not only one of the most enjoyable and beguiling of pastimes, but also to be one of the most fertile activities from which to harvest new stories (I do not advocate a literal interpretation of the word, however, for you could slip and fall). People may say that eavesdropping is rude and to them I say that we do not walk through town with our eyes closed, nor should we plug up our ears with cotton balls when there are good things to be heard. I overheard (*overheard* sounds so much more polite than eavesdrop, yet it also implies listening from an elevation), an absolutely fabulous anecdote the other day, but alas, I will not divulge it here for I am still writing a story born of that juicy tidbit (note that it is unwise to tell your stories before you have written them, for it diminishes your ability to make them fresh on the page).

One of the assignments I give my students is to go to a public place, say a restaurant, and eavesdrop on a conversation between two people. The students are to write down what is said as best they can. The assignment is actually a dialogue exercise explained later in this book, but it also allows the students the chance to realize the wealth of stories that eavesdropping affords.

Of course, there are also the stories we hear from friends and family, and they, too, can be seeds from which stories and even novels may germinate. A word of warning, though: if the story was about an event that occurred to someone you are familiar with, you might do well to avoid showing him or her your version for it will necessarily be different from what actually happened. This is because the story must *carry on the page*. In other words, it must be able to stand alone with an arc of its own and thus, it is almost always necessary to change what actually happened to what will work on the page.

An example of this type of story-genesis is Raymond Carver's "Why Don't You Dance?" Carver was sitting around with friends and fellow writers one evening when one of them told of how he had passed a driveway where all of the house's furnishings—bed, sofa, table, chairs, record player, lamps et cetera—were neatly arranged in the driveway as if someone lived *there*, outside. Then he asked the group which one of them was going to take this setting and write a story. Carver spoke up and the rest, as they say, is history.

Assuming that you never leave your house, and that you have no family, friends or acquaintances to draw from—and this all seems very postmodern and rather unlikely—then you may use the newspaper as a source of your stories (Robert Olen Butler wrote an entire collection of short stories, *Tabloid Dreams*, each story idea having been taken from a tabloid headline). Newspapers are full of intriguing stories. Taking the idea for a story from a newspaper article, by the way, is not plagiarism for you are simply basing a story on another account of something that happened to someone somewhere, and you are then making your own story from that kernel event. You may use the plot of the newspaper account and create new characters and maybe even a new setting.

In telling a visitor how he came up with stories, Anton Chekhov implied that the genesis of many of his ideas came from simple objects. He picked up the first thing he saw on a table, an ashtray, and told the visitor that he would have a story called "The Ashtray" by the next day.

The point to all this is to remind the writer that there are always stories, that we will never run out; one must merely keep one's eyes and ears opened. And if there were a finite number of stories we could tell, that would not matter in the least for in reality, we just keep retelling the same old stories anyway. "Romeo and Juliet" has been told hundreds and hundreds of times since Shakespeare's time; it is just that we put the star-crossed lovers in different settings in different times. That, and we change the names to protect the innocent.

One of a writer's greatest assets is his imagination. The English word "imagination" is derived from the Latin *imaginari,* meaning to form an image in one's mind and to create a picture for oneself. Thus, we create that picture in our mind and develop it into a story on the page, a story that will allow the reader another vicarious voyage wherein another shred, no matter how slight, of the human condition may be viewed. Yes, we do make up stories.

It is certainly useful to keep a writer's journal, for our memories are not infallible and though we think we will remember an idea or a phrase, more often than not that idea, no matter how profound, gets lost. I keep a journal of not only story ideas, but also of phrases and descriptions and characters' names—in short, I write down whatever I find interesting. When I have finished a story and am ready to move on to a new project, I look through the journal and inevitably, a story idea will come from its tattered pages.

You will find your stories. You will never suffer from Writer's Block, for it does not exist. There will be more stories than you will ever have time to tell.

Just keep your eyes and ears open. And remember: *We are surrounded by stories. We are surrounded by stories. We are surrounded by stories.*

Ron Carlson ─────────────────────────

THE SECOND STORY: HOW A PROMISING SINGLE EPISODE MIGHT FIND ITS FULLEST USE IN OUR FICTION

So many of my students' early stories are single moments, episodes, which are presented in the first person. The narrator, many times, appears to bear a strong similarity to the student. An example would be the "spring break in Mexico" story. In life spring break offers young people bonafide adventure, and if you go to college in Arizona many times these adventures are found south of the border. Three guys will pack up and head down to Rocky Point (*Puerto Penasco*), the town nearest Phoenix on the Gulf of California. There'll be camping and drinking and members of the opposite sex who are also camping and drinking, and all of this on spring break. A friendship will be tested by a decision made late the second night (never the first night) and the story will close on the ride home as the world and his best friend look different to the narrator. I'm being glib here, and such stories (the five or six I see every year) are never bad. There's always good humor in them and the imagery is mostly convincing, and because they are never quite bad, overtly shallow, or melodramatic, I've tried to wrestle with how the writer might get the next thing out of such a story.

In some way, such stories full of sand, sun, and Mickey and Doris far from home are stories we're just going to have to write. We went to the beach on our own for the first time and sat under the stars with people we'd just met, and we held our own in the conversations which were sophomoric and profound, and we made a mistake or narrowly avoided one, and we should write it down. I'm convinced that how we feel about the material, our emotional commitment to the material, is more important than the drama innate in the material; and by material here, I simply mean the data from the event we're using as basis for the story.

Do we write from our own experiences? Absolutely. But fiction, as all the big books have it, is different from recorded event. How? Somehow the teller changes, or we let the written record evolve from actual events in a process we call fiction writing. It evolves because we let go of the actual episode while we are writing it, the way you let go of the handlebars of a bicycle, and you follow as much as lead as you go forward. Your weight and velocity and angle suggest real good possibilities on how not to fall, and you listen to them. Writing a true story is often not about where you were going, but about how you didn't fall.

But the topic here is the single story, the episode which while pretty good, still could go farther. The craft exercise illustrated by the attached story could fall under the heading **narrative distance**. Narrative distance is how far the narrator is (in time and sometimes in place) from the story she is telling. When I recount my trip to Rocky Point it will be at the removal of twenty-five years, and there will be signpost transitions in the text to indicate that, such as: "In 1974 in a blue Volkswagen Bug Elaine and I crossed the border into Mexico . . ." Or: "Twenty-five years ago in a car my wife brought to our marriage, we drove south on the continent until we struck the first blue water bay . . ." et cetera, et cetera. Sometimes the distance is years and sometimes it is months or weeks, or most often it is an implied "recent past." The effect of distance like this is to shift the emphasis slightly from the episode to the effect of the episode and thereby, sometimes, get two stories where there might have been one.

I'm oversimplifying this, but for our purposes, that's fine. I'm speaking, I think, to the writer who has a hot episode and is not sure that it is enough of a resource to make a story out of, but wants to worry it north and south for a while just to see.

For that writer, I would suggest this jewelry metaphor: hold your gem and consider how it might be best displayed.

The more glittering your idea/event/episode, the more important it is to hold fire before starting. We see these one-note stories which are absolutely "on topic," stories which want to have a point, make a statement. This is limited fiction. Limited by being overtly neat, pat, smug.

My example is a student story that tantalized and ultimately stunned me, and I include the story of that story here.

My student, Bob Nelson, presented a story to me in consultation about a strange investment seminar. One evening a man, the narrator, goes to an elementary school to attend a generic mutual funds seminar. He's come into a little money and is thinking of learning how to invest. While he is waiting for the seminar to start, there is an act of violence. A man attending a parent-teacher conference in a nearby room, pulls a gun, threatens several people and then in front of the group, the distraught man kills himself. Our narrator leaves in a confused, bemused, philosophical state. The end.

Of course stories which end with the narrator in a bemused, confused, philosophical state are quite common, and in apprentice writers these stories usually end with what I call soundtrack, that is: natural symbols from the real world. Such as: *I left the building and began searching the dark parking lot for my old Camero under the cold stars.* Or: *The wind was strange now and urged me toward my car, my footsteps slapping the dry pavement.* These endings aren't bad. (A stark epiphany and full understanding of what had happened and how nothing would ever be the same would be a bad ending.) But, again, how can the moment be more, make a bigger splash, get some on us?

Nelson chose to wait to find another situation to couple his episode with. Lessons from literature show us that the broader and more overt/violent/extreme/melodramatic/magical the event, the better it is served by narrative distance. There is the story of a man who gets his face slapped, and then the story of somebody telling a story about a man getting his face slapped. In which is the slap louder? In which is the slap more resonant? (True answer: it depends. Suggested answer: the latter.)

You can check this out with the Slap Exercise. Write a first person account of slapping or being slapped (one slap please!) in one page. Then write a second short short story also in one page in which one person tells another a story of a slap or being slapped.

Bob Nelson waited and found his frame story after writing two other stories. He gave the seminar story to a character named Harley Sjostrand and had it emerge in an interview conducted by his new narrator, a young man looking back on the day he went out to see Harley in the village of Two Rivers. There is another story, of course, the story of the lost sister, and its shadow falls across Harley's seminar story to create a powerful and believable moment.

The story breaks down this way. The first twenty-five percent is the frame, the set up. The narrator tells us of a day years ago when he drove back to his home village to see Harley Sjorstrand. The connection between Harley and the narrator's sister Annie is established.

The main body of the story (more than sixty percent) is given to Harley and his telling of the seminar episode. This was Bob Nelson's original gem.

The return to the frame story composes fifteen percent of the story and goes on to earn a new surprise (beyond the bemused, confused, philosophical moment) when the narrator addresses what that day and those stories made him decide about his life. The catalogue of inventory in Harley's old truck from page one returns having collected meaning from the interview.

It is a simple and affecting story, built (it would seem) in layers, each having an echo for us. What I like best is that the lost sister is an aching gap in the narrator, but he never tells us that or asks for sympathy. It swims under the body of Harley's story, threatening us the entire time.

Mutual Funds

by Robert Nelson

It was raining when I left the dorm. I ran across the parking lot and tossed my dirty laundry into the car. On my way out of town, I stopped at Sears to buy a cheap tape recorder for the interview. The drive from Grand Forks to Two Rivers took an hour and a quarter; somewhere along the way, the rain turned to drizzle.

Harley Sjostrand's pickup was parked at the curb in front of Folke's Bar. I pulled in behind it. The tailgate was dented, the bumper flecked with rust. The license plate hung from a mess of twisted wire. Scattered about in the back were a dozen or so doubled-over Grain Belt Beer cans, a flat tire, a logging chain, hubcaps, a coil of rope, a rusty jack and a rain-soaked cardboard box. The windows of the pickup were rolled down, and since I had it in my mind to be a journalist, I looked inside. The truck stank of stale beer and cigarette smoke. The ashtray was piled high with butts. Others were scattered on the floor.

It was 1976. I was a sophomore at the University of North Dakota, and was taking a class called Special Articles Writing. It was this class, or an assignment for it, that brought me home to Two Rivers for the weekend. The assignment was to write an article about a character who seemed out of place. Out of place could mean anything, the instructor said, because place could mean anything. Place could be physical, temporal, spiritual. There was even a place exclusively defined within each one of us, the instructor said. After the class that day, I called Harley Sjostrand long distance and asked him for an interview. He asked me what I was after. I explained about the class. I explained about being out of one's place. "This isn't about your sister, then," Harley said. That subject, I told him, was ancient history; we wouldn't talk about Annie. "Off limits," Harley said. After I hung up I called my folks to say I'd be home for the weekend. "Bring your dirty laundry," my mother said.

I went inside the bar. Harley was shooting pool. Art Sorenson, an old man who had once been a farmer, stood behind the bar; he had a cup of coffee and a newspaper. Other than that, the place was empty. I ordered a pitcher of beer. When the old man brought it, along with a tall glass, I moved to a booth and sat down. Except for the occasional crack of the cue ball, the place was quiet. And then Harley said, "I been shooting stick since nine," and he slammed the eight ball in harder than it needed to go, but it stayed. He laid the cue stick on the table, grabbed his half empty glass off the bar, and walked over.

Harley was a tall, slender man, with a dinky round beer-belly that hung over his belt. His forearms were muscular, and still tan from a season of farming. He wasn't a farmer in the true sense of the word—Harley didn't own land nor did he rent it—but he was a hired man for a family that farmed on the Minnesota side of the Red River, not far from the old house Harley and my sister, Annie, had lived in.

I pulled the new tape recorder from my backpack.

"What you should do," Harley said, "if you really want to learn something, is ask me about my pool playing."

"This isn't a comedy piece I'm writing," I said, opening my "Reporter's Notebook."

Harley pushed his hat back. "A smart ass. Just like your sister." Harley's eyes were deep-set and blue and narrowly-placed. They could be piercing. He reached for the pitcher and filled his glass with beer.

I knew a couple of things about Harley already. He had left Minneapolis seven years earlier, and then, 360 miles later, he had picked up a hitchhiker standing on the outskirts of Two Rivers. That hitchhiker was my sister, Annie. She was unmarried and pregnant and had just moved home from college in the middle of the fall semester. It didn't last at home. She quarreled with my father and mother. Then finally there was a big blow out and Annie left. When Harley picked her up, she took him to the old farm house my father had just bought along with some land. Harley didn't just drop Annie off, he moved in with her instead.

"There's only one thing you need to know about pool," Harley said. "And that is that it's not a sport. It's a social event. You could go a long way in life just knowing that much."

I jotted down "pool, not a sport, a social event." I also noted that Harley was playing alone. What are the rules when you play pool by yourself? I wondered. Can you win? What's to keep you from losing?

"How old are you?" I asked, checking the level on the tape recorder.

"Thirty-four."

"And where are you from?"

"Minneapolis. Born and raised."

I wanted to tell him that you raised crops, that children, you reared; it was something I'd learned in my reporting class. But instead I asked him how a city boy like him ended up in a place like Two Rivers.

"Two Rivers is every boy's dream, isn't it?" he said.

Harley reached into the pocket of his t-shirt and pulled out a pouch of tobacco, a packet of cigarette papers and a matchbook. He snapped a paper from the packet and formed it into a trough. He laid a line of tobacco along the trough, smoothed it, twisted, then licked the glue. "My old man was dying," Harley said, looking at his handiwork. "And I was getting money, right? And all along he'd been saying, 'Mutual funds, boy, put the cash into mutual funds.' Hell, I didn't know squat about mutual funds. That kind of thing don't interest me. But then I saw this ad for a class in the newspaper so I signed up. Hell, I even went." Harley yanked a match loose and struck it. He lit the cigarette and exhaled a cloud of smoke.

"They had the class in this old school building off of Lake Street. Do you know the Cities?"

I said I didn't.

"Doesn't matter," Harley said, "the building's tore down now anyway."

I took a drink of beer. Harley spat a fleck of tobacco from the tip of his tongue.

"So what happened was the class started late and I sat there in the lobby waiting and there's this Indian—not an American Indian, an Indian from India Indian—sitting behind a desk in the lobby. He was all dressed up in a suit and he had on a vest and a tie and so naturally I figured he was the teacher, but I was hoping he wasn't 'cause India Indians are so hard to understand. You ever been around an India Indian?"

I said no.

"Most people around here haven't," Harley said. "Anyway, other people started showing up and when they did the guy behind the desk kept telling them the classroom wasn't ready yet and so please sit down and have a smoke. When the guy finally stood up and said something else, I was on my third cigarette and lost out in some daydream. So, when I finally did hear him talking, quick-like, the way they do, it was too late. But everyone else stood up and started down this hallway so I figured I better keep up for a change, I mean that was the whole idea of the class, to show a little gumption, do something with my money, with my life. I walked past the Indian. He gave me one of those looks. But that kind of thing don't bother me. If you know me at all, you know that much."

Outside the window of the bar, Harley's burnt-orange pickup stood in the rain. I wondered what kind of thing did bother Harley. He drank the last of his beer and poured himself another.

"We ended up standing around in this classroom full of kids' desks. You know, those little pink desks—or maybe blue—with fake wood tops and chairs that turn halfway around. Some of the desks were pushed to the side so a foldout type table, a lunchroom table, could be set up in the middle of the room. I remember there were clowns hanging all over the walls. Paper clowns, with strings scotch-taped to their palms and balloons tied to the string ends. The whole place smelled like paste.

"There was a little kid sitting in one of the desks. Otherwise, the place was empty. Except for us standing there. The kid's chin was on his hand and his wrist was bent like it was double-jointed and he had his head propped up against the wall. His little legs were stretched out. He didn't look at us but his foot kept tapping on the desk leg in front of him. The guy in the suit came in and said to find a seat at the table and sit down.

"I sat across from a blond. I scoped her out first, then I sat across from her. Then the Indian started heehawing around about this and that and then he said, 'Please refrain from smoking in the classroom.' He might have been looking at me when he said that but like I said, that kind of thing don't bother me. It turned out he wasn't the teacher anyway, so it didn't matter at all.

"I hadn't noticed it before but there was a closed door to a small room or office or something off to one side. I thought I heard talking coming from in there is why I noticed it.

"I turned back to the table and counted heads. There were eight of us. One guy was about sixty-five. He said, 'Are we all gonna learn to make money?' Then he smiled and looked around at us. He thought we needed perking up, I guess, 'cause we'd been hanging around so long. But I don't care much for perky or for getting perked up. Your sister was always trying to perk me up. 'Harley,' she'd say, 'perk up.' But she was the one in need of perking up."

"Help's what she needed," I said. I remembered the day she left, the day Harley must have picked her up. We were in the kitchen and my father told my mother to let her go, she'd be back. She'd be all right, my mother said. She just needed time. Time to think.

Harley took a swallow from his beer and set the glass down inside the ring of water it had made, then left behind. "So the old guy—Mr. Perky—he says, 'This is the class on mutual funds isn't it?' and about then I hear a noise coming from that small room. The noise was talking. I don't know if the guy just started talking in there or if he just started talking loud or what, but he said, 'Don't you talk to me about facing facts,' Then it was quiet, and then, 'I can't believe she's telling me to face facts.' Then it's quiet again. Then the door opened a crack and I heard the man snort, like maybe he couldn't believe what was happening. Then the door opened wider and he walked out.

"I can picture this guy even now. He was the kind that's short, but dresses tall. He had on a long tweed coat and he was wearing platform shoes. You know about platform shoes? There ain't no good reason for platform shoes 'cept to make yourself look taller than you are. If he was surprised to see us, he didn't let on.

"He started walking behind my side of the table and he's walking real slow and he says, real quiet this time, almost whispering, he says, 'Christ, she talks to me about facing facts.' Then he says, 'That's funny,' or 'That's not funny,' something like that, but real quiet, like maybe he's alone somewhere trying to figure it out, trying to talk himself into understanding it. But then I turned on the bench to get a better look and when I did the heel of my boot scraped along the floor and it made a sound something like a fart and then someone at the table laughed. It was a short, stupid laugh. I looked up. The man behind me looked pissed so I turned back to the table. Then he said, 'You got a problem?'"

Harley stopped his story and smiled at me and shook his head and laughed and said, "I looked at those clowns hanging on the wall and I smelled that paste and I said to myself, well here's ol' Harley in the wrong place again. And the guy said, and this is where it gets good I suppose, he said, 'I asked you, you got a problem?'

"I looked at that blond sitting across from me. Earlier, when the old guy was spouting off about it being a mutual funds class or not, I'd raised my eyebrows and the blond had smiled at me. It wasn't often I got smiled at. I was looking at her for another one. But she wasn't looking at me. She was watching the guy. Then her eyes swung to the right so I looked too and there was this woman standing in the doorway of that little room and from behind her, from inside, somebody was saying to let him go, but the one in the doorway? she's not worried about the man. She's worried about the kid.

"I heard movement back there then, rustling and scraping, and the guy said, 'A dying man don't care,' and I see the woman in the doorway's eyes get big and she ducks back and there's this roar and wood chips fly off the door frame, I mean the thing just explodes. I turn around and the guy's already yanked the kid out of the desk and he's jerking him around by his shirt and buttons are flying all over the place. He twists him around until he gets him facing us then points the gun at the side of his head, the side of the kid's head. Then the man looks at me because I'm standing now. Then he looks back toward the little room, then back at me because now I'm moving; I've decided to do something.

"'If you got to shoot somebody,' I tell him, 'shoot yourself.'

"'Maybe I'll just shoot you.'

"I figure it's not my time, so soon after the old man going, and if it is . . . well so what, I'm not heading anywhere special. And then the guy says, 'A dying man don't care.' And I said, 'What's this dying man don't care shit?'

" 'You tell me,' he said, and he sticks the gun in my face.

"I laughed. I mean it. I laughed right out loud.

" 'You think this is funny?' the guy says. 'What's funny about this?'

"I told him I didn't know.

" 'Laugh at this, then, funny man,' he says, and he puts the gun to his head and pulls the trigger."

Harley sat back hard in the booth and looked at me. His eyes were wide and dark but the whites were tangled in red.

"So what happened," I said.

"So he blew his brains out is what happened."

I looked away from Harley. Rain, rolling down the large front window of the bar, warped the orange pickup outside.

"Your windows," I said.

"Windows?"

"Your pickup. The windows are down. It's raining."

"It blew apart," Harley said. "The guy's head jerked and then it blew apart. Then he fell. The kid fell too. Then the woman ran out and grabbed him."

Harley slid out of the booth. He looked down at me sitting there. "The next day there was a story about it in the paper. The guy had cancer and his wife had left him. They were meeting with the kid's teacher."

Harley filled his beer glass. "The newspaper called but I had nothing to say. I've never told anyone about it, except Annie, until now. I guess that makes you quite the reporter.

"I took the money I was going to invest in a mutual fund and bought that pickup out there in the rain. A couple days later, I threw my junk in the back and left town. I was on my way west when I saw your sister hitching. And that's how I came to Two Rivers."

Harley set the pitcher down. He walked to the bar and sat on a stool. I switched off my tape recorder, closed my notebook, pushed it all into my backpack.

"And what about my sister," I said. "What did you say to her that night?"

"I never said anything to Annie," Harley said. His back was to me. "I wasn't even there when she did it."

"You were living with her."

"But I wasn't there that night."

Harley swivelled around on the stool and faced me. "Look, your sister was carrying a load of shit before I came along. It got to be more than she could handle. It gets that way sometimes. Someday you'll see."

Harley turned back to the bar. His fingers slid around his glass. He didn't lift it, he only held on. "I want to see that article when it's finished," he said.

I shouldered my backpack and walked outside. The rain had stopped. Water was dripping from the awning over the doorway. The air smelled like melted snow, a springtime smell, though it was late fall. Across the street, two grain elevators stood like giant gray markers against the clouds breaking up in the west.

I stepped off the curb into the space between the car my parents had bought me and Harley Sjostrand's pickup. In the box of the beat up truck was a flat tire, rope, a chain, two hubcaps, a jack, and several empty beer cans. In the corner behind the passenger's window lay a rain-soaked cardboard box.

I didn't stop at my parents' that weekend. I didn't rush back to the dorm to write an article for my journalism class. I wrote a story about my sister, instead. I've written other stories. But that first one, the one about Annie, that one started with the junk lying in the back of Harley Sjostrand's pickup.

chapter fifteen

POINT OF VIEW

One of the first decisions a writer must make in starting a new story is what point of view to use, and one of the most natural acts of an emerging writer is to start a new story with what is one of the most deceivingly complex points of view. I am alluding to the **first person point of view**, of course. In a beginning creative writing course, my students are not allowed to write their first story in the first person. The reason is that I want the students to separate themselves from the story itself, and I believe that is more easily done in the **third person limited**, **third person multiple** or **third person omniscient**.

While employing the first person as the point of view of a story is the most natural of acts, it is often the most difficult, because the writer must become the character of the story. Inherent in that task is a whole list of demands, not the least of which is that in order to adopt the character's psyche, the writer must shed his or her own identity, and that is no easy trick. Let's say the writer is an eighteen-year-old male from the suburbs outside of Portland, Oregon. He has chosen to write his first story about a rancher in Eastern Oregon who has shot and killed his neighbor because of a dispute involving the neighbor's cows that have been grazing on his land. So far, so good.

Now, when he starts writing the story in the first person, he must become that rancher, of

The choice of a point of view is the initial act of a culture.

Jose Ortega y Gasset

course, and to become the rancher he must think like the rancher, talk like the rancher, walk like the rancher, et cetera. He can no longer be an eighteen-year-old college student from the suburbs of Portland.

It goes without saying that in the third person limited he must also understand the rancher, but it will be easier for this writer to narrate in the third person; if he chooses first person, all of the exposition he writes as well as the rancher's dialogue must be written in the **persona** of the rancher.

With these introductory remarks having been made, let us take a look at the various third person points of view before discussing the use of the first person.

THIRD PERSON LIMITED

Third person limited is just that: it is the third person limited to *one* of the character's points of view (pov), often that of the main character, though not always. In a third person story with the characters Bill, Ed, Sally and Louise, we refer to the characters as he, she and they, of course. But in third person limited, we must decide which character will be our lens; in other words, to which character we will limit the point of view from which the story is being told.

If we decide that we will limit the point of view or pov to Bill's, we can only narrate when Bill is present. Thus, we might write the following: *They sat in Louise's living room playing four-handed cribbage. Bill got up from the sofa and went into the kitchen for more beer.* Using these two sentences as an example, the reader will see that if the point of view is limited to Bill, we cannot describe what the other three characters are doing when Bill is absent from the scene. We cannot write *Sally asked Ed to pass the nuts* because Bill, the lens through whom the story is being told in third person limited, is not present to be our witness. However, given the same scenario, we could write *Bill opened the refrigerator and though the cans of Budweiser were in plain view on the top shelf, he opened the vegetable drawer and rummaged through the sacks of fruits and vegetables until he found what he knew he would find: two bottles of Heineken safely hidden beneath the broccoli and lettuce.*

THIRD PERSON MULTIPLE

The third person multiple point of view allows us to have more than one character serve as the lens through which we view the story. Using the example above, if we had chosen Louise to be another lens through which to view the story, then we could have her ask Ed to pass the nuts while Bill is in the kitchen searching for the imported beer. But the writer has to make a conscious decision as to why he would want to use third person multiple, for while this point of view is often employed in longer works such as the novel, third person multiple can be jarring to readers in a short work as they bounce back and forth between characters.

Sometimes a student writer will have unconsciously chosen third person limited for his story, and halfway through the draft, I will find a scene in which the character whom the writer has chosen to be the lens is not present—a scene wherein we are viewing the action through the eyes of another character. This is what is known as a **shift in point of view** (of course, there are more egregious shifts such as from third person to first or second). A shift in point of view can tumble the reader right out of the hammock where she was quietly reading, leaving her somewhat dazed and confused.

Because of the sheer scope of a novel, we will often need scenes without our protagonist and thus, we will need to use a third person multiple point of view. That does not mean, however, that we must utilize the somewhat dated third person omniscient point of view.

THIRD PERSON OMNISCIENT

A third person omniscient narrator is not only third person multiple; such a narrator also knows what even the characters do not know, and hence is all-knowing. Stephen Crane's third person omniscient narrator in "The Open Boat" tells the reader that, although the characters in the life raft are in search of a life-saving station, "It is fair to say here that there was not a life-saving station within twenty miles in either direction." Although such narrators were often the norm in eighteenth- and nineteenth-century fiction, use of this kind of narrator is much rarer today (Brian Moore's novel *The Magician's Wife* is a contemporary example of this point of view). Henry Fielding's eighteenth-century novel *Tom Jones* is a good example of the third person omniscient personal wherein the author often editorializes and may even address the reader in **metadiscourse.** Fielding often digressed in the novel with this point of view: "Reader, I think proper, before we proceed any farther together, to acquaint thee that I intend to digress . . ." In this point of view where the author announces his presence, the reader is asked to believe the author to be, in a sense, one of the characters in his own book and today's readers find this intrusive and even incredible. Still, it is possible to use an impersonal omniscient pov wherein the narrator knows all but does not intervene in the text with casual asides to the reader.

FIRST PERSON

We are all well acquainted with the first person point of view for we employ it every day. As I mentioned earlier, however, the first person is deceivingly complex, for when we write *I* in the voice of a serial killer, we must remember that he is not me and we must sustain that separation from page one to the end of the story. In other words, we must not slip into our own natural voice. Once we fail to maintain that separation between our own voice and the one we have created, the reader becomes confused and may ascribe a possible mental disorder to either the character or the author.

If you were to write ten different short stories, each in the first person, each narrator would be inherently different and so would be his voice (see Chapter Twenty). The first person is not one point of view; it is several, and in any given story, you, the writer, have a choice of whom you could have narrate. You could choose to narrate the story through the voice of the protagonist, he who is central to the action, and thus be privy to the narrator's thoughts as he is engulfed in the action of the story, or you could narrate that same story through the voice of another character in the story, say a detached observer. Employing the latter point of view would allow the reader to make judgments along with the observer who narrates the story.

Another possibility with the first person is to have more than one narrator. Because of the length of a short story, this is often more manageable in a novel wherein the reader will have more time to make the transition between one narrator and another. William Faulkner uses this point of view in his tour de force *As I Lay Dying*, a novel in which he employs fifteen different narrators to tell the darkly comic story of a funeral journey. I call this technique "reality disjuncture" and find it a compelling point of view; we get a clearer picture of reality by having more than one person describe the same event, for each person has a different background from which to view that same event—in other words, your reality is different from my reality.

Whether you choose a first person point of view through the eyes of the protagonist, a detached observer, or through several narrators, you must decide upon your **narrative distance** (see Ron Carlson's essay "The Second Story" in Chapter Fourteen), that period of time between when the event occurred and the narration of its occurrence. If you have an adult narrator telling a story of something that occurred when he was a child, he will necessarily tell it in a different way as an adult than if he were a child narrator telling the story shortly after the event occurred. The establishment of the narrative distance gives the reader a clearer picture of the narrator, and it helps the reader ascertain the reliability of the narrator.

SECOND PERSON

The second person voice of *you* is given little attention in these pages for it seems a bit artificial, but Jay McInerney makes good use of it in his novel *Bright Lights, Big City*, a story of a drugged-up and totally disenfranchised young man in a lost society where alienation reigns supreme. McInerney sustains the point of view from the first sentence of the novel—"You are not the type of guy who would be at a place like this at this time of the morning"—until the last sentence some 182 pages later: "You will have to learn everything all over again." Although the second person often distances the reader from the work, it is successfully used in this novel because of the subject matter. The second person is another possibility for the writer to consider.

A NOTE ON VERB TENSE

One might note how verb tense affects the pace of the story. Most of our stories are written in the simple past tense, and this is in part because of narrative distance, because our narrators are looking back, but telling a story in the past tense also speeds up the action and increases the pace of the story.

Bobbie Ann Mason's story "Shiloh" is told in the third person limited point of view employing the present tense. Notice how using the present tense slows down the pace of the story: "Leroy Moffitt's wife, Norma Jean, is working on her pectorals. She lifts three-pound dumbbells to warm up, then progresses to a twenty-pound barbell. Standing with her legs apart, she reminds Leroy of Wonder Woman."

Notice what happens if we rewrite the paragraph using the past tense: "Leroy Moffitt's wife, Norma Jean, was working on her pectorals. She lifted three-pound dumbbells to warm up, then progressed to a twenty-pound barbell. Standing with her legs apart, she reminded Leroy of Wonder Woman."

Using the past tense, the action is already completed, but using the present tense, the reader is waiting for the action to be completed and thus, time moves more slowly. You can see that the action is slower in the first paragraph using the present tense, and Mason consciously chose this tense because everything in their lives has slowed down: Leroy, a truck driver, has been injured, and he now stays at home getting stoned. Only slowly is Norma Jean realizing that their marriage is falling apart.

Much of the reward in writing is that you are in control. You have hundreds of choices to make in any given story, and two of them are verb tense and point of view. There will be times when you will write a story and after a few drafts you will realize that the point of view is not working. This happened to a student of mine who wrote a twenty-page story in the first person. It was a haunting story of a disenfranchised and angst-filled man who was totally alienated from the world to the point at which he would drive to restaurants and ask to take his meals in his car.

The problem with the story was that in the first person voice, the narrator was too close to his own problems and it seemed as if he was explaining them to the reader. Thus, I asked Jacob to try writing the story in the third person limited and he took on the arduous task of doing so. The new draft, with that one step of removal from the character, was greatly improved: his alienation now seemed to be real.

Remember that when you begin a story using a point of view, you can always change it. In fact, that is one of the exercises I ask of my students.

Debra Earling

THE WAY I SEE IT: POINT OF VIEW

It is the beginning of the term. Students have been away for a long summer but now they have returned to school and summer still lingers at the windows, heavy summer, the summer of autumn, Indian summer, the last endless days of sleepiness and dreams, and the new writers sit in their chairs, some eager, some inattentive, most watchful and listening for magic. There must be a magic to writing, some clue, a key, and some of those students I am sure are convinced that I have the answer because I stand in front of the class and grab the marker to jot down on the white board: Point of View.

"What is point of view?" I ask, not looking for a particular answer but hopeful still.

Point of view. Point of view. Sometimes the class is silent. Not long. I have learned that students are most uncomfortable with silence. Silence suggests a grim awareness of all that is unspoken, a dense physicality of chairs shifting, quiet books, tapping of pens, the presence of every single person because every body is in view when silence slows the room. Students stiffen in their chairs, hoping someone will save them from themselves, from the glances of their colleagues.

Point of view is the way we look at things, one will begin. It is the way one person sees the world around herself. "What does it mean to have point of view in writing?" I say. And at this time I am always impressed that most of the students know the lingo. Terms arise and scatter about the room.

Point of view can be in first person as in: *Every Saturday I watch the woman hang her laundry on the clothesline and imagine she wears everything she is drying.* Point of view can also be in second person: *Every Saturday you watch the woman hang her laundry on the clothesline and imagine she wears everything she is drying, from the size forty-two panties to the small man's boxer shorts.* Point of view can also be in third person: *Every day he watches the woman hang her laundry on the clothesline and imagines she wears everything she is drying, from the ragged purple panties to the pink running shorts.* Or just this: *I wash my clothes. You wash your clothes. She washes her clothes.*

Simple enough. Point of view seems almost easy, doesn't it? But what does writing in first person suggest? What are the difficulties that arise in writing in first person? What are some of the problems we might encounter writing in second person? And what does it mean to write in third person? What responsibilities, if any, do we have to the reader?

I try to steer my students toward the discipline of writing in third person limited omniscient. Write with the great authority of an omniscient being, but rein your work in. Allow your reader to be in the mind of only one character even though you see everything. You understand that the woman hanging her clothing on the line is aware of the man watching her, that she even likes it, and has her own fantasies. I send my students off on their first assignment. Write a two-page beginning from third person limited omniscient. My students seem almost pained. They were looking for something more challenging, more exciting. I do not warn them about the pitfalls, the desire always to see just around the corner, to see beyond the fray. I do not tell them at first, because in a beginning level writing class or even at a more advanced level writing class, it is difficult to explain that the point of view you launch into carries its own immutable authority, an astonishing power that moves beyond your own ability to understand or control. The point of view you select, the character who carries the story, can suddenly take on a life of her own. But this sounds crazy to most students. It sounds crazy to me. And I do know writers who tell me there is only the craft of writing, that characters remain silent and are really always the author's thoughts flat on the page, invented. Still, perhaps it is the way I was taught, the way my mother shared her stories with me, that influenced my own stories to take on life. Stories that no longer seemed of my invention, characters that breathed on the page and whispered to me. Not auditory hallucinations, I tell my students, surely not that. But I cannot deny that some of my characters seem so real to me, I think in my stupored moments after putting down the pen for sleep that I could drive to the towns where they live, have a beer with them, recognize them in a crowd of people. Crazy, I know. And not something a student is too eager to embrace. I have found we look for certainty. We employ awareness of the world that grounds us. When I enter the stories I am writing, the ground shifts and the world pivots. My voice becomes another. How can this be?

I remember years ago, when I was a student at the University of Washington, I was taking a writing class with my friend Laura Stearns and she told me that she was writing late into the night. The story she was writing concerned a mother and her two daughters. These women were in an attic sifting through their grandmother's things, memorabilia, old photographs, lace gloves, button shoes, a long-dead child's pair of eyeglasses, dishes, a boxed wedding dress, the stuff of a long life ended. Laura told me she wished to keep the point of view centered on the mother but as she was writing, the elder daughter's point of view became stronger and stronger. "I couldn't shut her up," Laura had told

me. "When I tried to stop her altogether, she told her story through dialogue. It was her voice that dominated. Her voice was constant, high
pitched, nagging." Eunice was the character's name. Eunice could not be
silenced. Laura knew only one way to shut her up. She turned off her
electric typewriter and covered the keys. "As I walked down the hall,"
she said, "I felt her follow me. It was as if she wanted her story told so
badly she was after me. Even after I got into bed I could feel her in the
room," Laura told me. Does this happen to you? I ask my students when
we meet again. Some of my students look at me, I guess, in the same way
I looked at Laura. A little confused. A little frustrated. Others lean forward in their chairs as if confessing or sharing a secret. Something did
happen when they were writing. Something beyond their control. A character began to take on life, not just the main character they were focused
on, but suddenly other things began to happen in their stories. "I
couldn't get my character to enter the kitchen. She wouldn't go. Every
time I tried to write about her entering the kitchen she became stiff. It was
more like stage directions. And then it dawned on me. She didn't want to
go into the damn kitchen."

Others say they couldn't keep focused on one character. Other characters wanted to share their point of view. Other characters became more
immediate, more dramatic, more interesting. I guess you write your way
into the best point of view. Yes and no. Sometimes assuming the point of
view of a character that least interests you is the way to enter the story.
Sometimes the character that you know the least about has more to tell
you. But isn't this a little nutty? What about craft? Yes, what about craft?

And then there are always the students who don't have any dramatic
experience. The exercise was almost plodding to them. And yet when I
examine their stories I find many places where point of view has shifted.
Places where suddenly the primary point of view character becomes sec-
ondary or tertiary. When I mark the spots where the point of view begins
to stray the students are usually unaware of the tendency. Is it lack of vigilance, laziness, or something else?

So what is the difficulty we face when we try to hold to one point of
view, third person limited omniscient? Why does it take vigilance to hold
to one view? What spins in us? Shifts in us? What steers us off course?
What is the trouble we encounter in writing? What exactly is the "big
deal" anyway? I ask my students to think about the idea of where their
stories come from. How come I can give them an outline of a story, even
a character sketch to follow and they will all arrive the next week with
completely different characters and a hundred different stories? Easy
enough again. We are all different. But what marks us as different? Our
experiences. Experiences real or imagined. The way we see life, the way
we were reared, our backgrounds, our talents, the people we have
known, the people we imagine we will meet, what we want out of life,

the loves we have embraced, the stupidity we have endured, the part of the country we come from, culture, background, ideas, race, religion, no religion, heartbreak, heartache, how tall we are, how short we are, if we are a sweets person or a person who enjoys salt more, if we have traveled or have not traveled, if we read and what we read, if we are in love at the moment or moving out of love. The writing we tap in the deepest part of ourselves is like a memory beyond our knowing. A sharper memory than present because it is a memory that includes our whole life, and depending on what we believe, before life. And some of all that we have ever encountered but cannot access rationally or logically slips into our stories when the editorial self begins to fall away. Is this what we must contend with when we are writing and trying to control a singular point of view? I suggest to my students that it is. And the worst and best part of it is, as writers we have to shift from the great untamed world of all of our experiences to the tight discipline of craft and to the tighter discipline of our own varied voice put to craft. We have to limit point of view even if we choose an omniscient point of view. We have to focus the work, shape the story, press it into the point of view we have claimed for the story. And at our very best, we create a story that calls our characters to experience and witness change, a change of self, a change of the point of view that compelled our writing of the story and urged the reader to look down the path of the character's thoughts and actions and hope for that change.

I have often heard that a narrator exists only in first person. I have seen it written in craft magazines, in books on writing. After reading that idea and hearing it so many times I tried to believe that it is true. I tried to convince myself that in third person I was the narrator. If I made some off-center remark it was I, not the narrator. I would look at my stories sometimes and censor myself because I would not say even in third person what my story was saying. Now I know for myself, and I think it is a discovery and a choice, a rule you can choose to break if you wish to embrace a different idea; and the truth is, I embrace the idea that I am not the narrator of any of my stories, even when they are in third person. Somehow a smarter, wiser narrator steps in, sometimes even an idiot narrator steps in—a narrator that orchestrates a story I believe I have never heard or known but a story that belongs to the third person narrator almost as a story belongs to a screenwriter and not the director. Maybe I wish a disclaimer for myself and for my students. This is not I. This sometimes is not even my invention. I only craft the story that I hear. I like that idea. It is a grand excuse for bad behavior and I suppose as an excuse it qualifies as another story. You can ask any other writer for her opinion and you can choose what you prefer to believe. To me that is the freedom of writing.

If we choose to write in first person we have to be careful to select a narrator who can carry the story. A child in first person present tense or a child recalling recent events is deadly. I know it's been done. Break the rule, if there is a rule, but spare your readers a mommy-and-daddy-beat-me story. There must be more original drama in a child's life than the fear of the rod.

I like a story that challenges the writers in my class, a story that shoots from them like a screamed surprise, something that awakens in them a feeling of omniscience in the truest sense, a story beyond their ability to tell, an unrecognizable story, a story bigger than self. Try a point of view that moves you, I suggest, a point of view that shudders you. Don't write from your own experience I say, explaining that I am talking about the immediate idea of experience, the mundane idea of experience. When I say write from your own experience I mean write from every story you have ever heard, everything. And they look at me smiling, some guarded. But isn't that cheating? If it's not my experience, am I stealing someone else's story? And I remind them that when they write, even within strict guidelines, everyone writing on essentially the same story, it is always, always a different story and always will be a different story.

There is one more thing, I say, there is always one more thing. Be careful after you've spilled your story, to craft that story. Make sure that after you have pinned the point of view down, that the point of view doesn't loft away on you, that suddenly your Lazy Daisy waitress doesn't move from a mature point of view to a nonsensical point of view, that her ideas don't lapse into the monotony of stereotypes or become steeped in something so distant from her nature we are no longer willing as readers to suspend our disbelief. Your characters should be complex, as the world is complex, but not so complex as to suggest schizophrenia unless of course that is the point of your story. And that too I tell them, writing about crazy people or someone who is mentally unbalanced from the crazy character's point of view can also be problematic. A story that bends too closely to the mind and will of an unusual character runs the risk, I say (like there is impending physical danger in writing to those of us who are not Salmon Rushdie), of flapping on the idea of form becoming content, a lapse that can spiral a story into nonsensical dead ends. The reader is to follow the character through all the craziness, craziness is the story, the idea. Beware of form becoming an extension of content, but—and there is always a but—break even this "rule" because there are no rules, I tell them. Learn the ideas of craft, then reinvent the craft. Try to make those ideas work. Throw your stories into the workshop pile after you have given it your best shot and are at a loss. Does it work? Does it work? Does it work?

I don't say much about second person except to say I love the idea, the intimate idea. When a writer employs second person it is an invitation to the reader to enter the story as character. It is also too much a directive. Students are quick to see that they don't want to enter certain stories. The story can easily become too intrusive and their instinct is to put the story down. It is a challenge to write a story in second person, to engage the readers in such a forceful way that you take them places they would prefer not to go. If you want to write in second person, try to take your readers first to the places, emotionally and physically, that they might want to enter. After you have secured their interest, you can take them down to the depths, the heart of your story. Second person requires a constant awareness of readership. Many of us do not want to be thrust into a jockstrap or be stopped to admire for ourselves a particular warm shade of rouge. Some of us do not wish to be fourteen again or harbor the thoughts of a randy young man looking for a good time. Then again convince us that we would. Hook us.

And at the end of the semester, when the long classroom days disperse to holidays, to wide lanes of snow and new and old destinations, I ask my students, "Is there magic to writing?" And they look at me with bleary eyes that reveal writing and rewriting, weary, and some perhaps disdainful. And I pick up their own stories and I read to them.

> The air sticks to Bytom. I used to wipe my forehead with pieces of paper to see the hidden pollution rise up and off my skin. I had contests with other Americans. Whoever had the dirtiest sheet got pizza from the rest of us. Our skin never looked black, but the coal had gone into our pores. I never won, but it was a good excuse to get pizza. And in the winter, when the city's heart pulses with burning coal, it falls from the sky. In the frozen sky, flakes of coal fall like snow. Sometimes they glitter like snow too, because the street lamps try to fool you. The flakes sometimes have that obsidian sheen, and they flash as they pass the lamps.
>
> *National Geographic* sent American and Japanese scientists to Bytom. My friends in America sent me the issue. The scientists declared Bytom unfit for human life. People should not be able to live here. They'd be poisoning themselves if they did. That's what the scientists said.
>
> But that's not so bad. Nobody talks about the really bad stuff. Not even the whisperers. I rarely heard anybody open up and describe some tragedy. Sure, the Poles, the Bytom regulars, were more happy to say, "Very dirty. It's a very dirty place. It smells bad. Ugly city." But nobody said, "My grandmother died from the air, her lungs stopped working. They couldn't get air." Nobody sat with me in their tiny living room and whispered under their breath. "My husband, or my brother, or my father. He's buried deep down below the city. He called out to me over the radio, but the mine, the mine all caved in when the pockets of gas caught fire. It shot hot. It burned through all the tunnels. Just like a flash. And my love died under the ground." People don't like to talk about that sort of thing.
>
> *From "Bytom"*
> *Sean Pfunder, undergraduate writer*
> *(First Person Narrator)*

Her eyes, like winter, hold an empty stare. Bea stands alone at the window in her kitchen. The acid of ripe tomatoes stings the cracks of her cuticles, and the trash under the sink smells of old banana peels and coffee grounds. The red and green slices of tomatoes and cucumbers hug each other while they bathe in vinaigrette in a bowl on the counter. Her friends have been there for an hour and all she said when they walked in was, "Hi, how are you? Glad you came." Jack, her neighbor, has a glass of wine in his hand and listens to his wife tell a story. Bea hears just a little of it and walks to the sink to wash her fingers.

"Yesterday a man invited me to see pictures of his trip around the world."

"Where did he go?"

"He saw a woman drink the blood of a goat. And a man walk miles across the desert holding a newborn baby."

When Bea traveled to Egypt a year ago her mind came back to the same thing every day, a fresh glass of lemonade that existed in the states, miles and miles from where she was.

From "The Oscillation of Her World"
Erin Greenwood, undergraduate writer
(Third Person, Limited Omniscience)

The woman's eyesight was blurred and she fell against the stone walls of his house, out the door to use the toilet. She walked through his back door past the pig pen and into the wooden outhouse. She calmed herself, and tried to forget her childhood fear of falling into the toilet, hitting the ground and slush, and being forgotten there. She had been drunk with a man before, but not with this man, a stranger. She liked men as a habit. Her body, unlike most of the women here, had become natural to her. Sex, a way of getting to know somebody. After peeing, she got on her knees and prayed, banging her teeth together which were numb, the sign of a good high.

"Dear God, take my life, not that I don't want to live, but you know what I am saying. Just do something for me. If this is wrong then help me get out of this situation with the stranger. But I'm going to do it anyway unless some miracle happens. Sorry, I love you."

She stopped to look at the moon which drinking had ruined. Now it was just moving white light, nothing to hang one's life upon. Sometimes when she was sober, she saw the moon as a thing she had in common with all people that have ever lived, except the blind.

Inside the house she tried to make conversation with the stranger, but he took her wrists and tied them with rope to the bed posts. Things like this didn't happen here, she told herself. And with her arms above her, she chose to live upside down, no more choices. Things between them could just happen now.

From "Selfish Peasant"
Anna Baker, undergraduate writer
(Third Person, Limited Omniscience)

And they straighten in their chairs, look down at the floor, sideways to see if anyone can recognize their own particular brand of genius. And when I say this is all your work, your stories, your ideas, I see brilliance. I see a keen, fresh authority. And I see magic. I see magic. I know I do.

*   *   *

Exercises

1. Take a short story you are currently working on, and rewrite it in another point of view. For example, if it is in third person limited, you might try rewriting it in third person limited in another character's point of view. Or, try writing it in first person.
2. In the first person, write a paragraph describing your first kiss. Then describe that same kiss through the point of view of the recipient (again, first person). Then describe the same kiss through the third person limited point of view of either of the two characters. Note the changes in the way the kiss is described.

See the exercises under setting.

chapter sixteen

PLOT

In the evening, after a long day at school or at work, we gather at the dinner table with our families where we ask each other about our days. In asking "How was your day?" or "What's new?" what we are really asking is *What was the plot of your day?* In other words, what happened?

Plot is simply the *set of events of a story* and they can be relayed in any number of ways (note that plot is not necessarily *the chain of events* for this phrase seems to indicate chronology and plots do not have to be organized in chronological order although they often are).

If, though, we say that plot is the set of events of a story, that plot is quite simply the things that happen in a story, it seems obvious that what is important is *to whom* these things happen and/or *who* makes them happen, and that brings up another element of fiction, that of **character.** In other words, it is rather awkward to discuss plot in a separate section from character, especially given that in literary fiction character is almost always greater or equal to plot.

With that said, we will go on to discuss plot in terms of story structure before discussing the writer's search for plots.

As stated earlier in this discussion, the organization of a story may be chronological or it may be one interspersed with **flashbacks** and **flashforwards** (see William Faulkner's story "A Rose for Emily"). Regardless, a story's structure—its

> *There has to be a tension, a sense that something is imminent, that certain things are in relentless motion, or else, most often, there simply won't be a story.*
>
> Raymond Carver

arc—is an inherent part of plot, and it can be broken down into four basic components: the conflict; the escalation or rise in complication; the climax or the turning point; and the denouement and conclusion (one often thinks of these four components as the three even more basic components of beginning, middle and end with the middle consisting of both the rise in complication and the climax). It might be illustrated as follows:

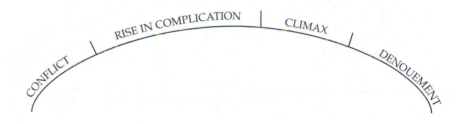

The above illustration outlines the arc of the plot. This plot, the set of events in the story, will go through the four components and we will call this the outer story. For example, CONFLICT: John wants to take a trip to Las Vegas, but his wife Heide does not. ESCALATION OF CONFLICT: John decides to take the trip alone and he buys a ticket. CLIMAX: Friday night Heide finds the airline ticket and hotel reservation for that weekend in his jacket, and she confronts him at dinner. John grabs the ticket from her, grabs his bag, and heads out the door. DENOUEMENT: Heide is on a plane to Las Vegas.

Now, with the above scenario, you could end the story any way you want: it could be a happy reunion or a bitter end. All we have done here is chart out the outer story. The key, of course, is the inner story, that subtextual arc lying beneath the outer story, Hemingway's seven-eighths of the iceberg that lies beneath the surface, and the key to the inner story is the characters. The following illustration outlines our outer story and a possible inner story.

You notice that we started this story of John and Heide with immediate conflict; in other words, we started *in medias res* or in the middle of things. All too often, a writer feels that his reader needs to know everything in a character's history before we even introduce conflict, and this is, of course, a mistake and will create a huge problem of **pacing** wherein the editor will quickly put the story down, for there are too many good stories to be read to spend time with those that bore us to death with long-winded exposition. A writer will, however, write his way into a story: A writer may sit down and start typing without a clear direction, and that is O.K. for writing is, in large part, a process of discovery. In working this way, the writer may discover the beginning of his story on page seven. What the writer needs to do, of course, is

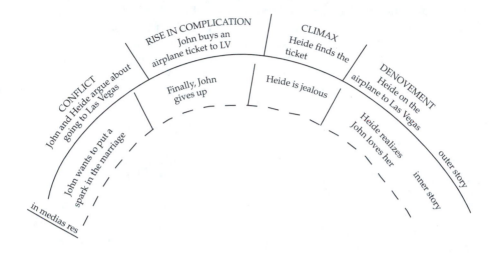

throw the first six pages away, and there is nothing wrong with that for his time was not wasted; what he did was work his way to the beginning of the story. (Writers who refuse to work their way to the beginning of the story and who, instead, sit and wait for the beginning to magically arrive, are those who often complain of writer's block. Again, there is no such thing as writer's block unless you refuse to write.)

The writer needs to know the character's history, of course, but he does not need to regale the reader with all of it. It is true that the more the writer knows about his characters, the more clearly defined they will be on paper, even though he does not include all he knows about them in the story. In other words, it is important for the writer to know his characters' backstory if the reader is to have some idea of their futurestory after the story ends.

From the illustration on page 153, we can see that a story certainly has a **backstory** which may, if necessary, be alluded to indirectly or directly through flashback, and the story has a **futurestory** which the reader should be able to at least partly discern; in between these two "stories" is the story on the page, one that you will have, after several drafts, plotted out either chronologically or otherwise.

If you are employing a chronological plot, then you are going to have a series of events in order of occurrence from page one to the last page of the story. After reading the story, the reader will be able to recount your outer story by stating what happened first, second, third, et cetera. As you, the writer, are working your way through these plot events, you will have to decide which of the events should be handled through **exposition** and which should be handled through **scene**.

This sounds like an obvious and easy task, but it is not necessarily so. First, remember the admonition to writers that has become a cliché: *Show, don't tell*. While this is often good advice, it is not always true. Exposition is

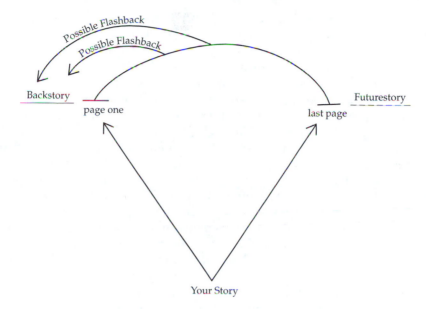

Your Story

telling and scene is showing, and there are times when the reader needs to be told some information or the story may not make sense.

In the plot we created at the beginning of this chapter, we have four plot events: John and Heide argue about Las Vegas; John buys an airline ticket to Las Vegas; Heide finds John's ticket in his coat pocket and confronts him and John leaves; and in the fourth and final plot event of this story, Heide is on an airplane to Las Vegas.

Of the four events, which should be done in scene and which in exposition and what are your criteria for making that decision? The first element would make a vibrant scene, of course, for we would watch the husband and wife argue about a trip to Las Vegas and in this *live action* scene, the tension would rise and grab our attention as the conflict escalates. Also, we would learn a great deal about each character (and about the state of their marriage) in this scene by the way they act toward one another.

The second plot event—John's purchase of an airline ticket—might be better handled in exposition, however, for although it is integral to the story that he do so, we would learn very little by watching him at the ticket office or on the phone.

The third event of this plot—Heide discovering the ticket—might also be best handled in scene for the reader would learn much about her and how she felt by watching her as she discovers the ticket; the same goes for the fourth event when she is alone on an airplane to Las Vegas: watching her on a plane and what she is doing—reading (reading what? *Mademoiselle* or a How-To-Play-Blackjack book?), looking out the window, conversing with a fellow passenger, drinking Scotch—the reader will be with her and experience some of what she is experiencing and therein gain the empathy for the character, the empathy that is so important in fiction.

In conclusion, then, we could say that the above story could be plotted chronologically as scene, exposition, scene, scene.

Exposition is also used to form narrative bridges between scenes so that in this example of four plot events, wherein the second event is handled through exposition, we may, indeed, have more exposition in the story. For example, there could be exposition serving as a transition between the last two scenes, wherein she has discovered the ticket and she is last seen on the airplane: there could be a paragraph or two of exposition describing her packing for the trip (what she is putting in that suitcase might be very important: a black negligee and a cotton nightgown pack different emotional weights).

How we plot a story depends on a great number of variables, many of which are discussed in the other elements-of-fiction chapters in this book. The **point of view** I employ will greatly affect the plot structure (if, for example, I chose to use **third person limited** through the character John, I would not be able to describe Heide on an airplane to Las Vegas, so while she may be on that plane, it would not be one of the plot events of the story).

The next question we should address is where our plots come from. The answer to that is quite simple. They come from all around us. We've all had compelling experiences from which to draw but even if we were to completely run out of our own experiences to write about, there are the experiences of others to draw from. Pick up the newspaper any given day and you will be sure to find a compelling plot.

I tell my creative writing students that, among other things, I will teach them to steal. What I mean by that is I will teach them to find plots, whether they be from the newspaper, from the lives of friends, from the lives of coworkers, or from other stories they've read. Jim Manuel, an exemplary student of literature and a fine writer, whose story "Jacob Boscoe" appears in the workshop section of this text, said that the genesis for this story was Franz Kafka's "A Hunger Artist." Did Jim steal something from Kafka? Of course not. But in reading Kafka's story, Jim thought of a plot for his own story.

Who among us does not eavesdrop? Many of my own plots come from others as I am an inveterate practitioner of the art of eavesdropping. My plots also come from my own experience and sometimes they are a composite of that experience along with ideas I've taken from stories I've read and stories I've heard. The point is, no writer should ever have to suffer from a shortage of plots, for although there may be a limited number of plots in the world, what writers do is recast those plots with new characters. How many stories of unrequited love have we read? How man stories of star-crossed lovers? David Guterson's fine novel *Snow Falling on Cedars* is in one sense a retelling of Shakespeare's *Romeo and Juliet*.

John Gardner said that there were really only two possible plots: either a stranger comes to town, or someone leaves town. We can literally disagree with Gardner, of course, but implied in his statement is that there is a finite number of plots and what matters most is who the characters are in those plots, for it is the characters who people the plot who help us understand the human condition.

H. Lee Barnes

FAIRY TALES ALWAYS COME TRUE: PLOT AND IMAGINATION

Is something or someone menacing your character? If nothing is, you probably don't have a plot. To some student writers the most challenging element of a short story is the plot, moving the action to a resolution that is satisfying. The reasons are several: the writer's concern with character development, the limited space of short fiction, the sense that plot is more artifice and less art than other elements, and even the desire by the writer to be "subtle." On the other hand, too much focus on plot or too obvious a plot or a surprising ending come off heavy-handed. Yet a story must have a plot. The plot simply fulfills the understanding the reader has that something is going to happen. The writer accomplishes her end by asking the right questions about what could happen and eliminating bad choices; the reader reads the story without questioning the choices made by the writer. It's a communion—two people sharing one imagination.

To move forward a story must present complications or obstacles for the protagonist, and reach a climax followed by a resolution, at which point the character or the character's life is somehow altered by the event. Note that I don't state that the character *must* be altered. A man's life changes if he's sent to prison or divorced or abandoned, but he may never change. The notion that characters must experience an epiphany leads some writers to focus on this aspect at the expense of plot, and consequently, story. A story may be so subtle that it is difficult to find. Writers should remember that a reader wishes for more than language and artfulness from a story. Sometimes the protagonist should just ride off into the sunset or catch a plane to Mali. A story does not need a complicated plot to be complex; in fact, a story's complexity comes through a layering of elements.

Long before Poe thought to compose his theories on short fiction, short prose existed in forms such as Viking romances and fairy tales. These early stories were structured around external conflict and obvious themes, usually good versus evil. They generally contained cultural parables and were intended to entertain and enlighten. I mention these tales because, like short stories, they are sustained by complication linked to resolution. Contemporary stories differ; the plot is layered. Conflict exists at two primary levels: external and internal. In addition, some conflicts are peripheral and some tangential. Think of plot as a chain towing a heavily-weighted object and being jerked back and forth. How much stress can the chain take? Only as much as its weakest link. What will it strike if it snaps? The tension in a story is built around the link that is under the most stress. If the writer finds the weak link in the character's life at the moment the story begins, the plot will almost write itself.

A character pushed by circumstances in two or more directions is compelling. Dramatic irony results when the reader sees a character's dilemma, but the character does not. The audience is compelled by Hamlet's circumstances because he avoids the inevitable decision he must make, and when he makes it, it's too late. A character's indecisiveness is the core to many stories. For the character the central issue becomes what course of action to take. As an example, we can use a woman who is in an abusive situation, a stock theme in the creative writing classroom. Many students treat this complication in an all-too-obvious manner. They fail to be persuasive. The woman is beaten and wants to forgive and makes excuses. He is a monster. The writer wants the victim to overcome, wants her to be strong. It is a decent impulse on the part of the writer but does not make for a very compelling story line. The question the writer should be asking centers on why the woman has remained in an abusive relationship. What behavior of her own has she failed to see? We know the woman must leave, but we must also deal with her reasons for not leaving. We must be exposed to her fuller humanity, including *her* weaknesses, to admire her strengths.

Another approach the writer may want to consider is to write the abuser's story. Try to see what the abuser experiences. An exercise that may help a writer to better understand conflict is to begin with the same character(s) and a central conflict and write drafts of the story with three different scenarios. One or all may or may not work, but the insight gained is worth the effort. It is important to remember that writing is an act of imagination, which translated for the purpose of plot means, imagine what happens if. . . .

Raymond Carver wrote "The Bath," a rather short story of a husband and wife whose son is hit by a car on the boy's birthday. The central complication is that the son goes into a coma. The parents keep vigil beside him. The peripheral complication occurs because the mother has ordered a birthday cake from a rather dour baker who menaces her with hang-up phone calls. The mother leaves her husband at the hospital and goes home for a bath. The story ends with the phone ringing and the mother picking the receiver up. The ending is open. It may be bad news or good news from the hospital, or it may be the baker. It stands on its own as a story, very Carveresque in terms of economy of language and action. But Carver saw another story in "The Bath." The second seems to begin with the question: What if the child dies? And the final question to resolve the story is: What if the parents confront the baker who continues to call? The answer here is that the baker feels deep remorse. He has forgotten the human contract, but rediscovers it by giving food and comfort to the grieving parents and sharing in their grief. I recommend reading and studying the way Carver develops this single complication into two stories.

To illustrate how a story has many potential paths, let us take the example of a girl, age fifteen, who's dating, against her parent's wishes, a boy of eighteen. The obvious external conflict is parental control over her freedom, and the internal conflict is the girl's desire to break free of these restraints. We can also add to the equation the intensity of young love and its inherent passion. This is the stuff of *Romeo and Juliet*—nothing new to literature. For the writer, the central complication is only the springboard. The writer dictates the circumstances. For our purposes, we will add that the girl is a Jamaican immigrant and the boy is a white, middle-class kid who has a drug problem. Is this getting to be too much for a short story? Is it novel-size material? This depends on the writer's ability to reign the story in and decide what complications best feed the plot. What the story needs is a critical moment. If the reader understands the central conflicts, the moment of crisis, the finite period of time that the characters exist on the page will spring to life for her. If the writer allows the story to get out of hand, it will become soppy and trite. The potential dies. Here are some possible scenarios: the boy is driving her to an abortion clinic where protestors walk the sidewalks; the girl is sitting in a crack house with the boy; the boy is pressuring her to have sex. Any one of these scenarios has potential to develop the conflict to a crisis. Each choice could result in a solid story or a limp story. But whatever choice the writer makes eliminates other possibilities.

A story is usually better discovered than predicted. More often than not, a character will tell me what he or she should do next. A writer is dealing with human frailty and human strength and everything in between. Thinking of a character as an individual helps. Is she or he willing to quit a job and walk away on a principle? Or is the character too weak or too rigid to quit? Will the character experience a profound change? Will she have an epiphany? The tactic to use is simply to follow a scenario and continue to ask, what if? Think, "What menaces my character?"

Emerging writers must be aware that a resolution is not a solution and guard against forcing fraudulent complications and circumstances into a story. Too often a writer wants to plot a puzzle because she has a clever ending in mind. This does not allow for spontaneity (events in life and on the page often result from impulse or spontaneity). By working toward a fixed end that reeks of solution, the writer is not solving the problem of the character but forcing pieces into a puzzle. The writer solves only the puzzle of the story itself.

When I get a student story that lacks imagination, that reads like an essay, invariably the student says, "That's how it is." Writing from life is a fine inclination, but a hindrance to the imagination. Ron Carlson wrote "Zanduce at Second," a story about a baseball player who kills fans in the bleachers with his powerful foul balls. A story such as Carlson's is metered by possibility, not reality. He asks the seemingly impossible, simply stretches the borders when he asks the "what if" questions. "What if Zanduce hit a ball so hard it killed a fan? What would he think next time he came to the plate?" Stories spring from such imaginings.

A creature that hinders novice writers (and may present a problem to established writers as well) is the adult mind and its sophisticated world view. It understands ambiguity and desires to weave subtlety and layering into a story so that it reflects concrete human experience. There it is looming over the shoulder, whispering, "That's not possible. That doesn't reflect experience." The inner voice wants the story to be "true" to life or something called "reality." Shut the voice off; it's censoring you.

How would Gabriel Garcia-Marquez ever have written "A Very Old Man with Enormous Wings" had he confined his imagination to concrete human experience? He begs the question: How might people react if confronted with a miracle? In essence, what Marquez wrote is a fairy tale, albeit an ironic one that probes human faith. The first complication is Pelayo's sick child; the second is the mysterious presence of an old man with wings. Of course the story takes ironic twists and turns after that as the skeptics seek Christ-like miracles from the old man, who is indifferent to them. What Marquez's gifted imagination does is blend the borders of the real with the fantastic, basic human nature with the enchanted, which is what fairy tales have always done.

A fairy tale contains elements of magic and usually relies on conflict that pits innocence against evil. Often evil comes in a disguise. I'm convinced that many contemporary stories are, whether consciously or not, rooted in the fairy tale. One would be Joyce Carol Oates's highly anthologized "Where Are You Going, Where Have You Been?" Could any contemporary character be more evil than Arnold Friend? He certainly comes disguised, and one could reasonably argue that his knowledge of

Connie and her friends is magic. Oates possesses a multitude of tools and tricks herself, and weaving plot is one of them. The tension in the story is wonderfully developed, and one of the reasons is that Connie, through her innocence and vanity, contributes to the drama. The reader sees what Connie cannot until it is too late. Probably no contemporary writer understands the enduring power of fairy tales better than Oates.

As an assignment, I ask students to write a fairy tale. For a variety of reasons, some respond well to the assignment, a few do not, but it's a useful exercise that results in some pretty imaginative writing. The fairy tale naturally provides a structure that feeds off complication and moves toward resolution if the writer only begins with "Once upon a time" and asks the obvious questions who, where, what, and then discovers how and why. I maintain that a writer who can write a fairy tale, can weave a plot. If a writer understands that plot is not a separate but an integral element of the whole story, that it exists because the characters exist and the setting exists, she can ask the necessary questions. A student, in writing a fairy tale, must separate herself from the anchor of "realism" and enter into the world of imagination.

In the student story provided for this chapter, Trinae L. M. Rivas begins with the classical opening line of *Once upon a time*, provides the where, Neider Valley, the who, Sara, and the what, a girl who was terribly lonely. Trinae immediately introduces magic into the story in the form of five fairies who arrive to solve Sara's problem, but Sara, of course, is not satisfied. Trinea's story is a fairy tale, but is the story, as structured around the first complication, much different from a contemporary story? What if Sara lived in Los Angeles with her mother and was lonely? What if a man came along who promised to end her loneliness? What if there was a catch? Take note of how skillfully Trinea handles Sara's request to become a fairy. Trinea's fairly tale doesn't end up "happily ever after," but then, for that matter, neither do many contemporary stories.

Wishes Come True

by Trinae L. M. Rivas

Once upon a time in a small far away place called Neider Valley lived a girl name Sara. She was a lonely girl, for no other people were allowed in the valley, and her parents worked two jobs so they could drive a Mercedes S.U.V. and vacation in Hawaii. Sara had but one person to talk to, a tutor named Calphurnia who spoke only in Latin and laughed at her own jokes before she got to the punch line. Sara was so lonely that for her birthday she wished for friends. A single tear rolled down her cheek as she blew out the candles on the cake that she herself had made. That night in bed she chuckled to herself as she thought about the wish. How silly for a girl to wish for friends where there are only three adults and no people.

In the morning Sara awakened to whispers and giggling. She opened her eyes to find five fairies fluttering about her head. They introduced themselves as Rose, Hyacinth, Daisy, Daffodil, and Lily.

Sara was excited. She jumped out of bed and nearly fell over her own feet. "This is so incredible!"

"Well, you wished, now we're here," they chimed in unison. They were obligated by Fairy Law to uphold the most sincere birthday wishes.

"O.K., so are you my friends forever?" Sara asked.

"Most certainly," they all said at once, their voices sounding like bells.

Sara danced around the room. Her new friends waved their wands, and the room danced around Sara. She seemed about to burst with happiness. She was smiling so widely that she was sure the back of her head was wrinkled from being pushed together.

Time went on. Sara played with her friends. At first they seemed the same, but Sara came to know each by the hum of her wings. And they were individual in other ways. Rose and Daisy were average fairies. They had wands and used their magic in moderation. Lily and Daffodil were sisters; that is why Daffodil wanted to be called Dilly. Dilly and Lily were regenerated from the same larvae, much like worms are, but it was not fairylike to talk about pre-wing days. Hyacinth was a very proper fairy. She considered herself a higher class fairy because she was cocooned way up in a tree where the air was fresh, rather than under rocks like the others.

Sara was very happy. Her friends fussed over her and played any game she chose to play, but she did not quite fit in with them. After all, they could fly and use magic. So being merely human, Sara wanted more. She decided she wanted to become a fairy, but never dreamed it might truly be possible. Then one day she was sitting in a patch of grass while her fairy friends were weaving marigolds into her hair. Marigolds were Sara's favorite flower even if they did not smell so good.

Sara sighed. The fairies flew around her to see why Sara was depressed.

"What's wrong, Sara. Aren't you happy?" Daisy asked.

"I am, but . . . Oh, I wish I could be a fairy," Sara huffed out.

"It's not all it's cracked up to be," Rose said.

"Don't be silly, Rose. You can fly. Anything you don't have you can conjure with your magic. The whole world is at your command. What could be better?"

"Being a little girl," Rose said, trying to discourage Sara from really wanting fairyhood.

The fairies hovered over her to see if she was serious. They didn't understand why Sara would want to be a fairy except for Hyacinth, who knew exactly what Sara was going through.

"I just want to be one of you," Sara stated firmly.

Once a long time ago Hyacinth was a girl named Helen who, too, had wished for friends and had been transformed into a fairy. She knew the way back to the human state, but at the moment it seemed a cruel knowledge.

After all, she did like Sara, truly, but there comes a time in a convert fairy's life when she just wants to die. Hyacinth had reached that point. She fluttered forward. "It can be done. Are you absolutely sure?"

"Hyacinth!" Daisy snapped.

"Ah-ha! You've never been human, any of you, so don't interrupt," Hyacinth said. "Sara, are you sure?"

"I am," Sara said.

Waving her wand, Hyacinth chanted, "I am the fairy; Sara's the girl. I'll forfeit my wand to switch our worlds."

In an instant Sara was wrapped so tightly she could hardly breathe. "What happened?" she asked.

Dilly said, "You're not Sara any longer. Hyacinth is Sara and you are Marigold, the pre-wing fairy."

"One thousand years before you emerge from your cocoon," the fairies chimed. "We'll stop in on you now and then."

"But I thought you were my friends."

"We will always be your fairy-weather friends," they said, giggling.

"If I'd only been satisfied with myself and my life before," Sara lamented. She hoped that Hyacinth understood Latin.

The End

Trinae says, "I wrote this piece to try to reaffirm to people that sometimes the life we are presently living, though it may seem bleak, may be far better than what we think." Many students set out to write a story incorporating this type of theme, and their stories fail because theme dominates the tale. Trinae's story, while thematically inspired, is driven by the plot, yet at the same time, she uses all the elements of fiction, blending them carefully so that the theme, which is stated by Sara at the end, is well earned. Plot cannot be isolated from the other elements, just as a a fairy tale cannot be totally isolated from realism; a reader understands a piece of fantasy only as it relates to some type of reality.

Except for the magic and the fairies, the rest of Trinae's story is firmly rooted in a sense of the real. Neider Valley could easily be Mill Valley or Lost Desert Valley, anyplace where a young girl is separated from playmates by circumstance. We understand that this is as much a place of the mind as it is a physical setting. Sara is an ordinary girl in most senses. We assume this because she does nothing extraordinary and the narrative voice reinforces this impression. I think it is important to note that Trinae keeps descriptions to a minimum. She keeps what is absolutely essential to the tale, using language that services the fictional form. The reader is never aware of the language. It could be the Brothers Grimm who wrote the piece.

What makes this story work is the unpretentious introduction of the extraordinary. Once Trinae decided to insert fairies to solve Sara's loneliness, the story began to write itself. The result was a fully-plotted story written in less than 850 words, a story that moves from external complication to solution, to internal complication, to final complication, to resolution. Sara goes from solitude to companionship, to dissatisfaction, to transformation, to regret. She is menaced first by loneliness, then her inability to accept herself, and forever by her impulsive choice.

Could Trinae have plotted a similar story reflecting realism? Undoubtedly. Let's make Sara's ambition to become a model instead of a fairy. Introduce an unscrupulous agent, the fast life of a fashion model, the need to stay thin, the competition to stay on top, and the ubiquitous presence of drugs and see what happens. Plots need not be complicated to appeal to a reader, but a character must confront complications. The secret to a successful story is that there is no secret. It's about creating engaging characters, finding a voice appropriate to telling the story, using the elements of fiction, and keeping the question "What if?" going until you know it's time to type "The End." And then you rewrite until it's right.

* * *

Exercises

1. Browse through a newspaper looking at headlines. When you come across one that is compelling, read the article. Then, write down the plot points in chronological order. For example, in a long article about a woman and her son whose car broke down in a snowstorm when they out looking for a Christmas tree, you might outline the plot as follows:

   First: car breaks down.

   Second: woman bundles up infant and sets out on foot.

   Third: she gets lost in the storm and digs a snow cave.

   Fourth: rescue workers find them the next day.

   Fifth: both the woman and her son have toes amputated in the hospital.

   While this is a true story I came across in the newspaper, it is not very compelling for I have only given you the five plot points. You can make it compelling, however, when you take the time to develop the character of the woman.

2. Take a story you have written and outline the plot points as you did with the newspaper article in exercise one. Ask yourself if you have established the conflict early in the story and if you have a rise in tension before some kind of resolution. Then ask yourself if any of the plot points can be eliminated or rearranged by using a flashback or flashforward.

3. Using a highlighter, highlight the scenes in one of your stories. Then spread the story out on a diningroom table or tape it page by page to the wall and look at the ratio of unhighlighted text to high-lighted text. If you have many more blocks of white text, you may be using too much exposition and too few scenes.

chapter seventeen

CHARACTER

Think back to the most memorable story you've ever read and chances are you remember it because of some unforgettable character. As mentioned in the previous chapter, character is almost always greater or equal to **plot** for it is *who made it happen or to whom it happened* that draws the reader's empathy. Plot, after all, that set of events, is a thing; character is a person. One cannot have empathy for a thing, but when we watch someone struggle, we struggle with him.

> *Sow a thought, and you reap an act;*
> *Sow an act, and you reap a habit;*
> *Sow a habit, and you reap a character;*
> *Sow a character, and you reap a destiny.*
>
> Anonymous

Aristotle wrote "Man is his desire." We can translate that as *people are their desires*. Now, think about this. What this means is that we can be defined by what it is we want. Everyone wants something. Even the most humble of gurus wants something, be it serenity or be it enlightenment, it doesn't matter; what matters is the fact that we all want something.

Who we really are can be most clearly illustrated when we cannot get what we want—that defines our character. As a writer, you give a character a desire—say, John, who wants to go to Las Vegas—and then you place an obstacle before him—John's wife does not want to go to Las Vegas—and see how John acts or reacts. This will help us understand John and it will help us understand a little more what it means to be human.

Etymologically, the word character indicates uniqueness in that the word comes from the Greek *kharakter* which means *engraved mark;*

hence, one particular stamp marked one thing as different from another and this difference could be referred to as its "character." With that in mind, we see the need for our characters to be realized as different from one another on the page, as they are in life. Think of five friends or acquaintances and it will only take a minute for you to outline some severe differences among them. The difference may lie in what it is they want, or it may lie in their individual mental attitudes. Readers expect the characters in the stories they read to be different from each other in these respects as well.

In a letter to his wife Alice in 1878, William James wrote, "I have often thought that the best way to define a man's character would be to seek out the particular mental or moral attitude in which, when it came upon him, he felt himself most deeply and intensely active and alive. At such moments there is a voice inside which speaks and says: 'This is the real me!'"

Creating a developed character with James' mental and moral attitudes is quite likely the most difficult aspect of writing fiction. Devising a plot—a path the character can follow—is relatively simple. In order to establish a character's moral or mental attitude, it is often useful to elucidate that character's inner turmoil. In other words, what is at odds with his mental attitude? With his moral attitude? When the character is torn apart by contradiction—by what he thinks and by what choice of action lies before him—we grow to understand his human dilemma, and in that, we are given a broader perspective of what it means to be human. Ralph Waldo Emerson said, "The key to every man is his thought." When he acts in conflict with his own thoughts, he becomes more human.

And act he must. The word drama is derived from "doing" and hence, you had better have your character do something—act—or there will be no drama. Any action is inherently a choice (one could, for example, refuse to act at all), and we learn about our characters by what choices they make, right or wrong, and how they react to having made their choices.

There are as many types of characters as there are people in the world, but it may be useful to think of characters in E. M. Forster's terms as either *round* or *flat*, the former being a developing three-dimensional character and the latter being a static and undeveloped character of two dimensions. A story's **protagonist**—she who is central to the action—must almost always be a round character while peripheral characters may often be flat. The criterion for deciding which characters should be round and which flat is relatively simple: if the character is central to the action, if he or she is one of the main actors, then that character should be round. If the character is peripheral, if he or she is not central to the action, then he or she often may be sketched as flat.

In Bobbie Ann Mason's short story "Shiloh," the protagonist is Norma Jean. She is growing both physically and mentally in the story and is portrayed as round—one who is developing. Her husband, Leroy, is the **antagonist** (someone who provides a contest with the protagonist) and he remains static and is essentially a flat character (although he desires change when it is too late, at the end of the story, as Norma Jean is leaving him).

Norma Jean's mother, Mabel, another character in the story, is a flat character and her lack of development suffices for she is a **foil** (a flat character who, by contrast, is used to enhance another character) against whom Norma Jean is contrasted.

A good exercise when reading a story is to ask yourself whose story it is you are reading: in other words, which character(s) is facing some conflict and choice. As a writer, you know whose story it is and thus, you know which character must be defined as round.

Developing a character as round can be done in many ways. Before one begins the writing, it is often useful to develop a character chart outlining the character's life. Start with the obvious vital statistics such as name, sex, age, family and move on to education and occupation before addressing moral attitude, religion, politics and desires. Once you have created such a chart that can be referred to during the writing process (it is especially nice to have such a chart during the process of writing a novel for it is easy to forget whether a character named Billy Freeman inhaled at age eighteen when you are on page 456 of the manuscript and Billy is now thirty-six), you might conduct an interview with the character, again recording it for future reference during the actual writing of the story or novel. For example, you might ask Billy why he did not inhale the marijuana. He might respond: "Because it was illegal and I was afraid of how I would act if I got high. But I pretended anyway, because I didn't want my friends to think I was a chicken." Such a response is insightful, is it not?

Obviously, you would never include the pages of information you have recorded about a character in this way, but your knowing the information—even though you never mention Billy's not having inhaled in the story—will make the character more developed in the story simply because you, the creator, know the character so well. Because you know so much about the character, you will be defining him subtextually on the page as well as textually.

But how do we characterize textually? Often, the best way to reveal character is to do so scenically. We learn about people through the way they act, and this is also true of characters in a story or a novel. In observing what the character does and how she does it, the reader will learn a great deal about her.

Another way we develop character is through **dialogue**. What the character says and how she says it reveals a great deal about her.

It does take considerable space to develop a round character through scenes and through the use of dialogue, however, and sometimes the writer needs to add additional information about a character. We can do this through **exposition** or summary. The adage *show don't tell* is often good advice, but it is clearly a faulty imperative in that most stories (and certainly most novels) have narrative bridges of exposition between scenes.

Depending on the plot you have devised and the setting you have drawn and the character(s) you have created, your characters may react to the world in one of four ways. They may see this society and its values and assimilate by adopting those values as their own; they may accommodate in that they do not like those values but will adopt them anyway if only to get along; they may rebel against those values in any number of ways; or, they may take flight from that society and, as did Huck Finn, head out to the new territories. Unfortunately, there are few new territories to head out to any longer.

As the writer, you do not consciously need to think of the four options, but after having finished a draft of a story, you might be very suspicious of a character who does none of the four, for it may be that the character is unaware of that world you have so painstakingly created.

I tell my creative writing students that one thing they will learn in my course is how to steal. In relation to character, I mean taking traits from people we know or know of, and using them in the creation of a character of our own. Sometimes a character becomes a composite or synthesis of actual people we do know, and we change their names to protect the innocent. (Speaking of names: avoid giving characters names that sound alike. And in searching for a name, you might try the telephone book or the obituaries in your newspaper.)

Finally, remember that these round characters of ours are three-dimensional as are we, and that if you have a "good" man, be sure to give him a flaw, just as you would give a "bad" man a good trait. This is contradiction however slight, and that is how the most interesting of people live: in a state of tension.

And remember what Heraclitus said: "A man's character is his fate." The futurestory of those men and women you create on the page will be determined by how deeply you have created them.

Tracy Daugherty

A CHARACTER'S SKIN

If I encounter the following character in a story, what do I know about her?

> The house fell silent, as it had every morning after Josie had gone, but today, as she watched her mother's gold Mercedes wink like a brooch rounding the corner, Jude was aware of the coffee aroma rising from Josie's still-warm demitasse on the countertop, and it seemed as if she had been vaporized: here one moment, gone the next. Maybe she hadn't been there at all. Maybe she would not come back. Jude twisted a magazine in her hands. A too-thick emptiness seeped into the kitchen, and she startled when

the coffeemaker exhaled a gurgle of steam. The loaf of bread under a tea towel on the counter seemed like a sleeping animal. The Swiss cuckoo clock above the doorway might explode any moment with chaotic birds. It was time to get out—not just out of the kitchen. Out. Away. Somewhere.

Immediately, I know that Jude is anxious, twisting a magazine, jumping at the coffeemaker's sounds, fearing a clatter of chaotic birds from the clock, seeing the loaf of bread as vaguely threatening like an animal she doesn't want to disturb. The strength of this writing lies in its attention to detail: the "still-warm demitasse on the countertop," the tea towel covering the bread. I see Jude clearly in a setting, a well-heeled domestic setting, in relation to her mother, and furthermore I have some idea of Jude's feelings about her mom. Jude watches her mother's car "wink like a brooch" (expensive? delicate? stately?—all are implied, and not about the car, which, after all, is a Mercedes and needs no further comment, but about the mom). Jude feels her mother's absence more strongly than her presence—"Maybe she hadn't been there at all"—a loss powerfully conveyed by the cup. The writer, Lisa Raleigh, has effectively used third person limited point of view to filter details through Jude, giving us not only the setting, but a sense of how the setting affects Jude.

Still, as strong as the writing is, I find myself aware of the writer *manipulating* details, calling attention, ever so slightly, to herself, and away from her character. The key to this, I believe, lies in my earlier statement: the details are *filtered through* Jude. This is exactly what young writers are taught to do with third person limited point of view—the reader perches on the character's shoulder, sees what she sees—and Ms. Raleigh does it well here, but something else is required, I think, for us to fully *experience* a fictional character. Rather than noting objects as they're distilled through Jude, we want to feel we're observing the world *as if we were wearing Jude's skin*. This is a subtle distinction, achieved by an exacting balance of rhythms, of distance and intimacy in the language.

First, what do I mean by "manipulating details"? We're told that the "coffee aroma from Josie's still-warm demitasse" made Jude feel as if her mother "had been vaporized." How do we get from the coffee cup to Josie's annihilation? As I read the sentence I connect the linguistic dots, perhaps subconsciously the first time through: the words "aroma" and "vaporized" echo one another, sensually. *Aroma* reminds me of steam, particularly if it's rising from a hot cup of coffee, and steam leads me to the *vapor* in "vaporized." From there, it's easy to imagine Josie disappearing the way coffee steam rises and vanishes into the air. The image, though it's only implied, is subtle, potent, and logical, and as "Jude was aware" of all this, it reveals a great deal about her character. It feels niggling of me to say, then, that this very admirable sentence nevertheless strikes me as *writerly*. For all its effectiveness, it finally reveals the author's presence more than her character's. The connect-the-dots game tends to leave us thinking, "What a clever imagination!" not "What a troubled young woman!"

Put another way: I can readily see, here, a writer working out the subtleties of imagery; I have more difficulty imagining Jude in her mother's empty kitchen, working out *aroma-steam-vapor-vaporization*. After all, the whole point of the sentence is that Jude feels bereft in this house, numbed, unable to think clearly, "as if [her mother] had been vaporized . . . [and] would not come back."

If I'm going to *experience* Jude, I need to be aware, not of details sketching unspoken connections, but of Jude's utter emotional devastation.

As the paragraph unfolds, a "too-thick emptiness" seeps into the kitchen. Here, the writer is strangely removed from her own character, not nestled inside Jude's skin, where the emptiness *really* simmers, ready to boil over and swamp the kitchen, but outside Jude, outside the kitchen, even, reentering it, imaginatively, only as the emptiness seeps in—from where, we never learn. I suspect Ms. Raleigh was still thinking about the cup—half-empty, "still warm," at any rate—rather than her character's emotional state, making another rational association instead of crawling inside the mess of Jude's heart.

The scene ends with another neat connection: watching the clock, Jude thinks it's "time to get out." But again, the neatness here is cerebral, not emotional. *Clock* means *time.* I follow the sentence's logic, but I've failed to feel the crushing despair driving Jude from her home.

It's not an *explanation* the reader longs for at this point, but an *experience*, a sense of living in the moment with Jude. *As* Jude.

I began by saying I know, from the scene's generous details, that Jude is anxious. But by the paragraph's last line, that's still all I know. The coffee's smell, the coffeemaker's gurgle, the lurking bread, the ticking clock, all point in the same direction: Jude is an anxious daughter.

Young writers are taught that every detail should count, and should illuminate a story's themes to its readers. Good advice, and Ms. Raleigh has taken it to heart here. But the problem is, illuminating a story's themes often *competes* with creating believable characters. People are multi-textured, never just one thing or another. For the sake of clarity and economy, Jude's anxiety may be the most important thing to know about her, but if that's *all* we know, she's not going to feel fully alive to us.

Ms. Raleigh, a student of mine in a graduate fiction writing workshop, was aware, after her first draft about Jude, that she hadn't gotten completely "under the character's skin." She wanted to "push deeper." Oddly, for all the intimacy implied by such talk, it was greater distance from the character that finally enabled Ms. Raleigh to enspirit Jude—or more accurately, greater flexibility, movement, a delicate dance of distance and intimacy.

Just as the various parts of a person's skin may be soft *and* hard—muscled from dancing, say—rough and smooth, familiar and surprising, public and private, the language a writer uses to inhabit a character's skin must be varied, rippling, unexpected. Not random; skin, after all, is whole, of a piece, a secure container—in that sense, *focused*. But startling.

In her second draft, Ms. Raleigh composed another scene with Jude and Josie in the kitchen. Here, Jude is somewhat younger than she was in the first paragraph. Again, what do we know?

> Jude's mother was fixing her own breakfast plate. Her hair was clamped in rows of hot curlers, giving her a vaguely robotic appearance—but this did not detract in the least from her elemental grace. Standing at the stove, her back to Jude, she scraped eggs onto her plate with a light-wristed turn of the spatula; she might have had a book balanced on her head. Perfect posture, proportions, effortless gesture. If anything, the spiky curlers made everything else about her more feminine by comparison. She wore her special bathrobe—fuzzy, plush, trimmed with satin collar and piping. Though it was pink, a much paler shade than the Berry Belinda table, Jude felt a soft, fluttering contentment in the presence of this robe, the way it flowed as her mother moved; she knew how it would feel to be hugged by those sleeves and she wanted to rise as if taking her plate to the sink, drifting over to her mother. But her mother would notice the pooled yellow yolk on her plate and remind her how many vitamins and minerals it had, what a waste of nourishment it would be.

To begin with, I suspect it's harder to say what we "know" from this paragraph, as compared to the first one, because—on the surface, at least—the details (beautifully observed) aren't all pointing the same way. Furthermore, the linguistic texture here is thicker, less logical, more sensual, moving from abstract formal phrases—"elemental grace"—that we wouldn't normally link with a little girl's perceptions, to specific details—"the Berry Belinda table"—firmly anchored in childhood. (I'll address, in a moment, what might seem to be inconsistent diction.) Still, I think we come away from this scene with a much fuller experience of Jude than we did the first time around.

We're not being told what Jude feels, nor are Jude's emotions described from the outside in, like the "too-thick emptiness" seeping *into* the kitchen the first time around. Here, we're working from the inside out—everything begins in Jude. There's a subtle, but enormous, difference between *filtering* details through a character, and actually *seeing* through a character's eyes. In the first case, we're told that "Jude was aware" of the objects in the room—in effect, we're invited to watch Jude watching. Then we get the details, the coffee aroma, the bread, the clock. Finally, we see how Jude responds to them. She twists, she startles, she imagines chaos.

In this second draft, we're automatically placed inside Jude's skin, watching her mother fix breakfast, just as Jude is watching her. We're not *directed* to see what Jude sees; we see it ourselves, experiencing first-hand Josie's every "effortless gesture." At the same time, the narrative voice is flexible enough to describe what Jude herself is probably not mature enough to articulate—her mother's "elemental grace." Certainly, a little girl wouldn't think those words, but she could be aware of the physicality behind them. The perception is followed by a fragmented sentence, "Perfect posture, proportions, effortless gesture," like a sudden memory of lessons Jude has likely heard from her mother. By solidly grounding each observation inside Jude, Ms. Raleigh allows herself a free range of expression, from Jude's conscious thoughts at the moment, to impressions she's only dimly aware of, which will come back to haunt her later, as an adult, when she remembers that morning in the kitchen.

We know Jude longs for connection with her mother, a longing conveyed in strong tactile detail. The "fuzzy, plush" bathrobe "flowed as her mother moved"—this is how a little girl learns "elemental grace," and it fills her with "fluttering contentment." Note, again, the voice's flexibility. The reader accepts the word "contentment"—a rather distant concept for a child, perhaps—because it is "fluttering," physical, tickling, and anxious, precisely the way Jude's skin would react at that instant.

In the first draft, Jude is left alone in the kitchen, absorbing her mother's actual absence. In the second scene, we endure Josie's loss, along with Jude, even as Josie is still fixing breakfast. Jude wishes to drift over to her mother, to be hugged by "those sleeves," but "her mother would notice the pooled yellow yolk on her plate and remind her . . . what a waste of nourishment it would be." These last lines begin with Jude's desire and end in Josie's scolding voice *as it's lodged inside Jude,* thwarting her desire. The mother is both here and not here, present but unavailable to Jude. No explanation is necessary. We have just experienced why Jude feels her mother's absence so keenly.

The language pays careful attention to rhythm as well as detail, moving far beyond mere logical connections. The long, sensory sentences in the paragraph's center, with their soft sounds (*f,s,sh*) give way, at the end, to the harsh, almost pounding insistence of one-syllable words, one after the other—"yolk on her plate," "what a waste . . . it would be." We slip from the rich, "fluttery" textures of Jude's need for contact to the slapslap of Josie's refusal. Literally, we're stopped short as we're reading. In this way, we share Jude's devastation. We inhabit her skin.

Language, after all, is the only skin a fictional character has.

In this second draft, Ms. Raleigh reached the heart of character. Usually, young writers are taught to build character through detail, to let a character's actions and observations reveal her emotions, her personality. But as we've seen from these examples, detail alone is not enough.

Sifting detail, like sand, through a character's mind is not enough. The language must act as the character's skin, *registering awareness* of detail through its rhythms. What do we know? We know what we feel. And feeling begins with the skin.

* * *

Exercises

1. First name each of the following characters (don't be too exotic or too mundane). Then give each character a trait opposite his presumed nature. In other words, characters who are inherently bad usually have some redeeming qualities just as those inherently good characters have some flaws.

    Example: An embezzler. Name: Roland Banks. Quality: A volunteer in the Big Brother Program.

    A priest
    A fire fighter
    An emergency room physician
    A PTA president
    A Peace Corps volunteer
    A drug dealer
    A bank robber
    A poacher
    A corrupt politician
    A mafia assassin

2. Now do the same with one of your own characters.

3. With a tape recorder, interview a character from one of your stories. As a newspaper reporter, prepare a list of questions to ask your character. As you will also be giving the answers, this will require you to wear two hats.

chapter eighteen

SETTING

All too often, the beginning writer pays too little attention to setting, the very foundation on which the character stands. Yet when we travel, it is the setting that is most often the focus of our attention. We don't backpack through the Himalayas with our eyes closed; rather, we walk through new worlds in awe, with all of our sensory organs barraged by new stimuli, for we are sentient beings with our senses even more aware when entering new territory.

The same goes for the reader—when she enters a short story or a novel for the first time, it is a new world for her, never before explored, and her senses are on alert for new sights, new scents, new sounds, new tastes, and yes, for something new to touch. The reader is as wary of a story without setting as a traveler is wary of a place totally devoid of sensory appeal. If there is such a place, I have never been there.

*The poetry of earth is
never dead.*

John Keats

Think back to the last time you traveled to a place where you had never before ventured. The place itself does not matter; it might be Mexico, Cameroon, France, Oregon, California. Close your eyes and recall your arrival in this new world. What was it that first struck you about the place? Was it the sweet aroma of plantains roasting over a charcoal fire? Was it the sight of young girls in green and orange *saris* walking barefoot through the market with pans of water precariously balanced on their heads? Was it the whinny of a horse as you walked by a Paris slaughterhouse? Was it hiking in Oregon's Coast Range through a spring rain storm, your soaking shirt wrapping you like some new and heavy skin? Was it pulling off the highway into the dust of a California roadside fruit stand, parched and tired from the long drive, taking a heavy strawberry as big as a thumb, and biting into an explosion of sweet, red juices?

All of these appeals to our senses are touches of setting. Setting can certainly be defined as place—again, Mexico, Cameroon, France, Oregon, California—but what is truly place? It is necessarily a combination of space and time for, quite simply, place changes as time passes. A short story set in Kansas City in 2000 would, quite obviously, have a different setting than would that same story set in that same city in 1910, for half of our equation of *place + time = setting* is now different. (It should be noted that while the mantra "write about what you know" is good advice, that doesn't mean the writer cannot learn more; if you want to write about Kansas City in the year of 1910 learn about that place and time by doing some research in the library.)

Setting, then, is necessarily a combination of space and time, and time has as much to do with the second, the minute, the hour, the day, the week, the month, and the year as it does with the character who inhabits your setting and what this character's particular **mood** is.

Example: *The place: Bangui, the capital of the Central African Empire. The Time: September, 1979.* I have established setting by indicating the place and the time. Or so it seems. But who is to people this setting? By asking this question, I have inextricably linked **character** and setting (and **point of view**, as well, for through whose eyes are we viewing this setting?).

Bangui is a beautiful city situated between rising hills and the wide expanse of the Ubangui River. Having lived there for some time as a Peace Corps Volunteer, there is much I could describe. As often suggested in advice on descriptive writing in textbooks, I could appeal to all of the reader's five senses, and I could focus on a dominant impression, the humidity, for example. But what criterion do I use for choosing which aspect of a setting to describe?

The answer is often, but not always, *mood.*

What first comes to mind is the mood of the character. Certainly, if a story is told in **third person limited** through the eyes of a young, naive Peace Corps Volunteer, a devout Catholic from Boston who is depressed at the poverty he has encountered in Africa, we might describe a section of Bangui's Centre Ville, where the New Palace Bar is situated across the street from several mango trees, like this:

> As Johnson walked up Avenue Boganda from the Peace Corps office, he stopped to watch two small boys throw rocks up into one of the green mango trees that lined the avenue. The boys' bellies were distended from a lack of protein, and they were dressed

only in tattered shorts. One boy had a goiter the size of a grapefruit growing from the back of his neck. Johnson tried to spy out a mango in the dense tangle of green leaves and branches, but he couldn't see a single one. He turned and walked on past the crowded veranda of the New Palace Bar.

The reader sees that Johnson is focused on the boys and their hunger— that is the setting Johnson observes. Yet in that same setting is the veranda of the New Palace Bar which Johnson ignores. Another character, we'll call him Smitty, is also walking up Avenue Boganda from the Peace Corps office. Smitty is from Arizona and is finishing his second year as a volunteer and will be going home in three weeks. He is excited about returning to the states:

Smitty walked up Avenue Boganda past the African boys who were throwing rocks into the thick foliage of a mango tree. He climbed the stairs to the veranda of the New Palace Bar. It was not yet noon, but the veranda was crowded with government functionaires and French expatriates drinking beer in the morning sun. It was the first of the month and the functionaires had been paid; the French, they were always there. There was laughter and shouting. Pops, the Cameroonian waiter who waddled his great bulk from table to table, waved to Smitty as he cleared a table for him. Smitty shook his hand and kissed both of his cheeks before ordering a beer and a Croque Madame. As he waited for his beer, he watched two boys throwing rocks at a mango tree across the avenue.

From the two examples, we can see that what we describe may greatly depend on the point of view employed by the writer; that what we describe may, indeed, depend on the mood of the character from whose lens we are watching events unfold.

However, when we use the word mood in relation to setting, we often are more concerned with the **theme** of the story. Granted, a writer very rarely goes into a story knowing its theme—in fact, a writer very rarely enters a story knowing its plot; one must remember that in first drafts, the writing of a story is very often a process of discovery for the writer—but after several drafts, the writer will have discovered what she wants the story to mean and she may then go on to write subsequent drafts in which she hopes to use the setting to help reflect that very meaning.

If one were writing a story focusing on the disparity of wealth in the Central African Empire, one might juxtapose the descriptions of the French expatriates drinking on the veranda with the two boys trying to knock down a meal from a mango tree. This visual image would, undoubtedly, help inform the reader of the writer's concern without ever having used any overt exposition—informing the reader, then, by showing, not telling.

Any aspect of setting can greatly influence the mood of a story, and James Joyce makes great use of light in his story "Araby." The narrator, a young school boy in Ireland, has fallen in love with a neighbor's sister. She tells him of a bazaar she would like to attend but cannot. He decides he will go to Araby where he will buy her a gift that will represent his affection for her. As he moves through the story, it grows progressively darker until, at the end of the story, the lights of the bazaar go out and it is completely dark. The story ends: "Gazing up into the darkness I saw myself as a creature driven and derided by vanity; and my eyes burned with anguish and anger."

What Joyce has done is to use the darkness to represent the boy's realization that his naive hope for reciprocal love was no more than a pipe dream and that having moved from this youthful naiveté, he has entered the darker realm of the adult (there is also the sense that the boy has lost his religious faith as well; the description of the bazaar is similar to that of a church and again, in the end, the lights go out).

Setting, of course, does not have to represent theme; it is just one of the many possibilities that setting possesses. Another possibility is one of choice. In Ernest Hemingway's story "Hills Like White Elephants," the setting plays as important a role as do the two characters. The setting is a railway station in Spain wherein a man and a woman are discussing whether to have an abortion. Actually, the man is manipulating the woman, trying to force her to make the choice to have what he calls "an awfully simple operation."

In this very short story, Hemingway describes the setting very clearly. There is a train station set between two lines of rails. On one side of the station, where the couple is sitting, the hills are big and barren; these are the hills the woman describes as being like "white elephants." On the other side of the station, there is a river, there are fields of grain, and there are mountains and trees. Obviously, the woman has a choice to make: near the end of the story, she gets up and walks along the platform, turns her back to the barren hills, and looks to the verdant fields beyond the river on the other side of the station. Hemingway has used setting to represent the choice the woman has before her: two sides of the station, two sets of tracks.

Sometimes a beginning writer will be so concerned with character or plot, she will forget to create a credible setting. In early drafts, that may be O.K., but eventually the setting will have to be painted in, for the reader needs to be grounded in a believable world. The setting does not have to represent the mood of the character, nor does it necessarily have to represent the mood of the story; those are just possibilities. What it must do, however, is represent a credible world wherein the character can make choices. And if the story is science fiction or fantasy, it is even more important for that setting to be credible, for if the writer wants the reader to believe that humans on earth can be vaporized in a millisecond only to reappear on Mars in human form one second later, then that writer had better have a detailed, concrete description of the machine that does it, or the reader will call foul.

As the writer Ron Carlson says, "Solve your problems in the physical world." And to the writer, that physical world is the setting.

Valerie Miner ———————————————————

TAKE *PLACE*

I don't know whether I am first a writer or a traveler, but I got interested in exploring and storytelling at the same time. In the kitchen, I listened to my mother's memories of her native Edinburgh: walks up Calton Hill, windowshopping along Princes Street, errands to the corner shop to buy chipped fruit and *The News of the World* for her father. In our back garden, I sat on the lawn while my seaman father tied up his beefsteak tomatoes, drank iced tea, and described brilliant fabrics he had seen in Argentina and the strange, tasty seaweed he had eaten in Japan. During the many months he was gone at sea, I awaited his return, eager for more stories and especially eager for the new doll he would bring dressed in a local fashion. Those dolls from Korea and Japan and Holland and Jamaica and the Dominican Republic now sit together on my bookcase. Just as I always knew each one had a distinct personality, I knew this personality was related to her place of origin.

Before I write a short story or teach a fiction class, I remind myself that "Place" is a verb as well as a noun. We're not talking painting or postcard description here. We're dealing with dialect, music, the angle of the sun, moisture in the air, historical kerfuffles, whispers of the spirits. Setting is action and being and states of being.

Grade school geography classes made me even more curious about people in their settings. Vividly, I remember photos of the Acropolis, vowing I would go to Greece when I grew up (and, indeed, I recently made my fifth trip to that country, this time to do research for a collaborative theatre piece.) Tungsten and soybeans—natural and agricultural resources of China—were still on my mind in the 1980s as I was escorted around literary salons in Beijing, Shanghai, and Guangzhou by members of the Chinese Writers' Association. Surely the precise, colorful maps I constructed of Morocco in the fifth grade later persuaded me to travel in 1975 on those rickety local buses from Tetuan through the Riff Mountains and down to the Sahara, where I met blue men of the desert carrying white sacks on camels. Although I didn't visit any of these places with the intention of writing about them, short stories eventually emerged from each experience.

Such traveling made coming "home" that much more fascinating because I now knew other places (settings) to which I compared familiar food and voices and climate. Home became something smaller and larger and far more complicated than the place I left. And I was never able to think about home again without seeing it on a map—in context—

home wasn't the center of the world any more, but it was finally *in* the world.

One of my favorite stories about "home" is "Presents," written by Julie Gard, a graduate student at the University of Minnesota. In fourteen compact pages, Gard reveals significant shifts in perception and action between Michael and Karen, a middle-aged couple living in a roomy suburban Philadelphia house. As her story opens, they are preparing for the visit of a twenty-five year old daughter and saying goodbye to a Japanese family who have been staying with them for a month as part of a cultural exchange program. Karen's appreciation of their home is external. "After twenty years she still can't get over it, how beautiful their home is surrounded by maple and oak. She'll often touch the stone and stand back to admire the deep green of the shutters, almost black. . . . The way the roads curve, the Welsh names of the streets, how everything is tucked behind azalea and rhododendron and hard to find. And the trees, the way they tower over the houses."

Meanwhile, Michael's sensibilities are all inside and right now they are focused on a beautiful old bookcase he is refinishing as a birthday present for his returning daughter. "Michael likes to work in the basement. It smells like sawdust down there, and turpentine. Often there is paint or shellac in the creases of his palms."

Unlike Gard, some students omit setting from their stories. Perhaps too much daily life is spent in our heads. Our idiosyncratic characters, forced to muck their ways through our tepid grey matter, emerge in consequent colorlessness. Technology validates the cerebral over the sensual. On the Information Highway, an e-mail from Sri Lanka looks like an e-mail from Ohio. And even when we leave town, it's easy to confuse one airport with another. If we're going to succeed as writers, we want to step away from the computer, escape the airport—well beyond the car rental satellite—onto the small streets where we witness climate, culture, geography, history, people mowing lawns, telling jokes, having fights, fixing dinner. We want to listen to their accents and diction and vocabulary. We want to smell what's simmering on the stove.

"Karen starts passing around the food: sushi, lasagna, French bread, green salad, a bowl of dumplings that Miki made fresh. Michael breathes in tomato and soy sauce. . . ."

Julie Gard's ability to write so precisely about her Philadelphia suburbs comes, in part, from the distance she has experienced living long periods in Russia and attending colleges in Iowa and Minnesota. In "Presents," Michael and Karen can compare home to places they've visited. Meanwhile, the Japanese family allow them to see their home in yet a different light.

Setting influences character. Sometimes setting is character. The pleasure Michael and Karen take from their home, mirrors their family love, and their risk in opening the house to international visitors is the best expression of their generosity and curiosity.

When I read Gard's carefully observed story, I wonder how some of her peers simply "forget" setting. Perhaps it's because so much of our celebrated literary fiction is character-driven. An almost pathological focus on the isolated individual's quest, combined with the "action-driven" nature of film culture encourages storytellers to overemphasize character and plot at the expense of setting. But whether we're talking about powerful scenes of home birth or gruesome portraits of mass murder—the setting of these scenes is important; all dramas take *place*. Setting is inextricable from character and plot (even if that setting is a fantasy or a mystery to the reader). The best writers allow themselves to be surprised by complications of place, derailments, astral projections.

Here are some common omissions my students and I have noticed: (1) Three pages of dialogue in which the speakers don't seem to move any body part except, possibly, their lips (Are they in the kitchen? the bedroom? the old tree house built when they were children?). (2) The long, grim narrative that gives us no city name, no history, no hint about the age or ethnic mix of local citizenry. (3) Elaborate lyrical passages in which every flower in the garden is sensually sniffed by a disembodied nose.

After we laugh good-humoredly at such encounters, I ask students to consider the *sources* of setting. We discuss: (1) Direct and careful observation (a form of reportage). (2) Memory (from yesterday, from childhood, from someone else's yesterday). (3) Imagination (the creation of a new planet or an underwater world). (4) Cultural mythology (Judeo-Christian scriptures, the oral history of Plains Indians). (5) Gossip (the legend of ancient Mr. Simplegreen who never left the house on the corner for fifty years; the rumor about the cheerleader and the basketball star murdered in lovers' lane a quarter-century ago). Once the list of sources begins, it expands, and students get excited about the wealth of their artistic inventories. We talk about how "writing the familiar" is the trickiest task because we assume too much, don't look closely enough, and thus the first-draft setting is often too implicit. Then we begin to do basic archaeology about the most familiar places—finding maps, photos, news articles, oral histories, of places students believed had *automatically* come alive in their first attempts. Suddenly setting is neither a supernatural gift nor impossible drudgery, but an aesthetic opportunity that opens our stories (and ourselves) to deeper sensual pleasure and emotional power.

Narrative place attends to time. We all live in history. To convey the spirit of a town in 1999, we need to know the skyline of ten years ago, eighty years ago. What was the village/town/city like when there were more trees and fewer people? How do the oldtimers relate to the incomers? Western Civilization has erected the aesthetic of the scaffold—on Fifth Avenue, at Notre Dame, the Sydney Opera House—which allows us to imagine the future through the protective brace of the present. Yet there's nothing to keep us from looking beneath the scaffold, around the scaffold, into our imaginations.

Today, here, now is perhaps the hardest to describe because we don't look at our costumes, hear our own music. But the dailiness of today can be just as provocative as the Czar's elaborate parties at the Summer Palace in the last century. On a sweltering August afternoon, we want to know that our hero is wearing army boots, a long, sheer red dress and tatooed arms. How many rings does her boyfriend wear in his nose? Does the antagonist dye his hair black or is that the natural color? Why does his mother insist on wearing those faded hippie skirts from twenty years ago? Perhaps these don't seem like historical costumes now, but think about describing them as a sharp-eyed feature journalist. If journalism is "literature in a hurry," perhaps literature is journalism with breathing space.

In "Presents," "Michael remembers when Jeannie and Rachel dressed up in Wonder Woman outfits, using their pajamas and bits of old Halloween costumes . . . his daughters decked out in red and blue, big Ws taped to their chests, Rachel in red snowboots and Jeannie in red magic-markered ballet slippers."

The historical moment of our fiction includes season and time of day. Each term, my students and I begin with a short short story in which I make only two requests—that all writers *subtly* convey the season and time of day in their narratives. Always, always, half the class forgets one or both assignments and we have an album of stories that take place at no particular time of day in no particular season!

Gard uses narrative time effectively when she shows that Michael is so excited about his daughter's return that he can't sleep, and he gets up in the middle of the hot summer night to finish the bookcase he is making for her. "The stairs to the first floor creak in the dark; his bare feet sink into the basement stairs, thick with old carpet. The mildew smells stronger at night. The dehumidifier has gone off again; he kicks it and the buzz starts up. . . . He starts from the top, pushing the rag into the twists and crevices in the wood. He works his way down the flat sides and cleans off a tar stain near the bottom. Soon his bookcase stands wet and dark in the pool of light, and he stands next to it. Around them, the room is all shadows."

The next assignment of the term is to take the same story and change just one element—either the time of day (dawn to noon or early evening) or the season (spring to fall). Usually people are astonished by the difference this makes in their characters' possibilities and behaviors. We discuss how a writerly attention to absence (such as the silence of traffic in a scene that has shifted from midday to midnight) as well as observation of such often overlooked details as temperature, the texture of grass, the intensity of the sun, the color of the sky, makes our characters feel different and act in new ways.

In Gard's story, we find that Michael's attitude toward the bookcase is very different during the midday buzz than it is in the quiet hours of the morning. It becomes a companion and eventually a sedative.

Setting, as Gard demonstrates, is inside as well as outside—the inside of a house, apartment, jail, makeshift cardboard box claimed by a homeless person. The interiors can be as dramatic as the features of the external world.

Some writers fret that their places will be too common or too exotic for readers. Several years ago, a graduate student asked me whether she should abandon her collection of New York stories because New York had been *done* before. "What can I add to Paley, Doctorow, Mailer?" None of these authors, to my knowledge, had written from the perspective of a young WASP woman from the Midwest camping out in Manhattan for a couple of years in the 1990s. Her New York would be a completely different location, perhaps an infinitely more fascinating city than their New Yorks, because of her foreignness, much in the way that nonnative speakers of English (Eva Hoffman, Joseph Conrad) often compose our most musical prose, for they are not frozen by conventional idiom.

Speech is a primary element of setting. Dialect and vocabulary hint at where our characters have been, where they think they're going. So do the rhythms of conversations, from the fast-paced, ever-interrupting chats one experiences in Greenwich Village to the slower, more collaborative exchanges one hears in the Big Horn Moutains. Randall Kenan's exemplary story, "Tell Me, Tell Me," opens with a middle-of-the-night telephone conversation between two women. From their vocabularly, we realize they are old white southerners ("grandboy . . . pickaninny"). We gather something about their social status when one of them suggests that the other has had a bad dream, "Probably those oysters you ate at the club. You had oysters that other night too. Remember? Oysters just don't agree with you. They didn't agree with my mama either." Although the story proceeds for many pages in a more conventional mix of dialogue, summary, and action, these first four pages of conversation are the key to our understanding of Bella and Ida's places in Tims Creek, North Carolina, in American social history.

Even when characters disguise their native dialect, readers' appreciation for place is enlarged. What's happening when the North Dakotan living in London pretends to be Canadian or even English? What do we intuit about a character's shame or ambition or dexterity when we hear him speak in an artificial accent?

When Miki Yamanaka speaks, we learn that she is comfortable in English if not completely fluent. Her speech is careful, unpretentious, communicative. "Miki is still working at the counter. She lays out strips of something green and wet, seaweed, he thinks, white rice, a pile of cut-up vegetables. 'I make sushi for tonight,' she says. 'Your wife make lasagna to go with it.'"

Ultimately, one wants to create, construct, divine a setting that is not only credible, but memorable, so palpable that we can't remember whether an image comes from a story or from our own lived experience. Gard ends her story memorably, in keeping with setting and character, as Michael stands on the front step of his cherished family home waving, "He wants to wave until Jeannie comes, until his goodbye to the Yamanakas is a greeting for his younger daughter. He wants to skip church and stand on the front step out in the sun, just stand there and wave all day."

It makes me want to wave back.

How do we discover or name or claim our own artistic home and how does this influence our practice writing in terms of setting? My Scottish mother and seaman father taught me that the difference between being a wanderer and a traveler is the gift of finding a particular home. My California cabin allows me to write about Norway, Kenya, India as much as it nudges me to evoke the American West. Setting comes from experience in a place, a retreat from that place, and a return to that place. While I'd never write about a location I didn't know, I find it's very helpful to get far away from the setting, at least for the first draft of the book. The physical separation allows memory to work creatively and ensures that the narrative swells from imaginative depth rather than from a more reflexive impulse to record or report.

Knowing my artistic home has not been confining. Quite the opposite, it has freed me to roam, sometimes forced me to travel that artistic distance to where I can no longer hear the quiet sound of the tall grasses dancing. But no matter where I am, I know that the Pacific Ocean creates the currents I imagine *against* and *with*. Have you found your artistic home? What are the currents that carry you onto the page?

* * *

Exercises

1. Print a draft of a story and with a highlighter, highlight all references to setting in the draft. Now go back and estimate the percentage of all references to setting as they address our five senses. You might come out with something like this:
   1% tactile
   3% taste
   5% olfactory

30% sound

61% sight

There is, of course, no correct ratio in defining a setting, but if your story is set in Fairbanks, Alaska, in January and after having done this exercise you see that only 1% of your setting falls in the tactile category, you had better go back and add some appeals to that sense. After all, Alaska can be cold in January.

And, after having done this exercise, if you see several pages with no highlighted material, I would be very suspicious.

2. What is described in a particular setting often depends upon the point of view of the story. Describe a real park you have visited, first in the first person pov through the eyes of a young man or young woman in love, and then through the eyes of an old widow or widower. After you have finished, note the differences in setting even though it was the same park. You can do the same exercise using third person limited.

chapter nineteen

DIALOGUE

The act of speaking is an act so natural to us that it would seem that writing dialogue would come just as naturally, but unfortunately it does not. It is not that writing dialogue is particularly difficult. Rather, the difficulty lies in choosing *when* and *how* to use dialogue to enhance your story by enriching your scenes.

Direct dialogue occurs when two or more people are speaking in a scene (see the chapter on plot for the distinction between scene and exposition) as opposed to **indirect dialogue** which is reported speech. Certainly, if what the characters say is important in developing the plot or in characterization, the conversation should be handled directly as follows:

> *"Las Vegas will be fun. Hell, you've never even been there," John said.*
> *"And I don't want to go for the first time," Heide said.*

If, however, we chose to handle this dialogue indirectly, it would appear as follows:

> *John told Heide that it would be fun to go to Las Vegas, but she said she did not want to go.*

The difference between the two is obvious; in the former, we have a scene, and in the latter we have exposition. In the interest of **pacing**, there will be times when you will mix the two, for there

Speech is a mirror of the soul: as a man speaks, so is he.

Publilius Syrus

will be instances in which the reader needs to know some information that may slow the story down and would thus be better handled indirectly:

> *"Las Vegas will be fun. Hell, you've never even been there," John said.*
> *"And I don't want to go for the first time," Heide said. She went on to remind her husband of how her own father had lost everything the family owned, including the house, when she was nine years old. She told him again of how her mother had divorced him and how her father had committed suicide. Then she began to cry.*
> *"It's okay," he said as he took her in his arms. "Relax now. It's okay."*

From this example, one can see how we can use both direct and indirect dialogue to advance the story and thereby keep up its pace. Notice too that the only tag verb used in the example is the verb *said*. It is a perfectly good verb that reports the action of speech without drawing attention to itself; the attention should be on the dialogue itself and not on the verb that reports it. *Said* is almost always the right verb for dialogue. Reading a passage like the following sours the stomach:

> *"Las Vegas will be fun. Hell, you've never even been there," John stated.*
> *"And I don't want to go for the first time," Heide exclaimed.*
> *"Oh, come on. Let's just go this one time," he pleaded.*
> *"I said no once and I meant it," she pronounced.*
> *"Well, the hell with you then," he barked.*

Ad nauseam.

One should also avoid the use of adverbs to describe the way someone says something, for what the writer is then doing is telling and not showing. To wit: *"And I don't want to go there for the first time," she said cleverly.* One can see that the adverb is meant to clarify the way she made the statement, but if the statement has been made the way the adverbs says it was made—cleverly—then it would be redundant to employ the adverb. And if the statement was not clever, but we wanted the reader to think it was, using the adverb is the lazy way out. Far better to take your time and think of something clever in the first place.

It is also important to realize that rarely do we have a conversation about one limited topic without talking about something else at the same time. In other words, if you are talking about your day at work while sitting at the dinner table with your spouse, you will probably also talk about the food.

> *"Las Vegas will be fun. Hell, you've never even been there," John said.*
> *"And I don't want to go for the first time," Heide said. "Pass the butter, will you."*

Sometimes writers will forget that our characters do not drop everything to have a conversation. In other words, they are physically active as they talk. It is important to embody the dialogue of your characters, for they should not be physically frozen as they speak. Again and again, I tell my students to avoid naked dialogue.

> *"Las Vegas will be fun. Hell, you've never even been there," John said as he poured wine first in his wife's glass and then in his own.*
>
> *"And I don't want to go for the first time," Heide said. "Pass the butter, will you."*
>
> *She took the butter from John without looking at him. As she buttered her bread, she went on to remind her husband of how her own father had lost everything the family owned, including the house, when she was nine years old. She told him again of how her mother had divorced him and how her father had committed suicide. Then she began to cry.*

There will be times when you have set your story in Mexico, France, or some other foreign local, and you want your reader to believe that the characters are speaking Spanish or French or some other language, yet you do not want to write the entire dialogue in that language for fear of confusing your reader—and/or because you do not know the language. Usually, incorporating a foreign word from time to time will remind the reader of the language the characters are speaking. Hemingway was a master at doing this.

Finally, it should be noted that we do not speak on point as people do who are being interviewed. Dialogue should not be done in a question and answer form, for that is not how we speak, and neither should our characters.

Diana Abu-Jaber

ON DIALOGUE

Dialogue can be just as slick and slippery as everyday conversation, but what sets it apart from conversation is that dialogue is *shaped* and that it exists to *advance* and *deepen* the story. Great dialogue-writers know that dialogue is a kind of sleight-of-hand: you create the illusion of eavesdropping on completely natural speech. What's not said is often as important as what is said, and when you combine the words and the silences with body language—gestures, tics, poses—then you have a fully-realized form of dialogue.

Well-written dialogue is one form of *action*, and action is what keeps readers close and involved in reading. Writing is, after all, a fairly abstract form of art: words on a page signaling the world beyond. While straight narrative is descriptive and informative, dialogue allows characters to speak directly for themselves. Suddenly things pick up; we break free from blocks of looking and thinking and shift into faster slices of listening. Run your eye down the page and you'll notice that passages of dialogue have more "eye-appeal." They signal a break from the hard work of concentration into a more performative and entertaining area. There's a sense of spontaneity and unpredictable freeplay about well-written dialogue that mimics the spark of real-life conversations. But, of course, that's all an illusion.

A writer has to exert close control over her characters' dialogue; it's easy to fall into the "Talkative trap" where dialogue lapses into the patterns of everyday blather, or worse, chitchat, small-talk, or speechifying.

So when Gary, a student in my fiction workshop, wrote the following lines in a story:

> "Have you heard bout, oh, ah, hey hi, you know bout the guy, what'sisname. Yeah. Wait. But I mean like have you?" Gary said.
> "Yeah? What? What guy?" Walter said. "Who? Him? Old Jones?"
> "Well, yuh, who else? I mean, who else would I even be wasting my time talking about, okay?"

he was erring on the side of realism. By faithfully recording the nuances of patterns of everyday talk, it might seem as if he'd created a wonderfully authentic piece of writing. But remember that (1) recording is not the same as writing, and (2) real-life can be confining to a story. In so-called real-life, we have more patience with conversation because we're all in the same boat: thinking on our feet. Have you ever seen courtroom transcripts? They're full of umm's and uh's and you-know's and assorted other stammers and stutters. We have much less patience with that sort of flotsam in literature because we want to read a story, not a transcript. And, unless for some postmodern reason your story is about the fragmentation of conversation—or something equally dull—it will not be advanced by that sort of detail.

Bear in mind that Dialogue should only SEEM spontaneous. Meanwhile, you should cut out all the filler. Sculpt it, bend it, mold it to reflect what's happening. Write it spontaneously, but go back and shape it up later. That's the secret beauty of *revision*: nothing is unfixable.

So the writer above tightened the little exchange to:

> "Have you heard about—what's his name—that new pharmacist?"
> "What guy?" Walter said. "You mean Old Jones?"

And the sequence was brisk and readable, with just a soupçon of realistic hesitation and misdirection. It receded back into the momentum of the story, which is exactly where it belonged, because it wasn't that important an exchange. A story is an organic entity—all its parts need to fit together. Readers should only really "see" the important moments, and that goes double for dialogue.

Hence, dialogue has to do a couple of jobs at once. It should never simply exist for filling in "local color."

My student Charmane wrote a long monologue for one of her characters, a bored corporate executive who spends a lot of time in one scene talking about a yellow coat she sees in a store window:

> "I'd love to get that coat. This time of year a woman needs a good coat, that's what I say, and that's what I'll always say. A good coat made out of yellow cotton and wool. A winter-into-spring deal. Just you wait. A good yellow coat like that, just waiting for me to come and get it. It's sayin' hello-dolly, come and get me!"

The problem, as I pointed out to Charmane, was that her story was not about coats. If anything, allowing a character to go on about a particular distraction or digression can become a bit of a **red herring**. Readers will resent feeling that they've been misled, that some sort of big clue or broad hint has been thrown out that really doesn't lead to anything more in the story.

But Charmane claimed that this passage lent a kind of depth to the character. The monologue was deliberately pitched to show the incongruity between the executive's personal history of growing up in poverty and her current station in the fast lane. Problem is, that's not enough. Even though this segment gave us some insights into the woman's character, it gave very little into the nature of the story. Remember, you can—and should—always make dialogue do double-duty. To paraphrase Heide Fonda, make it work for you. Not only should the monologue tell us about the character, it should give us important information about what's happening to her in the story. The monologue about the yellow coat would be fine if the yellow coat somehow figured into the overall scheme of things—or possibly if the character had a tradition of going off on tangents in order to avoid the main topic. Otherwise: make your dialogue MATTER.

Bear in mind that when I say dialogue should matter, that doesn't mean that the characters should be narrating, explaining, or describing the actual events of the story. Assuming that you're not Edgar Allen Poe and plan to have an obsessive-compulsive type sit down and reel off the creepy family history, and assuming that you're not writing a soap opera where characters need to catch each other up constantly ("So you're saying that Jeremaia is not, in fact, Scurval's second cousin once removed . . . that Norbert never really loved Tessie Mae or their father . . . and that you are the actually heir to the throne of Micronesia . . .") it's safe to assume that successful dialogue usually directs through indirection. As in this section of dialogue from my student Deborah Reed's short story:

"My lawyer said no way. He's one of the best you know. He said it was clear as the day is long that we could win so we took them on and boy did he know his stuff. You should have seen him in that courtroom!"

"Why? What did he say?"

"Oh I don't understand all that legal mumbo jumbo. All I know is he's a charmer and that was something the judge and jury just couldn't deny either."

"So what exactly did you sue for?" I ask her.

"Well, damages of course. You know how my back is. I'll be damned if I was going to let them slave drivers kill me. They had no idea who they were dealing with. I'm considered disabled now, you know?"

And so on. This is a mother and a daughter who *seem* to be saying one thing to each other on the surface, but manage to be saying many other things hidden beneath the literal meanings. The mother is slightly crazy and very manipulative and the daughter has been trying for years to escape her mother's emotional invasions. At first glance the conversation might appear to be civil, rational—if a bit intense—and friendly. But in the context of the story, their exchange gives us both *character information*— the mother is nuts and the daughter is fleeing—and *story information*—the mother is a scam artist and the daughter may get dragged into her mother's web again.

Ultimately, if you want to write great dialogue you have to learn how to *listen*. Deborah's dialogue captures the little bits of slang, *mumbo jumbo*, just the right amount of cursing for this mother, and the right sorts of silences and pauses for the daughter. Read authors who have a great "ear" for dialogue, like Raymond Carver, J. D. Salinger, and Louise Erdrich, and notice the way their dialogue is not only informative and textured, it's also shapely and interesting. If you learn to zero in on the key phrases, the hesitations, the parries and jokes, suggestions and intimations, and to express what needs to be stated as well as what needs to be unspoken, your dialogue will be eloquent indeed.

*   *   *

Exercises

1. The Dead Horse Exercise. Write a scene in the third person limited point of view where two characters are charged with the task of removing a dead horse from a field before morning (it is the neighbor's horse and he has asked them to remove it before his daughter wakes up on Christmas morning to see her favorite horse dead in a field). They can remove it any way they find possible. As they work, they will be talking about the huge task at hand, but they will also be talking about their own lives. The objective: to realize that whenever we have a conversation, we usually talk about

more than one thing at a time. And, we are usually doing something as we talk, and thus our dialogue is embodied.

2. Go to a public place such as a restaurant and get near enough to two people in conversation to enable you to transcribe what they are saying. (Don't be too obvious, for you could offend someone.) Do not describe what they are doing; just transcribe the dialogue. After fifteen or twenty minutes, you'll have several pages of notes. Type them up verbatim. Then type the conversation again, this time embodying the dialogue anyway you choose. Now, note the difference between the two sets of pages. The objective: To avoid naked dialogue. We move when we talk.

chapter twenty

STYLE, TONE, AND VOICE

I have never really heard a good definition of voice, but I have seen **voice** and **tone** and **style** so stewed together that one is hardly distinguishable from another, so that when one speaks of voice he really means style, and when another speaks of style he really means tone. Thus, let me endeavor to clarify the three here: If a writer's style is the way she uses language—her rhetorical strategy, such as variance of sentence length and word choice and punctuation—and if a writer's tone is her use of irony, understatement, and hyperbole and the like—when we put the two together we come up with the equation *Style + Tone = Voice.* Thus, your individual voice comprises both your style and your tone.

Many books on creative writing forgo a discussion of voice. It may be that they do so because voice is something that is honed from years of writing, not something that you pick up and utilize as you might an omniscient point of view after reading a chapter about the various points of view. But voice is as important as the other elements of fiction, for it is the voice that carries the reader through the story. Unless you are a disciple of Evelyn Wood and you burn through the pages to get to the end of the book, it is the voice of the writer that you hear as if she were sitting on your shoulder and whispering in your ear. When I am reading fiction, I often stop and read a particularly good paragraph two, maybe three,

Great writers leave their mark by the originality of their style, stamping it with an imprint that imposes a new face on the coins of language.

Jean-Joseph Goux

times. If the book is good, if the voice is compelling, I am the slowest of slow readers. This past winter, I read Jim Harrison's novel *The Road Home* as slowly as one possibly could because the understated voice was so enchanting that to no longer hear it would be, well, disenchanting. I am unsure of how many times I have gone back and reread passages such as this one that opens the novel:

> It is easy to forget that in the main we die only seven times more slowly than our dogs. The simplicity of this law of proportion came to me early in life, growing up as I did so remotely that dogs were my closest childhood friends. I've always been a slow talker, though if my vocal cords had been otherwise constructed I may have done well at a growl or bark or howl at scented but unseen dangers beyond the light we think surrounds us, but more often enshrouds us. My mother was an Oglala Sioux (they call themselves Lakota), my father was an orphan from the east, grayish white like March snow, under which you don't count on spring, intermittently mad as he was over a life largely spent on helping the Natives accommodate themselves to their conquerors. After his release from the Civil War (sic!) until December of 1890 he burned up body and soul in these efforts, fixing on botany as the tool of liberation and this in an area, the Great Plains, that is ill disposed to the cultivation of fruit-bearing trees, or berry-bearing bushes of an Eastern nature. The fact that he failed utterly in his life's mission only increases my reverence for him, though he was much easier to live with dead than alive, so powerful were the spates of irrationality that came upon him in the last twenty years of his life.

Harrison sustains this voice, never wavering, for some 446 pages.

A writer develops his style through years and years of practice, and while that style may be relatively constant, the demands of different stories may require different voices. Imagine that your writing career spans fifty years and that in those fifty years you write five-hundred short stories. Undoubtedly, you will have employed different points of view, but if you did write every story in the first person, you would have many different voices unless each story were narrated by the same character. If you write a story in the first person voice of an unemployed mill worker on the Oregon coast, that voice will necessarily differ from the first person narrator who is a lexicographer at a New York publishing house.

The very language you employ will also contribute to the voice of the story and using the idioms of your setting will help create a credible world and credible characters. Reading a group of stories by creative writing students from the South, Flannery O'Connor lamented that the stories lacked Southern flavor despite being set in the South. In her lecture "Writing Short Stories," she emphasized how important the use of local idioms is in creating a credible setting: "An idiom characterizes a society, and when you ignore the idiom, you are very likely ignoring the whole social fabric that could make a meaningful character. You can't cut characters off from their society and say much about them as individuals." In speaking of the students' individual stories, she pointed out that while all the stories were set in the South, "there was no distinctive sense of Southern life in them" because of their lack of employing Southern idioms, and though "a few place names were dropped, Savannah or Atlanta or Jacksonville . . . these could just as easily have been changed to Pittsburgh or Passaic without calling for any other alteration in the story. The characters spoke as if they had never heard any kind of language except what came out of a television set."

The proper voice adds credibility to a story and whether that voice is given life through a first or third person narrator, the use of the idioms of the setting and of the characters who people it will give the story that credibility.

It takes years to be comfortable in writing with different tones, and years to develop your own style, but it is a mistake to think that you have but one voice and through it your characters will always speak. Your voice—the voice you use in an individual story—will vary from story to story and experimenting with different voices allows you to learn as much from writing the story as the reader learns in reading it. And that, after all, is one of the reasons we write: to better understand the world we live in.

Amy Sage Webb

VOICE IN FICTION

A proper discussion of voice is difficult because the definition of voice, as it pertains to writing fiction, is difficult to create. We speak of authors having a distinctive "voice," by which we mean their tone and their original use of language. This is, of course, a function of narration, but voice is not the same thing as narration. The writer's notion of voice would seem to indicate that an author's voice or style would be recognizable whether the piece were in first or third person narration. In novels such as *The Sound and the Fury* and *Absalom, Absalom!* for example, William Faulkner uses different character points of view and narrative technique, but the combination of all of these is what would be viewed as Faulkner's voice. Similarly, though, Toni Morrison might write from the point of view of a male character in *Song of Solomon* and through a woman's point of view in *Beloved*, both novels are marked by what we might call Morrison's distinctive authorial "voice."

For our purposes as writers, then, what is voice, and how do we get it? How do we recognize and develop the voices we have? Should we ever change them to sound like something else? David Huddle writes in

The Writing Habit that one of the things we have to face as writers is the fact that our best voices may not be something worthy of great literature. This is in some respects true, for we all come to the art of writing with different degrees of learning and exposure, as well as different life experiences and perspectives, all of which color the way we tell a story. The telling of the story, for its own sake, is a redemptive act in that it puts into words the images and stories most crucial in our lives. For this reason, Nobel Prize-winning author Nadine Gordimer calls the writer's act her "essential gesture" as a social being. The writer's craft is her contribution to the world as she finds it. All of this seems to suggest that we are stuck with the voice we have, and that it is this voice which will inform the writing we create and which will be our contribution to the world of letters.

What if, however, voice were more supple than that? What if, rather than viewing voice as something innate, a gift from the muse and our lives' experiences, we viewed voice as something we could create at will? That if, as David Huddle points out, our best voice is not the best voice for the story at hand, we could change it? I find it more empowering to view voice as something we can create to suit a given piece or context, and I believe my students profit from this view. Rather than attempting to create their own style of writing before they have mastered the art of a good story, the students try to create voices which will enhance the stories they wish to tell. Through this process, of course, we usually discover that one particular voice seems more natural to us right now. Other writing seems forced. In this way, we discover what may be our true or natural "voice," but are not necessarily limited by it. We can also see that our true voice is likely to change and develop as we do, and that the later voice in which we write is not necessarily better than the first voice that felt natural to us; it is simply different.

Voice or language will not suffice to create good prose if a story lacks other fundamentals such as plotting, dialogue, or scene. When a story reads well and contains the fundamentals it needs, however, voice or original language can create magic, such that the piece shines where before it only read well. A student in my writing courses over the past few years, Lynnae Lewellen, finds that she has many different stories to tell, from many different perspectives. Some are nonfiction, some are highly fictional, even romanticized. Other stories are designed to feature vivid characters and situations. For each type of story, Lynnae faces the same dilemmas of plot, characterization, description, setting, dialogue, and scene. Each piece needs to strive for the shape and grace of story. She can use her voice, however, in different ways to highlight different aspects of these stories and create different moods.

Lynnae brings to her writing a sharp sense of humor and a strong regional dialect, peppered with colloquialisms of the Great Plains. Her life experiences have lent her a keen eye for character and plot, and a good ear for dialogue. Thus, Lynnae's natural writing "voice," we might say, is something closest to the voices of the point-of-view characters in "Save the Last Dance for Me" and "Jubilee." In "Save the Last Dance for Me," she writes from the point of view of a rural Kansas man in his seventies who is none too happy about celebrating his birthday with his wife and his newly-single best friend, H. J. Hawkins. Lynnae has lived in and around Kansas her entire life, listening to the language of people around her such that she can reproduce it fairly effortlessly. In this excerpt, the language is appropriate to the point-of-view character and his perceptions. He is both a jealous young lover, and a typically meticulous crank of an old man:

> He'd given the SOB one dance with her and already he was regretting it. Dave Boseman had been dancing with his wife, Carlene, most of the evening until he'd begun to feel they were neglecting Hawk. Now Hawk was doing one of those dip things with Carlene. Her back was bent over Hawk's left arm and when her head gave in to gravity, her throat showed pearly white under the dance floor lights. They had been married for fifteen years and Dave still felt cold-cocked every time she tipped her chin up for him and exposed that so-soft little pulse spot for his searching lips. . . . Dave thought birthday cake stunk, just like the booze. In fact, birthday celebrations were not his thing at all. . . . Carlene had brought the cake and Hawk had ordered the champagne. Dave thought champagne was a sissy drink. He'd get some nuts with that beer. Now nuts you could bite. . . .

In "Jubilee," Lynnae writes from the point of view of a Kansas girl whose domineering mother insists on packaging her in a too-tight dress for a school dance. The voice here is closest to the typical speaking voice Lynnae would use in conversation, with terms indicative of her (and the story's) generation such as "brassiere" instead of "bra" and "nylons" instead of "panty hose." The truncated sentences call attention to Carrie's halting, uncomfortable emotions. The mother's dialogue also demonstrates the kind of language Lynnae herself might use, but is carefully crafted to be emblematic of the mother's ability to see every external factor but not the girl, her daughter, in front of her.

> Carrie had breasts. Not normal breasts like the other girls in school. Carrie's breasts made her feel different. Made her feel humiliated when she received her first bras, in front of the family, in a Christmas package, a year earlier than her classmates but still much later than she should have received them. Her grandmother tried to soothe her. "You're lucky to have breasts like Jayne Mansfield, dear," she had said with a reassuring pat on the shoulder. Carrie knew she would never have to resort to stuffing her brassiere with nylons the way her mother did. But at fourteen, Carrie felt only that her breasts were like baggage, only there was no trip, and they were always in the way. Like right now.

Carrie studied her red-taffetaed reflection which seemed to fill the round mirror over her mother's dressing table. Her peripheral vision caught her mother's long, slender fingers picking over the top layer of a sewing basket, probing for a seam ripper. . . . "I swear, Carrie, I do not know where you got such a matronly figure," she said. "Size ten dresses are just not made for thirty-six inch busts! I wonder if Dr. Daniels would prescribe some of those new diet pills?"

When Lynnae wanted to write a magical realism piece called "Dreamboat," she found that her naturally factual, conversational voice did not lend to the story the necessary aura of mystery it needed. Once she had plotted the story and designed the scenes she needed, Lynnae began reading some Gothic horror stories to get a sense of the language used by authors such as Angela Carter and Edgar Allen Poe. She read some magical realism pieces by authors such as Gabriel Garcia Marquez. Then, armed with her greater reading background, she wrote "Dreamboat" in a voice all her own, but steeped in the traditions of the type of story she wished to create. This first paragraph of the story demonstrates the Gothic formality of diction and the distinctive, dreamy language appropriate for this narrator and such a time-period piece.

His was a devotion I did not suspect until he began disappearing from time to time a few weeks before our wedding. He was not gone long, usually just a day. This apparent secretive leaving left me devastated when he did not tell me where he had been and what he had been doing. Did not our love mean that we were now spiritually joined into one entity, moving in perfect unison in our universe, finishing each other's sentences, knowing each other's thoughts and desires?

Another one of Lynnae's great interests is nonfiction. Possessing as she does a rich family history of tales and characters, Lynnae wishes to preserve her family stories for future generations, as well as pass along some of her original perspective on those stories. The story of her great aunt Leila (Lee) is one of Lynnae's favorites, and in it Lynnae wished to pass along not simply the daring exploits of Lee, who was an aviatrix and successful single woman during the 1940s, but also her own admiration of Lee. Because she never met Lee when Lee was young, Lynnae could not rely on the voice of her own memory to describe her in her somewhat swaggering, younger days. In order to make Leila shine on the page, Lynnae needed to apply some of her fiction-writing techniques to the factual data that had been passed along to her so that she would seem to be observing Aunt Lee even though she was not there. Her natural voice is applied to information others have told her to make the third-person-omniscient narrative position more informal, a narration not of the story, but closer to it in voice. She has also interspersed the piece with dialogue from Aunt Lee and terms Aunt Lee would have used. Thus, the voice of the piece is observational and a bit detached, but filled with the essence and language of Lee herself.

> Fairly tall, raw-boned and lean, she could look down on my grandma, her little sister. If Grandma had not been such a little banty hen, Aunt Lee probably would have bullied her. As it was, when they would get into an argument, Aunt Lee would just roll her eyes, purse her lips, and toss her head back as she turned and walked away muttering, "I don't give a rat's ass what she says." Grandma usually got the last word, but it was a pretty limp thing by the time it had bounced off Aunt Lee's back. . . . She often wore halter tops and shorts with her midriff showing. She walked with her shoulders rolled toward herself, waist tucked in and hips thrust forward, probably from years of trying to appear less tall. There was a kind of saunter to her gait that told you she wasn't in much of a hurry for anything. She smoked a lot and often pulled her cigarette pack out of the front of her halter top. When she took a drag, her arm arced out sideways and the cigarette became a sort of lit baton, punctuating the highlights of her conversation.

Similarly, in the nonfiction essay "The Old School Bell," Lynnae again wished to remember some of the more vibrant women in her family, but this time she added her own interpretations. Here, she discovered that her tendency toward conversational voice did not allow her to create the wise authorial commentary she felt the piece needed. Notice the formality and distance in this piece, and how the greater distance and formalized language makes this "voice," describing the history of Great Grandmother Annie Mae, different from the voice which describes Aunt Lee above. This first-person-narrative position is definitely in and of the story being told, but the more formalized voice makes the narration seem farther from the events as it comments on them.

> These days I am a little mystified at the discrepancy between how unceremoniously I received the old bell, and the almost sacred importance it now has in my life. . . . It is this very touching of lives which makes me wonder about the old bell. For the most part, in our natural world, the old bell is now silent. But there are times when I wonder. Could it be possible that the old bell's clang was transformed into a serene call? Could sound have filtered through the many years that have passed since Annie Mae's hand wrapped around its handle and her arm swung up and down to ring the students into the school house? Could she and the bell have been unknowingly calling me to school before I was even born, its harsh clang necessary to break through the generational barriers of resistance I would encounter and my ensuing lack of confidence? Could she and the bell have even been calling other women in our family to teach for generations to come?

Think of how different the latter example, in first person narration, would have sounded with the voice of the former example, and vice versa. The difference is not necessarily a function of the narration, but the tone of language that narration uses. In both these essays, Lynnae modified her own voice, maintaining the conversational, mostly in-character perspective, and seeking for her historical/authorial voice something more formalized. She read essayists such as Barry Lopez and Edward Abbey to learn how they approached their subject matter in terms of voice. From Lopez she discovered a high seriousness, and from Abbey an ironic insight. She allowed herself to try on the voices of Romantic-era authors such as Nathaniel Hawthorne because such language lent itself to formal interpretation and commentary. In the end, Lynnae found that she was able to contemporize some of the formal language of other writing and eras with her own voice. She wanted more characterization than an essayist such as Annie Dillard would create, but less than would be apparent in a real fiction story. In this way, Lynnae created not just one, but *two* of her own nonfiction voices, both drawing from the voices of others to tell these stories.

It may seem that I am advocating a copy-cat approach to writing, and this is, in part, true. Every author we read teaches us something about the dilemma of writing. From our reading, we get a sense of the scope of language, and the ways other authors have employed it to create the tone of their best works, and, over time, the body of works which comprises what we know as an author's voice. Discovering voice is not as simple as grafting technique, however. As we read, we take in to our original perspective the play of another's language, and when we apply it to our own work, it becomes something altogether different, something at once traditional in tone and structure, and absolutely new, because it is filtered through our perspective. Herein, I believe, lies the magic of what we know as authorial voice. It is more than simply the language we bring, initially, to a piece. Voice is a function of an author's reading and study, her apprenticeship to the *right* language for a story's tone and purpose. Just as we move from one social context to another, employing a language slightly different at work from that we use at home, we must move from one story to the next, employing the language we think will best highlight the story we wish to tell. Both languages are ours. Both are learned. In both cases, too, an original magic takes place which is a function of the author's creativity. If genius is, as it has so often been defined, the ability to hold two seemingly contradictory ideas in tandem without confusion, then this thing we call the writer's voice may be a function of genius, for it is there that the author pieces together the seemingly disparate voices of her reading in order to create the new voice which is her own, a supple thing which bends and shapes itself to each story so artfully that, in the words of Coleridge, we "suspend our disbelief," and allow ourselves to be caught by and transported into the world of each new story, knowing all the while who has brought us there.

* * *

Exercises

1. As a young and aspiring writer, W. Somerset Maugham used to copy the work of writers he admired. This increased his facility with language. Take a couple of pages of a writer whose work you admire—Faulkner, for example or Flannery O'Connor, especially if you are not from the South—and copy the work verbatim until you begin to hear and feel the writer's voice supersede your own.
2. When you get together with a small group of friends some evening, tape record the conversations. Be sure and inform everyone of this, however. At first, your friends will be self-conscious, but eventually they will forget about the tape recorder (be sure and place it out of sight), and they will speak in their own voices. Listen to how varied the individual voices are and notice the idiomatic speech.

chapter twenty-one

CREDIBLE SURPRISE ON THE PATH TO RESONANCE

Without this playing with fantasy no creative work has ever yet come to birth. The debt we owe to the play of imagination is incalculable.

Carl Gustav Jung

As an editor of *Clackamas Literary Review,* a semi-annual national literary journal, I read hundreds of fiction submissions each year, and it is disappointing how similar in topic and utterly predictable so many of these stories are. I probably get forty stories each year of professors who are having affairs with graduate students and another twenty stories of graduate students who are having affairs with the students they teach in their capacity as Teaching Assistants. It would seem that life in graduate school is one big game we might call the Sexual Chain of Command. Each year I receive another twenty or thirty stories about parents who do not understand their teenage children and about the same number of stories of parents who are misunderstood. From the preponderance of these submissions, it would seem that everyone is either misunderstood or sexually promiscuous (it may be that when we are misunderstood we have affairs, or is it that when we have an affair we become misunderstood due to the necessity of lying?).

My point is that many of these stories are so haggard that in themselves they have become clichés. But is it possible to take one of these topics and breathe new life into it by making the conflict at least seem new and unique? By raising the stakes and escalating the conflict? By layering vibrant resonance in their endings? Yes, to all three.

To take such a tired topic and make it seem new greatly depends on the nature of *credible surprise*. Take a story of a mundane couple living in an apartment building, and then throw in a radio that picks up and transmits all the conversations of the neighboring tenants, with the owner of the radio listening to them daily, and what you have added is a credible surprise. John Cheever does exactly that in his story "The Enormous Radio," and he does so in such a realistic and credible fashion—by staying in the concrete and physical world—that the radio itself essentially disappears from the story as we begin to listen to the sad lives inhabiting the building. It is not the *transmitter* that we focus on; it is what is *transmitted*. And that is the nature of good stories.

We all want to read something new, but essentially all of our plots have been exhausted. I tell my creative writing students that what we are doing as writers is telling the same stories again and again, and I add that there is nothing wrong with that. Because our plot supply has become exhausted, does that mean there is no longer a need to write a story, a play, a novel, a poem? Of course not. As has been mentioned again and again, writing is a process of discovery for the writer as well as for the reader, and that alone makes the practice of writing worthwhile. With each story we write, we gain more human empathy just as we do with each story we read. But if we are to have readers, we had better make the story of *unrequited love* or *betrayal* or *first love* or *revenge* new and fresh so as to engage our reader; we can do so by offering some small but credible surprise like the peacock that enters the dining room as two couples eat dinner in Raymond Carver's story "Feathers" or as when Kenny shoots the dog in Tobias Wolff's story "Hunter's in the Snow." As a reader, your mouth drops and you turn the page to read on, for the writer has given you something you did not expect, and oh, how we love the unexpected as long as it is not a **red herring**.

In the chapter on Plot, we discussed the arc of a story and the need to establish conflict and escalate it before realizing a climax and a denouement, but we did not discuss **resonance**. Resonance is that vibration a reader feels, that chill on the spine, that hair bristling on the back of the neck. Do not confuse credible surprise with the resonance at the end of the story, however. Unearned surprise endings are cheap and facile. What we want is an ending with resonance that is credible due to the evidence inventoried earlier in the story. In Mary Robison's very short short story "Yours," it is autumn and a woman dying of cancer returns home to her husband with a car laden with pumpkins. They carve the pumpkins and then go to bed. In bed, she seems to be dying as her "pulse cords were fluttering under his fingers." And the story ends:

> At the telephone, Clark had a clear view out back and down to the porch. He wanted to get drunk with his wife once more. He wanted to tell her, from the greater perspective he had, that to own only a little talent, like his, was an awful, plaguing thing; that being only a little special meant you expected too

much, most of the time, and liked yourself too little. He wanted to assure her that she had missed nothing.

He was speaking into the phone now. He watched the jack-o'-lanterns. The jack-o'-lanterns watched him.

With that haunting image of the pumpkins within which votive candles burn in the night, the resonance is as palpable as fingernails dragged across a chalkboard.

Finding the right place to open a story is difficult, and sometimes that opening is not found until page two, three, or four; escalating conflict in the middle of the story and incorporating credible surprise is also a challenge; but finding the right ending where the resonance rings true may be the most difficult task of all. Sometimes your ending will come from some physical object found earlier in the story such as the jack-o'-lanterns in "Yours."

Craig Lesley

MYSTERY AND SURPRISE

"Surprise me," I frequently suggest to workshop participants. Try creating a character who is both original and mysterious, one who displays power and is capable of surprising both the reader (and the writer) after we discover all the facts. Spare me the hackneyed middle-aged professor churning through a midlife crisis with a tawdry affair. Stay away from spinsters in purple who "discover" rather late in life that their ennui resulted from being molested. If you must, pitch those sorry tales to Drs. Ruth or Laura. Consider writing for television where all improbably-loose ends get wrapped up in a single hour.

Also bear in mind that real mystery and surprise have nothing to do with characters who are also witches, vampires, warlocks, or were-wolves. King and Rice do it more successfully (at least commercially) than you ever will. Their pale imitators have gotten to be rather tiresome. Nor is surprise a masked misfit springing from the closet with a snarling chainsaw. When I want drive-in movie fare, I'll drive to one and stuff myself with hotdogs and greasy popcorn.

I'm asking for original, believable, and human characters tinged with mystery and capable of surprise. Geronimo Tagatac has given the reader exactly that kind of character in Augustine, the Filipino godfather of the young narrator in his story named for the mysterious fieldworker. Mr. Tagatac begins his narrative: "One Sunday a month, when the men slaughtered a pig, Augustine would fry the chopped intestines, garlic and vinegar, with the pig's blood, to make the black *deneguan* which we ate over rice. In the evenings I would hear the lisp of steel sharpened on stone coming through the darkness from his shack. When I thought of him, I thought of blood, earth and steel."

From the beginning, Augustine and submerged violence become associated in the narrator's and reader's minds, yet one of the surprises in the story is that no violence actually occurs on the page. In addition to violence, Augustine, a cropworker who came to California after the Asian exclusion laws were dropped following World War II, has an association with the earth and crops. The narrator recalls, "He was at the far edge of my sight and hearing, walking down the rows of a field, the whispering leaves and stalks brushing against the stiff twill of his khaki workpants, his boots making marks in the soft earth between the rows of squash and beans."

Part of Augustine's mystery arises from the camp stories circulating about his past. "Stories about Augustine, about fights and killings were whispered out of his hearing. More than one killing." These rumors have the force of scripture for the young narrator, especially when his Uncle Valeriano tells of a time he witnessed Augustine's power. On that occasion Augustine accidentally ran over lettuce crates with a tractor and the boss called him a "stupid, slant-eyed, black, son of a bitch" in front of the other men. As a result, according to Valeriano, Augustine's face became like "dark metal," resembling the "thick coarse steel that goes into the heavy blades of bolo knives."

Here, a less talented writer than Mr. Tagatac might choose to follow the bolo knife imagery with a physical attack on the boss. However, instead, the author presents a fine surprise that heightens Augustine's aura of mystery:

> That same afternoon, all of the lettuce leaves in the field began to turn brown at the edges. The next day, the crop, all nineteen acres, had begun to wither and was useless. By the third day, the whole field looked as though it had been burned black, and the men who had to walk its dying rows spoke in whispers. On the afternoon of the third day, Augustine turned to Valeriano and said in his quiet, accented English, "The boss don't need those crates now."
>
> "Plant disease," the boss said.
>
> "Augustine," said Valeriano, smiling.

Augustine's mysterious powers are further suggested by the fact that he always wears a long-sleeved workshirt and never washes with the other men in the bathhouse. He always washed "alone, late at night, and no one dared intrude on his privacy." Camp rumors claim he'd been badly scarred with knives and bullets, so badly scarred that his wife left him, and he had to pay women to sleep with him.

Mysterious rumors have enormous force in our own lives and in our fiction, an idea Mr. Tagatac applies in his story. Thinking of Augustine caused me to recall the stories I heard about the solitary men who roomed in my grandparents' house where I grew up. Reuben, a heavy smoker, had recurring tuberculosis and had spent six years in a sanitarium before being released. Whenever I had to change his bedsheets, I looked for bright spots of blood and covered my mouth with a bandanna so I wouldn't inhale "toxic spores." Dalton had killed dozens of enemy soldiers in Korea and had lost his toes due to frostbite. Sometimes, I'd open his closet, smelling cold steel and gun oil, then touch his rifles for a terrible thrill. I also carefully inspected his shoes and socks to see if they'd been altered in any way to accommodate his stumpy feet. Everett had robbed several banks in Tennessee and spent time in Leavenworth. All his visitors were shadowy suspects, and I camped outside his room, hoping to catch word of the next big heist. Once in a while, I'll employ one of my grandparents' roomers (or his close cousin) in a story.

When Mr. Tagatac's narrator is nine, he learns Augustine's power firsthand after a violent argument between Valeriano and one of the new men in camp. Furious, the new man retreats momentarily to the bunkhouse, then returns with a pistol:

> Everyone stood in the thick, red light and listened to the quick sound of the new man's footsteps coming out of the bunkhouse. His revolver's blue cylinder snapped closed as he walked toward Valeriano. Everyone stood frozen, waiting for the crack of the gun, waiting for the hard sound of Valeriano's body hitting the ground.
>
> Then, "Hssst!" Everyone's head turned, knowing that the shape coming out of the fading light was Augustine, drawn from across the field into the lethal vacuum. I remember seeing the stillness in Augustine's face. I saw his eyes, looking into the new man's face, his presence blotting out Valeriano and the other men, until I could see nothing but Augustine's face and eyes. Augustine's dark hand, with its hard, blue-black veins, reached out to the man. The man's gun hand rose to meet Augustine's as though drawn by the gold ring on his finger, and then the new man's hand was empty. Augustine held the revolver, then turned and was gone. He went into the new darkness so swiftly and quietly that I thought I could hear the air sliding into the space behind him as he strode across the field.

Augustine's intervention is especially remarkable as the reader recalls the stories of his scars from knife- and bullet-wounds. In this episode, he creates an uneasy peace. However, the displaced violence emerges in the new man's screaming nightmares, horrible dreams that infect the entire camp: The narrator's father believes his own father is whipping him for spilling a sack of rice. Valeriano dreams he's being bayoneted by Japanese soldiers. The narrator dreams Augustine's ring bites him as he tries it on.

After ten days, when the new man's dreams become unbearable, he leaps from bed one morning and drives away, naked and screaming, in an old green Hudson.

That car is a great detail because its specificity makes the surrounding events all the more probable. I've discovered that one way to convince readers as to the authenticity of a mystery or surprise is to link that event to a specific, concrete detail or place. If we believe in a Ford Taurus, we more readily accept the bizarre contents of its trunk. If we see the attractive young widow across the street wearing a Kansas State sweatshirt, we accept the rumor that both her husbands committed suicide.

Part of Augustine's power lies in his visionary storytelling. On the surface, he seems a simple fieldworker who drinks boiled coffee and eats beans and rice. However, on several occasions, he reveals a poetic imagination as he tells the narrator his versions of the natural world:

> Sometimes, after dinner, I would walk across the freshly plowed fields with Augustine. Once, he told me that the stars were fires in the mouths of faraway caves and that, if I looked carefully enough, I might see the faces of the people who lived in those sky shelters. He said that if I were ever lost in the forest and knew how to sing a special song, they would take me up into their caves and keep me safe for the night. But he never taught me the song.

When Augustine takes the boy to the beach, the powerful waves remind the narrator of Augustine's coffeepot coming to a boil, and the older man explains that the ocean's sounds come from "all the souls in heaven."

In addition, Augustine's power results in his always getting what he wants. He asks the narrator's father to be the boy's godfather and gets his request. Years earlier, when the father was courting the narrator's mother, Augustine made the father return with him to the Philippines, to the little village of Bataac. Both the reader and the narrator are left to speculate as to the sources of Augustine's power over people (everyone except his former wife) and events.

Mr. Tagatac leaves Augustine's greatest surprises until after his death. The narrator, now a young man, learns the details of Augustine's death from his father, who informs him that the old man had thousands of dollars in a savings account and that when he went to the morgue to identify the body, it bore no scars.

Much of Augustine's life has to be rethought, in the light of this new information. How much of his mystique was the force of rumor, gossip, perhaps superstition from the old country? Why did Augustine and the father journey back to the Philippines and why did the father go away from his bride-to-be? One of my students offered the left-field suggestion that perhaps the men had a sexual relationship or even that Augustine was a woman—hence the desire to always wash alone. That's pushing the edge perhaps, but the story is so rich with possibility, even that theory has a sliver of credulity. Of course only the father has seen Augustine's body, and he may not be telling all he knows.

One surprise remains. When the narrator receives Augustine's ring in the mail, he shows it to a woman friend. As she examines the face on the ring, she notes, "It's your face. But then you know that, don't you?"

As a reader and editor, I'm thankful to Mr. Tagatac for creating such a vivid and memorable character, and I'll remember Augustine's mystery, as well as the surprises in this fine story for a long time. Like the remarkable story telling itself, the character at first seems simple, but when we're finished, he's as elusive and awe-inspiring as those star-dwellers in the fiery mouths of their faraway caves.

* * *

Exercises

1. Look at a story you have written and ask yourself wherein lies the resonance in the ending and what accomplishes that resonance. For example, in the aforementioned story "Yours," the resonance is derived from the haunting image of the jack-o'-lanterns, with the burning votive candles connecting the reader to the wife's death. Could a physical object (such as the jack-o'-lanterns) be incorporated in your ending to amplify the resonance?
2. Make a chronological list of all of a character's actions in a story. For example, first she arrives home with the pumpkins; second, she suggests that she and her husband carve them; third, they carve the pumpkins; fourth, they go to bed. Then ask yourself if you could insert a more surprising action into the story that would heighten the reader's awareness without being a **red herring**.

chapter twenty-two

THEME

When someone speaks of the word theme, I think of bearded men in tweed jackets smoking pipes, black berets atilt, in mad and pedantic discussion. Sadly, theme is one of the most loaded words in literature, yet it does not have to be, for theme is really the simplest element of fiction and the element that demands the least discussion in a book such as this. Here, then, is the definition of theme: *what the story means*.

Should a writer embark upon a story knowing its theme? No, almost always not. As the reader is given the sweet opportunity to learn something new, to be fair, the writer should have that same opportunity. Remember, writing is, indeed, a process of discovery, and if the writer learns nothing new, chances are the reader will not, either. Another reason I say *almost always not* is that if you go into a story knowing its theme, chances are the story will come out as a didactic treatise devoid of subtext. If you have so little trust in your readers as to hammer them with overt theme, turn your efforts to nonfiction. Fiction is a much more subtle art, one that demands the reader to experience what the characters experience and thereby gain empathy for them, and it is from this human empathy that the readers learn of the story's thematic concern.

Once the writer finishes several drafts of a story, she may come to learn what her story means and this knowledge allows her to clarify

> *The truth about any subject only comes when all the sides of the story are put together, and all their different meanings make one new one.*
>
> Alice Walker

this meaning in subsequent drafts if it is too mute. But with this said, some-times a story's theme is too amorphous a matter to extract and define in a lim-ited number of words. This is what Flannery O'Connor was alluding to in "Writing Short Stories" when she wrote:

> Meaning is what keeps the short story from being short. I prefer to talk about the meaning in a story rather than the theme of a story. People talk about the theme of a story as if the theme were like the string that a sack of chicken feed is tied with. They think that if you can pick out the theme, the way you pick the right thread in the chicken-feed sack, you can rip the story open and feed the chickens. But this is not the way meaning works in fiction.
>
> When you can state the theme of a story, when you can separate it from the story itself, then you can be sure the story is not a very good one. The meaning of a story has to be embodied in it, has to be made concrete in it. A story is a way to say something that can't be said any other way, and it takes every word in the story to say what the meaning is. You tell a story because a statement would be inadequate. When anybody asks what a story is about, the only proper thing is to tell him to read the story. The meaning of fiction is not abstract meaning but experienced meaning, and the purpose of mak-ing statements about the meaning of a story is only to help you to experience that meaning more fully.

O'Connor is correct in saying that the meaning of a story permeates the entire story from the first word to the last, but she is being somewhat disin-genuous as well, for in her essay "The Element of Suspense in 'A Good Man is Hard to Find,'" she writes that the story is about a person's ability to per-sonify grace. Yet, even though slightly contradictory, her point is useful: The theme of a story, its meaning, is not something as easily extracted as a tooth. It is like water beneath the surface that flows throughout, and trying to dis-tinguish it from the water that rides above it is no easy task. The key is to jump in and get wet.

As a writer, I would never embark on writing a new story overly con-cerned about theme. You will discover what your story means; allow your-self that pleasure, for to deny yourself of it is to dilute one of the greatest joys of writing, and that is the discovery of what it is you are really writing about.

There will be occasions when you know exactly what you want to expose in your writing and that is fine, but pay close attention to how you relay that message to the reader, for you are in danger of waxing didactic as did Upton Sinclair in his novel *The Jungle*. Much of the book is good, but in the last third or so, Sinclair gets on the pulpit and preaches to the reader about the sins of the meatpacking industry, all the while greatly detracting from what art he had created earlier in the novel.

Remember that writing fiction is creating a subtle art of experiential par-ticipation: The reader is to walk in the shoes of your characters, go where they go, see what they see, do what they do, and through this vicarious action the reader should be allowed to proceed unfettered by your overt manipulation.

So, keep your hands off the readers. Leave them alone. Don't worry about theme. Just tell a good story.

And theme will take care of itself.

Exercise

When you have finished a story, complete the following sentence: This story means . . . Have friends and classmates read your story and have them complete the same sentence. It is not important that all the answers be the same, of course, but they should be in the same ballpark. For example, it would be disconcerting to the author of a story about lost childhood if one person wrote *This story means the transition from childhood to adulthood is difficult at best* and another person wrote *This story means that choosing a major is difficult and counselors should be more helpful.*

chapter twenty-three

REVISION

Perhaps if writers enjoyed a fuller experience of the private gratifications of artmaking, we would be less intimidated by the rigors of revision.

Valerie Miner

The word revise, along with the word visit, came to English from the Latin *videre*, meaning to see, and the Latin *visitare*, meaning to go to see. In that context, then, to revise a story is to go back to visit it and see it again. I mention this because all too often we think of revision as changing something, when we must first realize that to revise is to pay another visit to the story wherein we will see it again, and in that sense it is entirely and literally possible that we could revise an entire draft without changing a single word.

The key to writing, any writing, is revision. Certainly, writing that first draft is an exhilarating process, but it is just the beginning of a much longer process. A first draft is only the first leg of the journey. If our destination is a story as finely polished as we can possibly make it, then each draft we write is a step towards that destination.

When I was much younger, I loved writing first drafts, to the exclusion of revising them. Thus, I started many journeys, but I never arrived anywhere. Several years later I learned to love revision as well; it is an entirely different process, but when you realize how playful a process it can be, then you will enjoy it as well.

It has been said that time is a luxury, and it is, but in writing it is also a necessity. One must take time off between drafts. If I finish a first draft on Tuesday and try to revise it on Wednesday, I will make a muddle of things; I cannot *re-see* my story so soon after having written that first draft because it is still in my head as well as on the page. If, however, I take a week away from the story, working on another project, maybe, then when I revisit the story I will see it with fresh eyes and with those new eyes I will see areas that are unclear. Thus, *leave a draft alone for at least a few days before going back to revise.*

Whenever I do a public reading, whether a reading of a published or an unpublished piece of fiction, I can hear areas that need to be revised. Reading my work aloud alone, however, is less effective for there is some connection between the audience and me that allows me to hear the work with new ears; it is almost as if I am hearing the work for the first time with *their* ears, seeing it for the first time with *their* eyes. If you have no one to read your work to, try reading before a mirror with pencil in hand. For some reason, that seems to work, too. Be sure to make plenty of eye contact with that face staring you in the eyes; besides helping you hear your story—where it rings true and where it hits a sour note—reading aloud before a mirror is good practice for reading before an audience. Words are meant to be heard, after all, and when you have composed particularly beautiful sentences and paragraphs, reading them aloud allows you the full pleasure they afford as the words roll off your tongue to be retrieved by your ears. Reading silently is something akin to standing in the kitchen of Maxim's in Paris with your nostrils pinched shut.

Rewriting a story without a specific sense of direction can get you lost in the woods, for you may not know where to go, but if you go into a new draft knowing that you are only going to rewrite for one thing—temperature, for example—then you will avoid the pitfalls of trying to do everything at once. For example, if you are writing a story set in Alaska in midwinter, you may devote an entire draft to lowering the temperature wherever possible. That's what Ron Carlson did in his story "Blazo." If you are in Phoenix, Arizona, some hot August afternoon, reading this story will ice you down.

You might write another draft focusing on the dialogue of one particular character, and another focusing on a heightened sense of setting, and another on tone, and another on language. Gustave Flaubert coined the term *Le mot juste* meaning the exact word, and in rewriting for the exact, the precise, word, you may spend countless yet enjoyable hours. There is the story of Flaubert having met a friend at lunch who asked him how he had spent his morning. Flaubert told him he spent the entire morning trying to decide whether to keep or delete a comma. The friend asked what he finally decided, and Flaubert told him that he took the comma out. Later that evening, they met for dinner and this same friend asked Flaubert how he had spent the afternoon. Flaubert asked him if he remembered that comma he had taken out in the morning and the friend said yes, he did. "Well," Flaubert said. "I decided to put it back in."

Apocryphal or not, the story illustrates how careful we need be as writers. It sounds daunting, but if you enjoy the process of writing, this slow, painstaking revision is great fun. And as you can see, it is no surprise that a writer may go through twenty or thirty drafts before he feels he has arrived at the destination he sought from the beginning: the polished story.

As writers, we use different mediums: some of us use pencils and yellow legal pads, some of us use pens, others use typewriters and still others of us use computers, as do I. Before I begin a revision, I always print a hard copy on which I can take notes as I read. In this first reading, I am not revising for anything specific such as temperature; rather, I am looking for any problems in any element of the story. Maybe I have changed a character's name in one area, but not in another; maybe I have the time of day wrong in another area; maybe I have a character say something she need not say. In this first step of revision, I use black ink with which to make marginalia, and on the second reading I use red ink, and the third, green ink. In this fashion, I can see how my decisions have been changed with subsequent readings.

Next, I go back to the computer, and as I refer to my hard copy and all the notes I have made in three different colors of ink, I begin to make changes. Once I have done this, I print another hard copy and take the story before the mirror where I read it aloud with pen in hand, making changes on the manuscript as I read.

After making any changes on the hard copy during my "public reading," I go back to the computer and type those changes in, and then I begin the process of rewriting for a single aspect of the story I feel is weak. For example, I may feel that I have not quite clarified an individual character, so I go back through the hard copy and make notes where I feel I can heighten that character. And once I am done, I go back to the computer and type in the new changes. Next, I print another hard copy and begin the process again, this time focusing on a different element.

As one can see, I am probably going to make more changes in the earlier drafts. By the time I am on the fifteenth draft, it is not unusual that I may be making only one or two changes before I feel the story is as polished as I can make it. Then I leave the story alone for a week, print a new hard copy, and read it again. If I still feel the story is as polished as I can make it, then I consider it done.

Once I am at this stage, I give the story to friends and colleagues whose opinion I value. In the event that they suggest changes, and I agree with them, then I go back and do another draft.

Finally, I *think* that I am done with the story, but the fact of the matter is that I may not be done. At this point I'll submit the story to a magazine, and it may be that the editor will suggest changes, and again, if I agree with them, I will certainly make them.

And if the editor accepts the story, he accepts it because I *am* done. If the editor rejects the story, I'll send it somewhere else until some other editor does accept it—or until I realize the need to revisit the story and see it again through fresh eyes.

The process I have outlined may or may not work for you. If it doesn't, fine; you will come up with your own. What is important is that you have your own process of revision. And I promise you this: if you don't already, you will learn to love the art of revision.

chapter twenty-four

PARTICIPATING IN THE WORKSHOP

There are many ways to orchestrate a writing workshop, but no matter how the instructor handles it, it can be quite daunting for the student-writer the first time she is *on the block*—a rather disheartening metaphor for having your story critiqued by your instructor and fellow-students. If the class meets weekly, you have provided enough copies of your story to the instructor, who then distributes them to the other students; they take them home and read them and write critiques of them. That next week you walk into class both excited and horrified: excited that your instructor and your fellow student-writers will have loved your story; horrified that they will have hated it.

But if the instructor has prepared the students in the proper decorum of the workshop, it does not have to be this way. In this chapter, I will explain how I conduct a workshop and what I expect from the student-writers.

First of all, I explain that every story we workshop had better have some problems, for if the stories are perfect, then the student-writers should be teaching the class, and I should be out playing golf. When we go to the doctor because of an ache in the knee, we expect a diagnosis of what is wrong with suggestions of how to cure the problem. The same goes for a writing workshop: If we are realistic, we know there will be problems with the stories we have written, no matter

> *People ask you for criticism, but they only want praise.*
>
> W. Somerset Maugham

how slight or large, and we expect a diagnosis from the instructor and the student-writers so that we can fix the problem and learn how to avoid it in the future. Thus, if we are going into the workshop with this attitude, we will be less likely to have our feelings hurt. I do not believe the workshop should be a place of unmitigated nurture. Unconditional love is something your family can provide. The workshop is where we come to learn of problems in our writing and to learn how to avoid them in the future. And it is a place to learn of new possibilities. If you write a story based on your personal experience of having been codependent to someone suffering from something, you will have my sympathy, but if it does not carry on the page as a story should, I'll tell you why.

The student-writers are required to do their best in leaving their personal likes and dislikes at home. Admittedly, this is hard to do, but if you are against abortion and we are critiquing a story wherein the protagonist has an abortion, and you can't keep your feelings out of the discussion, then you might as well stay home.

I ask the student-writers to read each story twice before coming to the workshop. They may make notes in the margins and correct punctuation mistakes and errors in spelling and the like, but we will not discuss those matters. After they have read the story twice, they write a critique of the story focusing on the elements of fiction as they have been discussed in this book. Thus, if there is a shift in point of view on page six of the story we are workshopping, I would expect that many of the students would spot it and mention it in their critique. Remember, the effort here is to help the writer. If I have shifted points of view in a story—and I have—and I do not notice having done so, I hope someone would come to my aid by pointing out my error.

During the workshop, we do not critique the story haphazardly with anyone speaking up about anything at any time. Rather, I conduct the workshop as a conductor of an orchestra: I decide what we will focus on and then ask different students what they feel about it. For example, I might say that story A is told in the first person, and then I would ask a student what the effect would be of changing the point of view to the third person limited. Or, I might ask a student whether we needed all five characters in a particular story, and what would happen if we eliminated the character Dolores completely.

In this fashion, there is a sense of direction in the workshop. The writer of the story we are workshopping is not allowed to talk. She must remain silent and take notes. I tell her that we are editors at *Harper's* and that she has submitted the story and is presently in Paris sipping an espresso in a sidewalk café on the Rue de Vaugerard, and that her emissary is in the room to take notes on our discussion. The reason she is not allowed to talk is that inevitably someone will say that something is not working in the story and she will want to say, "But that's the way it really happened!" We don't care if that's the way it happened. What matters is how it happens on the page. In other words, it has to *carry on the page*.

After we have finished the discussion, we give the stories to the writer along with the critiques we have written—me included—and the student-writer takes them home and studies them. Of course, not everything we write will work or necessarily be "correct," but we have diagnosed some problems in her story that should help her in the rewrite. We will start the next class with her being able to ask us questions about what we wrote in our critiques of her story, and she may want to sound us out on new ideas for the story. Then she will be on her own to work on a rewrite.

At this point, I always collect the critiques so that I can evaluate them (later I will give them all to the writer for her keeping). If I feel a student-writer is being mean-spirited in her critique—and I have had students like that, though not many—I will have a talk with them and thus endeavor to resolve the problem.

The reason a workshop is such a good learning tool is twofold. One, you, the student-writer, are getting direct criticism of your work. In other words, you have worked hard and written a story in which inevitably you will have made some mistakes, and it is from mistakes that we learn and grow as writers. Two, you are being asked to write direct criticism of your fellow-writers' work. Undoubtedly, it is easier to see a flaw in someone else's writing than it is to see one in your own. This is because in our own writing we have the story in two places: in our head and on the page, and sometimes we get the two places confused. In looking at the story on the page, the perfect story in our head gets in the way and we cannot see where we have erred on the page. Thus, in seeing a problem in a shift in point of view in another student-writer's story, you may learn how to avoid doing the same in your own work.

We do not focus only on the negative, of course, but that is our main concern; if I have cancer, I don't want the doctor telling me what a great personality I have and how fine my hair looks. Still, we can learn from where a writer succeeds. For example, if we see a student-writer make great use of a flashforward when no one else in the class has tried the technique, we will stop and discuss why and how it is being used so successfully, then consider when we might use it as well.

So, remember, we are here to work together and to learn from each other, and there is nothing personal involved in our discussing each other's work. After all, we are crafting art and crafting art is not a competition like the one-hundred-meter dash. Instead, we are all moving forward together one step at a time. If we remembered what literature was all about, creating human empathy and clarifying this human condition of ours, we would more clearly see the irony in acting as though a workshop were some kind of contest where there were winners and losers. The only losers will be people who embrace such an inane attitude towards the noble effort of creating art where there had been none before.

chapter twenty-five

WORKSHOPPING A STORY IN THE FIRST PERSON

As you read the first draft of Toni Morgan's story "Benedictions," consider the following:

1. The setting: Do you feel as if you are there? Why or why not? Where do you think the setting is most clearly drawn? How does she achieve that? To what senses does she appeal? Where is the setting undeveloped?
2. The characters: How well do you come to know them? Which do you feel you know best? Whose story is it? What do the characters want?
3. The plot: What is at stake for whom?
4. The dialogue: Is it a close approximation of how these people would speak? Is it sufficiently embodied?
5. The point of view: How would the story be different in another point of view? What is the narrative distance? How does that affect the story?
6. Voice: What is the narrator's voice? Is it affected by the time in which the story takes place?

There is then creative reading as well as creative writing.

Ralph Waldo Emerson

Benedictions

by Toni Morgan

Here we are the four of us, bouncing along a dirt and gravel road, in Mexico to show Jack the cotton growing potential of the western and central regions. Tucker is driving. His bald head is pink and peeling despite the sun lotion he rubs into it every morning. I'm always amazed that he burns so easily since he was born in Tucson and raised on the desert. Wouldn't you think the skin would eventually build up a tolerance? But there it is in front of me, looking more like an onion than ever. Tucker procures for the Army what the Army needs to feed and clothe its soldiers. The Army needs cotton for uniforms.

Dust rolls out from beneath the station wagon like a tail dragging along behind us. It lies thick on the dashboard, over the seats, and coats our luggage and the extra fuel cans piled up in the back. My lips are dry and chapped and all I want at the moment is a long soak in a hot tub with plenty of soap. I wonder again why I agreed to come on this trip. Tucker seemed indifferent when he'd first mentioned it, appearing not to care if I came along or stayed home. We've been together for six months, but I'm not sure we'll ever have a permanent relationship. Or if I want one. My mother, who lives with me, was dead set against my coming. We argued for days.

"I just don't understand you, Virginia. I'm going to ignore the fact that you'll obviously be sleeping with that man," she never refers to Tucker by name. He's been married twice before and she views him with suspicion and some scorn. "But how can you go off and leave Richie for six weeks? He's only five. What if he gets sick? What if I need to contact you?" But the trip sounded like a lark, and Jack and Kay can be fun, so I promised I'd call frequently. Besides, Richie loves being with her. He probably doesn't even notice I'm not there.

Northeast of us is a range of mountains. San Ignatio, where we plan to spend the night, is located in the foothills. The last village we passed was three hours back and there is no sign of a village or even a house ahead of us. As far as I can see in all directions are sage and mesquite. The mountains are the only things that interrupt the flat landscape under its azure blue dome.

"According to the map there's another road we have to take to get to San Ignatio," says Tucker. "It can't be too much further."

"Let's roll up the windows," Kay says. "The dust is so thick in here I can hardly breathe."

Kay is from Texas. "Amarillo, Honey," she tells people in her flat, nasal drawl. We all met in Phoenix where so many people have moved since the war started, looking for excitement or jobs. Jack comes from the

Central Valley of California. His family owns a large cattle operation there. He came to Phoenix partly for business opportunities and partly to get away from his wife. I'm from a small town in Nevada nobody's ever heard of. The only thing different about me is they were born rich.

"It's too hot," Jack says.

"Well, I'd rather be hot than choke to death, Sugar."

"Put out your cigarette. Maybe that will help." Jack is always complaining about Kay's chain-smoking. Kay ignores him, but she doesn't say any more about putting up the windows.

"This must be the turn off," says Tucker. He pulls to a stop and we all look at the words *"San Ignatio"* with an arrow painted on a piece of wood nailed to a stake that has been pounded into the ground, pointing to the mountains.

"Jesus, that road looks worse than the one we're on."

"I knew we should have stayed nearer the coast."

"Well, what do you all think? Should we turn off here or keep going?"

Kay is for keeping to the road we're on, but the rest of us vote for the turn off, so Tucker puts the car into gear and points it toward the mountains. After a while the road begins to climb into hills that are rounded and undulating. The land is still covered in sage and mesquite, but now there is an occasional solitary juniper. I can see the road in front of us go up one side of a hill, disappear at the top, reappear on the hill beyond and again beyond that. When we reach the top of the last hill I look down at a valley below. At its bottom is a dry creek bed strewn with rocks and boulders, with clumps of oak and willow along its edges. On the other side of the creek I can make out tracks leading up the side of yet another hill and again disappearing over the top. The car grinds down to where the road runs into the creek bed. Tucker drives slowly forward maneuvering around the boulders. I hang onto the door handle to keep from being pitched sideways into Kay. When we reach the other side Tucker stops the car and we all climb out.

"Well, what do you think, Folks?"

"I think we're fuckin' lost, Honey," Kay says.

Jack pulls out the map and lays it across the hood of the car. Kay wanders over to a large boulder, sits down and lights another cigarette. Her sleek brown hair falls forward as she leans into the match, cupping the flame with carmine tipped fingers. She blows out a long stream of smoke and ignores the two men arguing over the map.

My blouse is sticking to my back, and my linen shorts have ridden up in a bunch between my legs. I am stiff from sitting in the car all day. I start to follow the tracks up the hill, partly to work out the kinks and partly to get away from everyone for at least a few minutes. When I reach the top I yell back to the rest. "There's a town. I can see it."

A church and several small buildings are silhouetted against the sky as we approach, dark against lavender, and lights are beginning to flicker in the windows of houses scattered down the hillside. We enter by one of what we later learn are two roads leading to San Ignatio. The back one, which we took, is seldom used. "The creek crossing is not dependable, Señora," our landlady tells me. The other road leads from the coast, crosses the road we'd traveled much of the day, passes through San Ignatio and continues over the mountains, eventually leading to the Gulf.

We have no trouble finding rooms. Apparently it is not unusual for motorists to be stranded here during the winter when the road through the mountains becomes impassable, although there are fewer travelers these days, they say, with the war going on and fuel harder to come by. But most everything is available in Mexico if you have the money to pay for it, and the industrious villagers are happy to care for unexpected guests.

The room Tucker and I are offered is nearly bare. There is a double bed with a bright magenta blanket covering it. The intertwining roses and vines on the wooden headboard are delicate but crudely carved, and I think of the unknown, unskilled artist who carved them and wonder if he thought about the people who might eventually sleep in his bed. Above it, as though in blessing, a cross hangs on the wall. Under the single window is a carved and painted chest. There is no rug on the smooth, wood planked floor and no curtains hang at the window. The simple beauty of the room appeals to me. Tucker appears not to notice.

"Let's go find a bar and get a drink."

"I want to see if I can find someplace to take a bath."

"You can do that later. Right now I want a drink."

Jack and Kay are already sitting at a table when we walk into the cantina. Drinks are in front of them along with a plate of sliced lemons and a dish of peppers. They look to be arguing when Jack sees us and waves us over.

"The tequila isn't bad," Jack says.

A woman comes to take our order. She's wearing a black cotton, gathered skirt and a white blouse. Her dusty, bare feet are thrust into leather sandals. She doesn't smile, but stands silent, waiting. Tucker orders a beer for himself and a glass of tequila for me. The ceiling is low and a single bulb dangling on a short, black cord at the center of the room casts a weak light that doesn't quite reach into the corners. Besides the smell of beer and cigarette smoke, the air is rich with cooking odors.

There are two men sitting at a nearby table. The ashtray between them is overflowing with stubbed out cigarettes and there is a bottle of beer and a glass in front of each man. One man is wearing a dark suit. His thin black tie hangs loose at the collar of his white shirt, but otherwise he looks tidy, as though someone who cares about his appearance has tended him. His companion is thin and dark, with pockmarked skin drawn tight over his narrow face. His dark eyes stare out from under thick bushy brows. The two men are speaking so quickly and softly I can't follow their Spanish, but the thin one is drawing lines in some beer spilled on the table and in between is jabbing his finger at the man in the suit.

The waitress brings our drinks. I sip the tequila and enjoy the sharp taste on my tongue and the spreading warmth as it hits my belly. Jack pulls the map out of his pocket, unfolds it and lays it out on the table, the plate of lemon slices and the dish of peppers pushing up the paper in the middle like small mountains. Jack and Tucker discuss the next day's route. I try to make conversation with Kay. She answers my questions in one or two words, lighting one cigarette from the end of another.

Suddenly Kay sits back in her chair and folds her arms across her chest. "Well, you'll know soon enough. I'm pregnant."

"Oh, for Christ's sake, Kay. Do you have to blab everything you know?" Jack looks disgusted and takes another swallow of tequila.

"Well, I think it's important for our friends to know that I'm knocked up, Sugar. Aren't you just thrilled for me, Honey?" she asks me. "What do you suppose it is, a boy or a girl? I'd love to have a little girl, I think. But then, again, a little boy would be nice, too." She lights another cigarette then quickly stubs it out and starts to cry.

"Just shut-up, Kay," says Jack. "God dammit, can't we just finish this trip and think about our problem later? Where's the waitress? Let's see if we can get something to eat."

"I don't want anything to eat. Besides, it isn't your problem, it's my problem. You already have a wife and son." Kay pushes herself back from the table and stands up. "I'm going back to our room," she says.

"Go ahead, then. Go," says Jack. Kay turns and, as she hurries past his table, stumbles against the man in the suit. He stands up and grabs Kay's elbow, steadying her. He looks at her and then at Jack before sitting back down and letting Kay pass.

"I'm going with Kay," I say to Tucker. "I'll see you later." I turn and follow after Kay, running a few steps before I catch up with her on the road outside the cantina. She doesn't stop walking.

"He wants me to have an abortion."

"An abortion. How? Where?"

"Oh, Jack will arrange something. Tucker probably knows somebody. They perform abortions all the time in the border towns. It's just that it's so squalid and lower class."

As I lie under the magenta blanket thinking about Kay I hear Tucker and Jack coming up the stairs, bumping into walls.

"Shit."

"Shhh."

The door opens and closes and I hear footsteps going down the hall and then another door opens and closes. Tucker sits down heavily on the bed. I pull my feet back just in time. Shoes fall to the floor one by one. Tucker mutters under his breath as he struggles to pull off his slacks and shirt. When he climbs into bed he pulls me to him. His arms and face are cold and there is the smell of stale beer and tequila on his breath. I turn my head and pull back. He pulls me to him again and thrusts his hips against me. I can feel it poking my thigh. He thrusts at me again and his shiny bald head hits me on the cheek bringing a stinging pain and tears to my eyes.

"Quit it, Tucker. I'm not in the mood."

"Too bad. I am."

"I mean it, Tucker. I'm tired. It's been a long day. Let's get some sleep."

"I mean it, Tucker," he mimics.

The foul smell of his breath nauseates me and I pull away from him again.

"Come here, dammit. I didn't bring you along to tell me you're not in the mood. I'm in the mood and that'll have to be enough." He grabs my arms and rolls on top of me.

I slip off the bed and search along the floor for my nightgown. I pull it on and tie the straps where they're torn. I roll a snoring Tucker over and wrap myself in the magenta blanket. Toward dawn I fall asleep.

Tucker is ignoring me this morning as he re-packs the small suitcase he brought from the car yesterday. After a while he leaves the room. When I come downstairs he's sitting at the table with Kay and Jack. The three of them are laughing about something. There's a hammered silver coffeepot and several ceramic mugs on a small table near a door I think leads to the kitchen. Next to the coffeepot is a tray of rolls and a pot of butter. I pour a cup of coffee and go over and sit down.

"Where's your bag?" says Tucker. "Aren't you packed yet? We want to leave here right after we pay the bill."

"I'm not going," I say.

"What do you mean, you're not going?"

"I mean I'm not going with you. I'm staying here."

"Don't be ridiculous. Of course you're not staying here. Now go get your things together and stop playing games."

"I'm not playing games with you, Tucker." Kay and Jack are watching us, but neither of them says a word.

"How are you going to get back to Phoenix then? We're not coming back here for you."

"I don't know. I'll find something. A bus maybe." I have no idea, but surely there must be busses that go through this town to somewhere I can get transportation.

"You're crazy. I mean it now. Are you coming with us or not?"

"I'm not."

"Suit yourself then." He stands up, pushes the chair back and walks away. Neither Kay nor Jack look at me, but stand and follow Tucker.

Immediately I want to say "Wait, I've changed my mind," but I don't. I go back up to the room and wait for them to leave.

"There is a bus to Leone on Wednesday, Señora, but it is not so nice. Maybe you can hire Mr. Lopez to drive you in his auto." I'm surprised to find the waitress at the cantina is so helpful. Her name is Otilia, and she serves me a breakfast of fresh melon and the most delicious oatmeal I've ever tasted.

"Who is Mr. Lopez?"

"He was here last night sitting at that table over there with his brother-in-law."

"I remember the two men. Which one is Mr. Lopez?" If he's the thin pock-faced man I'll take the bus.

As though she can read my mind she says, "Mr. Lopez is the mayor of San Ignatio, Señora. He always wears a fine suit." She tells me he comes to the cantina every afternoon and she will tell him about me. She knows where I am staying and she will send him to me.

I finish the melon and decide to spend the rest of the morning exploring San Ignatio. By the time I've climbed the hill to the church I'm sweating and out of breath. The church stands at the top of the hill, the rough stone roads of the town leading out from it like spokes. It has a rounded dome, stained glass windows and whitewashed adobe walls, and I guess it's more like a cathedral than a church. I peer through the wide opened carved wooden doors. After the bright sunlight, it's hard to make out anything except for splashes of colored light that fall on the stone floor and the rows of wooden benches. As my eyes begin to adjust I see a crucifix hanging on the wall at the front of the church above a tall altar. The thin body and face of Christ look sad and tormented, and I wonder how this figure brings comfort to so many. In several niches along the walls there are carved figures painted in vivid blues, yellows, reds and gold, as though drenched in the colors from the glass in the windows. I recognize one of the figures as Mary and another as Jesus, his arms outstretched, but I have no idea which saints the rest of the figures represent. I see no one inside the church, but still I sense a presence. Perhaps it's all the statues. Or perhaps it's the ghosts of the hundreds of petitioners who have knelt before Mary's statue, seeking her intervention to solve the problems in their lives.

The shade offered by the spreading branches of ancient oak trees in the park across from the church draws me to it. There is a large fountain in the center of the park and water cascades into a rough stone bowl surrounding its base. Tables piled with fruits and vegetables and other tables of merchandise line three sides of the park. I stroll around to examine what is for sale. I am offered an embroidered tablecloth, dishes, cooking pots, tortillas, shoes, brooms, gum, magazines, cigarettes, a silver framed mirror, belts, beans, aprons, lace, pencils, pens, scissors, knives, gloves, hats, hoes, picks, shovels, barbecued chicken, chickens live and squawking, a pig with a rope tied around its neck, squash, lemons, oranges, leather purses, wallets, balls, rings, books and ball bats. Each item is offered with an eager smile and soft words assuring me of its value and uniqueness as I make my way around the tables. There are children playing and several young babies are in baskets near their mothers' stalls. Dogs dart in and out and dodge half-hearted kicks as they nose around the tables with food. Two small boys run up to me. One elbows the other who says, "You Norte Americano?" I say yes and they both laugh and run off.

The oleanders at the foot of my garden sway in the late evening breeze sweeping down off Camelback Mountain, over the manicured gardens of the hotels and resorts, over the stuccoed walls of the newly rich and the old rich, on its way to the desert stretching east of Scottsdale. I sit on the still warm patio, an old woman now, watching the sky turn from pink to lavender to gray and remember the colors of the sky in Mexico that summer.

Mr. Lopez did drive me to Leone. On the way he told me about his brother-in-law and their dispute over some property left to Mr. Lopez and his sister by their parents. The problem was irrigation. Mr. Lopez said his brother-in-law was a good man, but wretched in his luck and had little skill as a farmer. In Leone I caught a bus to Guadalajara, then another that traveled up along the Sea of Cortez, turned inland to Nogales, Tucson and home to Phoenix.

Jack finally divorced his wife, I heard, and married Kay. After the war they spent time in Saudi Arabia, where Jack did something with the government and growing cotton, then they moved to California. There were never any children though, and when Jack died his son by his first wife inherited everything. Tucker and I ran into each other from time to time, but after a while I didn't see him any more.

The End

Before continuing, consider the following questions once again:

1. The setting: Do you feel as if you are there? Why or why not? Where do you think the setting is most clearly drawn? How does she

achieve that? To what senses does she appeal? Where is the setting undeveloped?

2. The characters: How well do you come to know them? Which do you feel you know best? Whose story is it? What do the characters want?

3. The plot: What is at stake for whom?

4. The dialogue: Is it a close approximation of how these people would speak? Is it sufficiently embodied?

5. The point of view: How would the story be different in another point of view? What is the narrative distance? How does that affect the story?

6. Voice: What is the narrator's voice? Is it affected by the time in which the story takes place?

When you have finished, look at this same draft with marginalia, and then the critique that follows the draft.

Benedictions

by Toni Morgan

Here we are the four of us, bouncing along a dirt and gravel road in Mexico to show Jack the cotton growing potential of the western and central regions. Tucker is driving. His bald head is pink and peeling despite the sun lotion he rubs into it every morning. I'm always amazed that he burns so easily since he was born in Tucson and raised on the desert. Wouldn't you think the skin would   *Pov?* eventually build up a tolerance? But there it is in front of me, looking more like an onion than ever. Tucker procures for the Army what the Army   *Time?* needs to feed and clothe its soldiers. The Army needs cotton for uniforms.

Dust rolls out from beneath the station wagon like a tail dragging along behind us. It lies thick on the dashboard, over the seats, and coats our luggage and the extra fuel cans piled up in the back. My lips are dry and chapped and all I want at the moment is a long soak in a hot tub with plenty of soap. I wonder again why I agreed to come on this trip. Tucker seemed indifferent when he'd first mentioned it, appearing not to care if I came along or stayed home. We've been

together for six months, but I'm not sure we'll
ever have a permanent relationship. Or if I want
one. My mother, who lives with me, was dead set
against my coming. We argued for days.

"I just don't understand you, Virginia. I'm
going to ignore the fact that you'll obviously be
sleeping with that man," she never refers to   *Nice Transition.*
Tucker by name. He's been married twice before
and she views him with suspicion and some
scorn. "But how can you go off and leave Richie
for six weeks? He's only five. What if he gets sick?
What if I need to contact you?" But the trip
sounded like a lark, and Jack and Kay can be fun,
so I promised I'd call frequently. Besides, Richie
loves being with her. He probably doesn't even
notice I'm not there.

Northeast of us is a range of mountains. San
Ignatio, where we plan to spend the night, is
located in the foothills. The last village we passed
was three hours back and there is no sign of a village or even a house ahead of us. As far as I can
see in all directions are sage and mesquite. The
mountains are the only things that interrupt the
flat landscape under its azure blue dome.

"According to the map there's another road
we have to take to get to San Ignatio," says
Tucker. "It can't be too much further."

"Let's roll up the windows," Kay says. "The
dust is so thick in here I can hardly breathe."

Kay is from Texas. "Amarillo, Honey," she
tells people in her flat, nasal drawl. We all met in
Phoenix where so many people have moved since
the war started, looking for excitement or jobs.
Jack comes from the Central Valley of California.
His family owns a large cattle operation there. He
came to Phoenix partly for business opportunities and partly to get away from his wife. I'm
from a small town in Nevada nobody's ever   *Why not name town?*
heard of. The only thing different about me is
they were born rich.

"It's too hot," Jack says.

"Well, I'd rather be hot than choke to death,
Sugar."

"Put out your cigarette. Maybe that will help." Jack is always complaining about Kay's chain-smoking. Kay ignores him, but she doesn't say any more about putting up the windows.

"This must be the turn off," says Tucker. He pulls to a stop and we all look at the words *"San Ignatio"* with an arrow painted on a piece of wood nailed to a stake that has been pounded into the ground, pointing to the mountains.

"Jesus, that road looks worse than the one we're on."

"I knew we should have stayed nearer the coast."

"Well, what do you all think? Should we turn off here or keep going?"

Kay is for keeping to the road we're on, but the rest of us vote for the turn off, so Tucker puts the car into gear and points it toward the mountains. After a while the road begins to climb into hills that are rounded and undulating. The land is still covered in sage and mesquite, but now there is an occasional solitary juniper. I can see the road in front of us go up one side of a hill, disappear at the top, reappear on the hill beyond and again beyond that. When we reach the top of the last hill I look down at a valley below. At its bottom is a dry creek bed strewn with rocks and boulders, with clumps of oak and willow along its edges. On the other side of the creek I can make out tracks leading up the side of yet another hill and again disappearing over the top. The car grinds down to where the road runs into the creek bed. Tucker drives slowly forward maneuvering around the boulders. I hang onto the door handle to keep from being pitched sideways into Kay. When we reach the other side Tucker stops the car and we all climb out.

"Well, what do you think, Folks?"

"I think we're fuckin' lost, Honey," Kay says.

Jack pulls out the map and lays it across the hood of the car. Kay wanders over to a large boulder, sits down and lights another cigarette. Her

Who is speaking?

There would be more tension with two men and one woman.

sleek brown hair falls forward as she leans into the match, cupping the flame with carmine tipped fingers. She blows out a long stream of smoke and ignores the two men arguing over the map.

Too eloquent for our 1st person narrator.

My blouse is sticking to my back, and my linen shorts have ridden up in a bunch between my legs. I am stiff from sitting in the car all day. I start to follow the tracks up the hill, partly to work out the kinks and partly to get away from everyone for at least a few minutes. When I reach the top I yell back to the rest. "There's a town. I can see it."

A church and several small buildings are silhouetted against the sky as we approach, dark against lavender, and lights are beginning to flicker in the windows of houses scattered down the hillside. We enter by one of what we later learn are two roads leading to San Ignatio. The back one, which we took, is seldom used. "The creek crossing is not dependable, Senora," our landlady tells me. The other road leads from the coast, crosses the road we'd traveled much of the day, passes through San Ignatio and continues over the mountains, eventually leading to the Gulf.

Narrator speaks Spanish? More tension if she has limited ability.

We have no trouble finding rooms. Apparently it is not unusual for motorists to be stranded here during the winter when the road through the mountains becomes impassable, although there are fewer travelers these days, they say, with the war going on and fuel harder to come by. But most everything is available in Mexico if you have the money to pay for it, and the industrious villagers are happy to care for unexpected guests.

Chronology.

The room Tucker and I are offered is nearly bare. There is a double bed with a bright magenta blanket covering it. The intertwining roses and vines on the wooden headboard are delicate but crudely carved, and I think of the unknown, unskilled artist who carved them and wonder if he thought about the people who might eventually sleep in his bed. Above it, as though in blessing, a cross hangs on the wall. Under the single window is a carved and painted chest. There is no rug on the smooth, wood planked floor and no curtains hang at the window. The simple beauty of the room appeals to me. Tucker appears not to notice.

More description of cross—one more beat—it will be important later.

"Let's find a bar and get a drink."

"I want to see if I can find someplace to take a bath."

"You can do that later. Right now I want a drink."

Keep bar in same building—we gain nothing by shifting locales.

Jack and Kay are already sitting at a table when we walk into the cantina. Drinks are in front of them along with a plate of sliced lemons and a dish of peppers. They look to be arguing when Jack sees us and waves us over.

"The tequila isn't bad," Jack says.

A woman comes to take our order. She's wearing a black cotton, gathered skirt and a white blouse. Her dusty, bare feet are thrust into leather sandals. She doesn't smile, but stands silent, waiting. Tucker orders a beer for himself and a glass of tequila for me. The ceiling is low and a single bulb dangling on a short, black cord at the center of the room casts a weak light that doesn't quite reach into the corners. Besides the smell of beer and cigarette smoke, the air is rich with cooking odors.

Make her the landlady—same as before. The fewer the characters the better.

There are two men sitting at a nearby table. The ashtray between them is overflowing with stubbed out cigarettes and there is a bottle of beer and a glass in front of each man. One man is wearing a dark suit. His thin black tie hangs loose at the collar of his white shirt, but otherwise he looks tidy, as though someone who cares about his appearance has tended him. His companion is thin and dark, with pockmarked skin drawn tight over his narrow face. His dark eyes stare out from under thick bushy brows. The two men are speaking so quickly and softly I can't follow their Spanish, but the thin one is drawing lines in some beer spilled on the table and in between is jabbing his finger at the man in the suit.

Narrator should have only rudimentary knowledge of Spanish.

The waitress brings our drinks. I sip the tequila and enjoy the sharp taste on my tongue and the spreading warmth as it hits my belly. Jack pulls the map out of his pocket, unfolds it and lays it out on the table, the plate of lemon slices and the dish of peppers pushing up the paper in the middle like small mountains. Jack and Tucker discuss the next day's route. I try to make conversation with Kay. She answers my questions in one or two words, lighting one cigarette from the end of another.

Suddenly Kay sits back in her chair and folds her arms across her chest. "Well, you'll know soon enough. I'm pregnant."

Why would they wait until Mexico to discuss this?

"Oh, for Christ's sake, Kay. Do you have to blab everything you know?" Jack looks disgusted and takes another swallow of tequila.

"Well, I think it's important for our friends to know that I'm knocked up, Sugar. Aren't you just thrilled for me, Honey?" she asks me. "What do you suppose it is, a boy or a girl? I'd love to have a little girl, I think. But then, again, a little boy would be nice, too." She lights another cigarette then quickly stubs it out and starts to cry.

I like this, but it detracts from the narrator's story—whose story is this?

"Just shut-up, Kay," says Jack. "God dammit, can't we just finish this trip and think about our problem later? Where's the waitress? Let's see if we can get something to eat."

Wooden dialogue.

"I don't want anything to eat. Besides, it isn't your problem, it's my problem. You already have a wife and son." Kay pushes herself back from the table and stands up. "I'm going back to our room," she says.

"Go ahead, then. Go," says Jack. Kay turns and, as she hurries past his table, stumbles against the man in the suit. He stands up and grabs Kay's elbow, steadying her. He looks at her and then at Jack before sitting back down and letting Kay pass.

"I'm going with Kay," I say to Tucker. "I'll see you later." I turn and follow after Kay, running a few steps before I catch up with her on the road outside the cantina. She doesn't stop walking.

You'll change this if you locate bar in hotel.

"He wants me to have an abortion."

"An abortion. How? Where?"

"Oh, Jack will arrange something. Tucker probably knows somebody. They perform abortions all the time in the border towns. It's just that it's so squalid and lower class."

Clarify time of year.

As I lie under the magenta blanket thinking about Kay I hear Tucker and Jack coming up the stairs, bumping into walls.

"Shit."

"Shhh."

The door opens and closes and I hear footsteps going down the hall and then another door opens and closes. Tucker sits down heavily on the bed. I pull my feet back just in time. Shoes fall to the floor one by one. Tucker mutters under his breath as he struggles to pull off his slacks and shirt. When he climbs into bed he pulls me to him. His arms and face are cold and there is the smell of stale beer and tequila on his breath. I turn my head and pull back. He pulls me to him again and thrusts his hips against me. I can feel it poking my thigh. He thrusts at me again and his shiny bald head hits me on the cheek bringing a stinging pain and tears to my eyes.

What would she call it?

"Quit it, Tucker. I'm not in the mood."

"Too bad. I am."

"I mean it, Tucker. I'm tired. It's been a long day. Let's get some sleep."

"*I mean it, Tucker,*" he mimics.

Nice!

The foul smell of his breath nauseates me and I pull away from him again.

"Come here, dammit. I didn't bring you along to tell me you're not in the mood. I'm in the mood and that'll have to be enough." He grabs my arms and rolls on top of me.

I slip off the bed and search along the floor for my nightgown. I pull it on and tie the straps where they're torn. I roll a snoring Tucker over and wrap myself in the magenta blanket. Toward dawn I fall asleep.

Tucker is ignoring me this morning as he re-packs the small suitcase he brought from the car yesterday. After a while he leaves the room. When I come downstairs he's sitting at the table with Kay and Jack. The three of them are laughing about something. There's a hammered silver coffeepot and several ceramic mugs on a small table near a door I think leads to the kitchen. Next to the coffeepot is a tray of rolls and a pot of butter. I pour a cup of coffee and go over and sit down.

> *Wrong mood—Kay would not laugh now. Have them sober.*

"Where's your bag?" says Tucker. "Aren't you packed yet? We want to leave here right after we pay the bill."

"I'm not going," I say.

"What do you mean, you're not going?"

"I mean I'm not going with you. I'm staying here."

"Don't be ridiculous. Of course you're not staying here. Now go get your things together and stop playing games."

"I'm not playing games with you, Tucker." Kay and Jack are watching us, but neither of them says a word.

"How are you going to get back to Phoenix then? We're not coming back here for you."

"I don't know. I'll find something. A bus maybe." I have no idea, but surely there must be buses that go through this town to somewhere I can get transportation.

"You're crazy. I mean it now. Are you coming with us or not?"

"I'm not."

"Suit yourself then." He stands up, pushes the chair back and walks away. Neither Kay nor Jack look at me, but stand and follow Tucker.

> *Kay or Jake or both would say something.*

Immediately I want to say "Wait, I've changed my mind," but I don't. I go back up to the room and wait for them to leave.

"There is a bus to Leone on Wednesday, Senora, but it is not so nice. Maybe you can hire Mr. Lopez to drive you in his auto." I'm surprised to find the waitress at the cantina is so helpful. Her name is Otilia, and she serves me a breakfast of fresh melon and the most delicious oatmeal I've ever tasted.

> *Use a little Spanish in following dialogue—Have the narrator a bit confused as to what is being said—and the reader, too.*

"Who is Mr. Lopez?"

"He was here last night sitting at that table over there with his brother-in-law."

"I remember the two men. Which one is Mr. Lopez?" If he's the thin pock-faced man I'll take the bus.

As though she can read my mind she says, "Mr. Lopez is the mayor of San Ignatio, Senora. He always wears a fine suit." She tells me he comes to the cantina every afternoon and she will tell him about me. She knows where I am staying and she will send him to me.

Same hotel.

I finish the melon and decide to spend the rest of the morning exploring San Ignatio. By the time I've climbed the hill to the church I'm sweating and out of breath. The church stands at the top of the hill, the rough stone roads of the town leading out from it like spokes. It has a rounded dome, stained glass windows and whitewashed adobe walls, and I guess it's more like a cathedral than a church. I peer through the wide opened carved wooden doors. After the bright sunlight, it's hard to make out anything except for splashes of colored light that fall on the stone floor and the rows of wooden benches. As my eyes begin to adjust I see a crucifix hanging on the wall at the front of the church above a tall altar. The thin body and face of Christ look sad and tormented, and I wonder how this figure brings comfort to so many. In several niches along the walls there are carved figures painted in vivid blues, yellows, reds and gold, as though drenched in the colors from the glass in the windows. I recognize one of the figures as Mary and another as Jesus, his arms outstretched, but I have no idea which saints the rest of the figures represent. I see no one inside the church, but still I sense a presence. Perhaps it's all the statues. Or perhaps it's the ghosts of the hundreds of petitioners who have knelt before Mary's statue, seeking her intervention to solve the problems in their lives.

Here's the key to your story— make it look like it was carved by the same guy as the one above the bed.

The shade offered by the spreading branches of ancient oak trees in the park across from the church draws me to it. There is a large fountain in the center of the park and water cascades into a rough stone bowl surrounding its base. Tables piled with fruits and vegetables and other tables of merchandise line three sides of the park. I stroll around to examine what is for sale. I am offered an embroidered tablecloth, dishes, cooking pots, tortillas, shoes, brooms, gum, magazines, cigarettes, a silver framed mirror, belts, beans, aprons, lace, pencils, pens, scissors, knives, gloves, hats, hoes, picks, shovels, barbecued chicken, chickens live and squawking, a pig with a rope tied around its neck, squash, lemons, oranges, leather purses, wallets, balls, rings, books and ball bats. Each item is offered with an eager smile and soft words assuring me of its value and uniqueness as I make my way around the tables. There are children playing and several young babies are in baskets near their mothers' stalls. Dogs dart in and out and dodge half-hearted kicks as they nose around the tables with food. Two small boys run up to me. One elbows the other who says, "You Norte Americano?" I say yes and they both laugh and run off.

Have a man who carries crucifixes here i.e., T.S. Eliot's objective correlative.

Big jump! End the story in Mexico.

The oleanders at the foot of my garden sway in the late evening breeze sweeping down off Camelback Mountain, over the manicured gardens of the hotels and resorts, over the stuccoed walls of the newly rich and the old rich, on its way to the desert stretching east of Scottsdale. I sit on the still warm patio, an old woman now, watching the sky turn from pink to lavender to gray and remember the colors of the sky in Mexico that summer.

Mr. Lopez did drive me to Leone. On the way he told me about his brother-in-law and their dispute over some property left to Mr. Lopez and his sister by their parents. The problem was irrigation. Mr. Lopez said his brother-in-law was a good man, but wretched in his luck and had little skill as a farmer. In Leone I caught a bus to Guadalajara, then another that traveled up along the Sea of Cortez, turned inland to Nogales, Tucson and home to Phoenix.

Jack finally divorced his wife, I heard, and married Kay. After the war they spent time in Saudi Arabia, where Jack did something with the government and growing cotton, then they moved to California. There were never any children though, and when Jack died his son by his first wife inherited everything. Tucker and I ran into each other from time to time, but after a while I didn't see him any more

No, not after rape. You are trying to tie up everything too neatly.

Critique

Dear Toni,

There is a lot to like in this draft. You do a good job of capturing much of the setting here so that we get a sense of Mexico, and you do a good job of establishing conflict early on and then raising the tension right away. And the flashback to the narrator's mother on page two is handled very smoothly; the reader rides right back in time with the narrator without a bump in the road. Good work in that.

What I want to do here is go through this page by page, drawing attention to my marginalia, and then I want to focus on some of the bigger issues that you may want to address in your next draft.

In the first two words, you have established the point of view. Great. Sometimes we will read the first two pages of a story and think that it is in the third person, and then the word *I* magically appears and we feel either dumb or duped. So good work, here. But in the same paragraph, you write *Wouldn't you think the skin would eventually build up a tolerance?* I realize this to be a rhetorical thought on the narrator's part, but it is also jarring to see the word *you* as if the narrator were addressing the reader and thus, I would eliminate that.

On this same page, we are told that they are on the trip to show Jack the "cotton growing potential" of the area, yet it never becomes clear why Jack wants to grow cotton in the area; it is Tucker, we are told, who procures supplies for the army. I would clarify just why they are all on this trip together.

On page two, you slide into the aforementioned flashback smoothly. To help you leave it and reenter story time just as smoothly, I would include a space break before starting the paragraph *Northeast of us . . .*

On page three, I do not know why the narrator would not name the town in Nevada where she is from. Place names are great for grounding the reader in a story, and *Elko* is far better than *a small town in Nevada nobody's ever heard of.* Farther down on this page, I am confused as to who is speaking in those three lines of dialogue I marked. A couple of tag lines with attribution will clear that up.

On page four, two large issues occur to me. First, I wonder if we could eliminate Kay. I wonder about this for several reasons, not the least of which is that the fewer characters you have in a story, the less confusing it is. Before we get to the end of this story, we wonder whose story it is. At one point, it seems to be Kay's story as she is discovered to be pregnant. At this point, we consider this possibility and conclude that the narrator is a detached observer. Of course, by the time the narrator is raped by Tucker, we realize that we were wrong and that this is, indeed, the narrator's story, but you do not want the reader to be confused to that extent.

Eliminating Kay would certainly raise the stakes, increase the tension, in that there now would be three characters—two men and a woman—traveling in Mexico where she would not have any resources for "escaping" from these men. Thus, I would suggest that you consider eliminating Kay.

My other concern on page four is one of point of view. I like the first person narrator's voice here, but I wonder about her describing Kay as *Her sleek brown hair falls forward as she leans into the match, cupping the flame with carmine tipped fingers.* Of course, that is beautiful writing, Toni, but (1) would the narrator have that ability in using such language; and (2) would she take the time to make such descriptions considering the circumstances? Thus, I am wondering if a change to a third person limited point of view might be more appropriate (by the way, I would mention the narrator's name more than once in the story; the only place I recall seeing her name was in the flashback, and by the end, I couldn't remember that her name was Virginia).

On page five, you have a minor problem with chronology in that you have the narrator speaking to the landlady and then the narrator makes the statement "We have no trouble finding rooms."

I would work on clarifying the setting here so that we see the church as they enter town. Then, I would make it clear that there is but one hotel in the town where they can find rooms. And then we can meet the landlady. I make these suggestions because the smaller the town, the fewer the resources for the narrator, and this raises the tension when we see her left behind.

On this same page, the landlady speaks to the narrator, but in which language? I would suggest that our narrator have only the most rudimentary knowledge of Spanish, again raising the stakes when she is left behind. The reader will wonder how she will ever get along. This can be clarified when they are in the *cantina,* drinking. And I would make the *cantina* in the same building as the inn with the landlady serving as hostess. Again, we don't gain anything by having them go to a *cantina* that is not in the hotel where they are staying (and having Tucker and Jack getting drunk in such close proximity to where our narrator is sleeping raises the tension as well).

You help yourself as a writer in inventorying the hotel room, and it is wise to have that cross above the bed in that the church will come into the story later, and the bed itself is where the rape occurs—directly beneath the cross. I would add one more beat to the description of the cross here on page five, however. Later in this critique, I will mention the cross again and it will be important to have this cross clearly described. It would probably be a good idea to give the carving one odd twist that the reader will recall. Physical objects can carry a terrific emotional weight, and this cross could do so and thereby be of more significance in the story than it is at present. (For further reading, see T. S. Eliot's "Hamlet and his Problems" in *The Sacred Wood*, wherein he coins the term "objective correlative," meaning a set of actions or objects that when seen by the reader evoke an emotion.)

If you agree that the bar should be in the hotel, you'll have to change the dialogue on page six. Maybe: "Let's go downstairs and get a drink." And again, I would have the waitress be the landlady whom we have met before. Give her some feature on first reference that we will see again here on page six, thus helping us recall her image. It could be something as simple as a slight limp.

I like the tension on page seven with Kay and the pregnancy, but as I indicated earlier, I think we should eliminate Kay because now it seems that this might be Kay's story. In other words, you have Kay's pregnancy competing with the narrator's rape, and the reader must decide where to vest his focus. (This also seems an odd place for Kay to discover she is pregnant; and if she already knew, why does it seem that this is the first time it has been discussed?)

Earlier on this page, I'd have the narrator struggle with some broken Spanish when she orders drinks (italicize the Spanish as we do with all foreign languages). This will increase the tension when she is left behind, stranded in Mexico with an inability to communicate.

If you have agreed to the suggestion of putting the bar in the hotel, then you'll have to make the necessary changes on page eight.

Page nine is certainly the pivotal point in the story. You do an excellent job at understating the rape. The mistake would be to draw it out with graphic detail. That last paragraph before the space break is just stunning and the reader is left shuddering. Earlier on the page, however, I would use whatever word our narrator would use for penis instead of using *it*. And italicize "*I mean it, Tucker*" when he mimics her. By the way, that mimicking is terrific characterization.

On page ten, I believe the mood has undeservedly shifted with the three of them laughing at the table when the narrator arrives. I do not believe they would be so happy with Kay in or not in the story. Instead, I would have the two men hung over and taciturn as they drink their coffee.

At the top of page eleven, I believe Jack would say something (as would Kay if she were to remain in the story) when Tucker leaves the *cantina* after the narrator says that she is not going with them.

On the same page, use a space break to indicate a temporal (time) and spatial (space) shift when she is talking to the landlady about transportation (the landlady if you take my suggestion of reducing the number of characters and places in the story by having the *cantina* in the hotel). And when the narrator is speaking to her about Mr. Lopez on this page, I would insert some Spanish and break up the speech more so that we can see she is having trouble communicating with the woman. As it is, she seems to be perfectly fluent which reduces the tension; again, if she is left behind and knows very little of the language, the tension is magnified. Tension, tension, tension.

Page twelve has huge potential for resonance, and that potential lies in the crucifix in the church which will remind us why she is here, so I would give the crucifix in the church the same malformation as the one in the hotel so that the reader will connect the two. Maybe the local crucifix carver has a trademarked scar on Christ's forehead that the narrator first notices in the bedroom and then notices again here in the church. Something like that to connect the two, so the reader will go back to that horrible moment in the bedroom.

Still on the same page: the narrator goes outside to a market of sorts where you have inventoried many, many items. I would reduce the number of items, thereby giving more weight to each, and—you can see where I am going now—have a table where a craftsman is busy carving various figures, and on his table the narrator sees the crucifixes with the same malformation. What would she do? Would she stop and touch one? Would she buy one?

In the ending you have here, you are trying to wrap everything up too neatly, I think. And having the story end back in Arizona so many years later when she is an old woman is a problematic **narrative distance** in its enormity. If we end our stay in Mexico at the market and then jump to Arizona many, many years later, one wonders what it was at the market that caused such reflection, and frankly, as it is, I don't know. Thus, I would greatly reduce the narrative distance. (And with the narrative distance that you do have, I would write this in the past tense. Notice that you shift from present tense to past tense when the narrator is an old woman back in Arizona. The present tense, by the way, slows down the action as we wait for events to unfold.)

I think you need to end the story in Mexico with her waiting for a bus or whatever transportation it is that will take her out of Mexico. This story needs to be more open-ended. Your last line is a throw-away line: *Tucker and I ran into each other from time to time, but after a while I didn't see him anymore.* So what? I think you were just looking for a way out here, Toni, and although you didn't find a plausible way out, you broke out just the same.

The key to the story is the undercurrent in the narrator that is not yet here. What was it that happened to her husband? Why would she go on this adventure with a man like Tucker? Why leave her son behind? In other words, I don't think you know enough about your narrator to provide the subtext to the story that would make the ending resonate for the reader. And the key question is why she would abandon the safety of Arizona for the dangers of traveling with a man like Tucker. Clarify that in your own mind and we will find a good ending in Mexico.

As I get to the end of this critique, Toni, I realize that I did not comment on the time. We are told that the story is taking place during the war—presumably World War II—but there is little evidence of the time in the story. In other words, it could be contemporary from the evidence in this draft. Is it important that the story take place during World War II? Why? How? How would it be different—to the narrator—if it were set in the same town today? Not very different, I would say.

The setting is stronger in the beginning, when they are traveling, than when they arrive. I would rewrite one or two drafts just for setting. Make it more Mexico.

O.K., Toni. Enough. This is a very good draft, one full of potential. In your next draft, rewrite for one thing. The key to the story is Virginia. Just who is this woman?

I look forward to seeing what decisions you will have made in rewriting the next draft.

—*Tim*

Revision

Benedictions

by Toni Morgan

Here we are the three of us, bouncing along a dirt and gravel road in Mexico to show Jack the cotton-growing potential of the western and central regions. Tucker is driving. His bald head is pink and peeling despite the sun lotion he rubs into it every morning. I'm always amazed that he burns so easily since he was born in Tucson and raised in the desert. But there it is in front of me, looking more like an onion than ever. Tucker procures for the Army what the Army needs to feed and clothe its soldiers. The Army needs cotton for uniforms.

Dust rolls out from beneath the station wagon like a tail dragging along behind us. It lies thick on the dashboard, over the seats, and it coats our luggage and the extra fuel cans piled up in the back. My lips are dry and chapped and all I want at the moment is a long soak in a hot tub with plenty of soap. I wonder again why I agreed to come on this trip. Tucker seemed indifferent when he'd first mentioned it, appearing not to care if I came along or stayed home. We've been together for six months, but I'm not sure we'll ever have a permanent relationship. Or if I want one. My mother, who lives with me, was dead set against my coming. We argued for days.

"I just don't understand you, Virginia. I'm going to ignore the fact that you're obviously sleeping with that man." She never refers to Tucker by name. He's been married twice before and she views him with suspicion and some scorn. "But how can you go off and leave Richie for six weeks? He's only five. What if he gets sick? What if I need to contact you?" But the trip sounded like a lark, so I promised I'd call frequently. Besides, Richie loves being with her. He probably doesn't even notice I'm not there.

* * *

Northeast of us is a range of mountains. The town where we plan to spend the night is located in the foothills. The last village we passed was three hours back and there is no sign of a village or even a house ahead of us. As far as I can see in all directions are sage and mesquite. The mountains are the only things that interrupt the flat landscape under its azure blue dome.

"According to the map there's another road we have to take to get to San Ignacio," says Tucker. "It can't be too much further."

The three of us met in Phoenix where so many people have moved since Pearl Harbor, looking for jobs or excitement. Excitement mostly. Practically as soon as war was declared, Tucker came up from Tucson. Jack comes from the Central Valley of California. His family owns a large cattle operation there. He moved to Phoenix partly for business opportunities and partly to get away from his wife. I'm from a small town nobody's heard of. Elko, Nevada. A ranch town in the Ruby Valley. My father worked in the Elko Pharmacy. There was never enough money. Jack and Tucker were born rich.

"Let's roll up the windows," I say. "The dust is so thick in here I can hardly breathe."

"It's too hot," Jack says.

"Well, I'd rather be hot than choke to death," I tell him.

"Put out your cigarette. Maybe that will help." Tucker is always complaining about me smoking. I ignore him and roll up my window. It doesn't help.

"This must be the turn off," says Tucker. He pulls to a stop and we all look at the words *San Ignacio* with an arrow painted on a piece of wood nailed to a stake that has been pounded into the ground, pointing to the mountains.

"Jesus, that road looks worse than the one we're on," says Jack.

"I knew we should have stayed nearer the coast."

"Well, what do you all think?" Tucker says. "Should we turn off here or keep going?"

I'm for keeping to the road we're on, but Jack and Tucker vote for the turn off, so Tucker puts the car into gear and points it toward the mountains. After a while the road begins to climb into low, rolling hills. The land is still covered in sage and mesquite, but now there is an occasional solitary juniper. I can see the road in front of us go up one side of a hill, disappear at the top, reappear on the hill beyond and again beyond that. When we reach the top of the last hill, I look down at a valley below. At its bottom is a dry creek bed strewn with rocks and boulders, with clumps of oak and willow along its edges. On the other side of the creek I can make out tracks leading up the side of yet another hill and again disappearing over the top. The car grinds down to where the road runs into the creek bed. Tucker drives slowly forward maneuvering around the boulders. I hang onto the door handle to keep from being pitched side-ways. When we reach the other side, Tucker stops the car and we all climb out.

"Well, what do you think, folks?"

"I think we're fuckin' lost," says Jack.

Jack pulls out the map and lays it across the hood of the car.

My blouse is sticking to my back, and my linen shorts have ridden up in a bunch between my legs. I'm stiff from sitting in the car all day. I wander over to a large boulder, sit down and light another cigarette, knowing I should try to cut down. I blow out a long stream of smoke and try to ignore the two men arguing over the map.

The sound of their voices is getting on my nerves. I stub out my cig-arette and go back to the car to get a drink of water from the sweating, canvas bag hanging off the driver's outside mirror. I can tell Tucker is get-ting angry, and I decide to follow the tracks up the hill. When I reach the top I yell down to them. "There's a town. I can see it."

It's dusk. A church and several small buildings are silhouetted against the sky as we approach, dark against lavender, and lights flicker in the windows of houses scattered down the hillside. We enter by one of what we learn are two roads leading to San Ignacio. The back one, which we took, is seldom used. "The creek crossing is not dependable, Señora," our landlady later tells me. The other road leads from the coast, crosses the road we'd traveled much of the day, passes through San Ignacio and con-tinues over the mountains, eventually leading to the Gulf.

We have no trouble finding rooms. Apparently it is not unusual for motorists to be stranded here during the winter when the road through the mountains becomes impassable, although there are fewer travelers these days, they say, with the war going on and fuel harder to come by. But most everything is available in Mexico if you have the money to pay for it, and the industrious residents of San Ignacio are happy to care for unexpected guests.

The room Tucker and I are offered is nearly bare. There is a double bed with a bright magenta blanket covering it. The intertwining roses and vines on the wooden headboard are delicate but crudely carved, and I think of the unknown, unskilled artist who carved them and wonder if he thought about the people who might eventually sleep in his bed. Above it, as though in blessing, a cross hangs on the wall. Under the single window is a carved and painted chest. There is no rug on the smooth, wood-planked floor and no curtains hang at the window. The simplicity of the room appeals to me. Tucker appears not to notice.

"Let's go find a bar and get a drink."

"I want to see if I can find someplace to take a bath and I need to call home."

"You can do that later. Right now I want a drink."

Jack is already sitting at a table when we walk into the cantina. A drink is in front of him along with a plate of sliced lemons and a dish of peppers. He sees us and waves us over.

"The tequila isn't bad."

A woman comes to take our order. She's wearing a black, gathered skirt and a white blouse. Her dusty, bare feet are thrust into leather sandals. She doesn't smile, but stands silent, waiting. Tucker orders a beer for himself and a glass of tequila for me. He grew up speaking Spanish.

The ceiling is low and a single bulb dangling on a short, black cord at the center of the room casts a weak light that doesn't quite reach into the corners. Besides the smell of beer and cigarette smoke, the air is rich with cooking odors.

There are two men sitting at a nearby table. The ashtray between them is overflowing with stubbed out cigarettes and there is a bottle of beer and a glass in front of each man. One man is wearing a dark suit. His thin black tie hangs loose at the collar of his white shirt, but otherwise he looks tidy, as though someone who cares about his appearance has tended him. His companion is thin and dark, with pockmarked skin drawn tight over his narrow face. His dark eyes stare out from under thick bushy brows. The two men are speaking so quickly and softly I can't follow their Spanish, but the thin one is drawing lines in some beer spilled on the table and in between is jabbing his finger at the man in the suit.

The waitress brings our drinks. I sip the tequila and enjoy the sharp taste on my tongue and the spreading warmth as it hits my belly. Jack pulls the map out of his pocket, unfolds it and lays it out on the table, the plate of lemon slices and the dish of peppers pushing up the paper in the middle like small mountains. Jack and Tucker discuss some property they plan to see the next day.

"The problem will be getting water to it," Tucker says.

"I have a little experience with that," says Jack. "We've done some irrigating on the ranch. This is the eastern edge of the three parcels, right?" He taps a spot on the map with his finger. "And the river is here at its closest point. That's what, five miles? It shouldn't be too hard to lay pipe that far. Mostly it'll depend on the terrain."

"If we could," says Tucker, "I think we'd produce as much cotton here, in one spot, as all the fields they've put in around Phoenix. And a lot cheaper." The two of them continue talking about their plans for the next day and the route we will take.

I turn to watch the two men at the other table, wondering if there will be a fight. But they seem to have calmed down, and the man in the suit stands. I hear him tell the other man goodnight. As he turns to leave he nods to me and says "Buenas noches, Señora."

"I'm ready to go back to the room, Tucker," I say. "I still want to get a bath and wash my hair tonight."

Tucker looks at me and then at the back of the man in the suit who is near the door, then he looks back at me, his eyebrow raised. "Lowering your standards a bit, aren't you?"

"That doesn't deserve an answer, Tucker."

I turn and walk out.

The landlady has told me I can go to the town hall tomorrow to make my phone call. There is only one telephone in town and it works between ten and twelve o'clock, she says. As I lie under the magenta blanket, wondering if Richie is missing me and picturing him asleep in his bed, little fingers still pinching the faded silk binding of his old baby blanket, I hear Tucker and Jack coming up the stairs. One of them trips and falls against the wall.

"Shit."

"Shhh."

The door opens and closes and I hear footsteps going down the hall and then another door opens and closes. Tucker sits down heavily on the bed. I pull my feet back just in time. Shoes fall to the floor one by one. Tucker mutters under his breath as he struggles to pull off his trousers and shirt. When he climbs into bed he pulls me to him. His arms and face are cold and there is the smell of stale beer and tequila on his breath. I turn my head and pull back. He pulls me to him again and thrusts his hips against me. I can feel it poking my thigh. He thrusts at me again and his shiny bald head hits me on the cheek bringing a stinging pain and tears to my eyes.

"Quit it, Tucker. I'm not in the mood."

"What's the matter? Your little Mexican bandito wear you out?"

"I mean it, Tucker. You're drunk. I'm tired. It's been a long day. Let's get some sleep."

"I mean it, Tucker," he mimics.

The foul smell of his breath nauseates me and I pull away from him again.

"Come here, dammit. I didn't bring you along to tell me you're not in the mood. I'm in the mood and that'll have to be enough." He grabs my arms and rolls on top of me.

I slip off the bed and search along the floor for my nightgown. I pull it on and tie the straps where they're torn. I roll a snoring Tucker over and wrap myself in the magenta blanket. Toward dawn I fall asleep.

*   *   *

Tucker is ignoring me this morning as he re-packs the small suitcase he brought from the car yesterday. After a while he leaves the room. When I come downstairs he's sitting at the table with Jack. Neither of them looks very happy. I think they may have been arguing. There's a hammered silver coffeepot and several earthenware mugs on a small table near a door I think leads to the kitchen. Next to the coffeepot are a tray of rolls and a pot of butter. I pour a cup of coffee and go over and sit down.

"Where's your bag?" says Tucker. "Aren't you packed yet? We want to leave here right after we pay the bill."

"I'm not going," I say.

"What do you mean, you're not going?"

"I mean I'm not going with you. I'm staying here."

"You can't stay in this God forsaken place," says Jack.

"Of course she's not staying here," says Tucker. "Now get your things together, Virginia, and stop playing games."

"I'm not playing games with you, Tucker." I light a cigarette, hoping they don't notice my hands are shaking.

"How are you going to get back to Phoenix then? We're not coming back here for you."

"I don't know. I'll find something. A bus maybe." I have no idea, but surely there must be busses that go through this town to somewhere I can get transportation.

"You're crazy. I mean it now. Are you coming with us or not?"

"I'm not."

"Suit yourself then." He stands up, pushes the chair back and walks out of the room.

"Virginia, why are you doing this?" Jack asks. "I know Tucker can be a total prick when he wants to, but we can all get separate rooms after this if you want. You don't have to stay here. Your Spanish is no better than mine is, and it won't be easy getting back to Phoenix."

I tell him I've thought about it and I won't go on with them. He doesn't press me any further, but asks if I have enough money to get home. I tell him yes.

"Here's some extra, just in case." He hands me some folded bills and turns to go.

I want to say wait, I've changed my mind. But I don't. I go back up to the room and wait for them to leave.

"Virginia, I can't hear you. What did you say?" My mother's voice is faint and tinny.

"I said how is Richie?" I shout to be heard over the pops and crackles.

"When will you be home?"

"Soon. Maybe next week. How is Richie?" I hear more wheezes. The lady behind the desk looks up at me, then down again at the ledger opened in front of her.

"What? What did you say? Virginia, I can't hear you. You need to come home. Richie misses you, and he's started . . ." The line goes dead.

"The line went dead," I tell the woman.

"I'm sorry, Señora. Let me try again." After forty minutes without success, the woman tells me the switchboard is closed for the day. Frustrated, I walk up the road to the cantina.

"There is a bus to Leone on Wednesday, Señora, but it is not so nice. Maybe you can hire Mr. Lopez to drive you in his auto." I'm surprised to find the waitress is so helpful. Her name is Otilia, and she serves me fresh melon and rolls.

"Who is Mr. Lopez?"

"He was here last night sitting at that table over there with Pedro Gutierrez."

"I remember the two men. Which one is Mr. Lopez?" If he's the thin pock-faced man I'll take the bus.

As though she can read my mind she says, "Mr. Lopez is the mayor of San Ignacio, Senora. He always wears a fine suit."

"And the other man?"

"He's Mr. Lopez' brother-in-law. They always argue, those two." Otilia tells me that Mr. Lopez and his sister inherited property from their parents. It is a very small holding, she says. "The brother-in-law, he is a good man, I think, but it is well known he has little skill as a farmer. Mr. Lopez, he worries about his sister."

She tells me Mr. Lopez comes to the cantina every day at two o'clock, and if I want to speak to him I should return at that time.

I finish the melon and decide to spend the time until two exploring. I awakened this morning to the clamoring of bells, and when I looked from the window I could see the dome of the church. I'm curious to see inside. As I climb the hill there are some shops, the doors opened and inviting, but I pass them by. I must watch where I step on the uneven stones, as there is evidence of the dogs that run free, darting here and there, nosing around wherever there is food. I look inside an opened gate set into a high wall and see a courtyard and a house with a long, covered patio. Bright red bougainvillea climb up the posts. I hear water tinkling somewhere.

When I reach the church, I'm out of breath and sweating. The church stands squarely at the top of the hill, the rough stone roads of San Ignacio leading out from it like spokes. Across from the church there is a plaza surrounded by ancient oak trees. The sounds of birds fill the air, but I don't see them. Then, as though one of the trees explodes, hundreds of birds fly up, only to disappear again into the branches of another tree. Their noise doesn't diminish. In the center of the plaza is a large fountain, and water cascades into a rough stone bowl surrounding its base. In my mind young courting couples stroll along the walkways on Sunday afternoons under the watchful eyes of duennas who sit on benches in the shade of the oak trees, gossiping. Do they still do this, I wonder?

The church has two bell towers, a rounded dome and whitewashed adobe walls, and I guess it's more like a cathedral than a church. I peer through the wide opened carved wooden doors. After the bright sunlight, it's hard to make out anything except for splashes of colored light that fall from the stained glass windows onto the stone floor and the rows of wooden benches. As my eyes begin to adjust, I see a crucifix hanging on the wall at the front of the church above a tall altar. The thin body and face of Christ looks sad and tormented, and I wonder how this figure brings comfort to so many. In several niches along the walls, there are carved figures painted in vivid blues, yellows, reds and gold, as though drenched in the colors from the glass in the windows. I recognize one of the figures as Mary and another as Jesus, his arms outstretched, but I have no idea which saints the rest of the figures represent. I see no one inside the church, but still I sense a presence. Perhaps it's all the statues. Or perhaps it's the ghosts of the hundreds of petitioners who have knelt before Mary's statue, seeking her intervention.

The interior is cool. I sit down on one of the worn benches and let the quiet wash over me. It is so very quiet. And peaceful. I wonder why I'm not frightened of being on my own in a foreign country. I told Jack I had enough money to get home. In truth, it will be close. I wonder what I'll do for money when I do get home. Without Tucker to pay the bills. And I think about Richie. What was my mother trying to tell me? I can't try calling again until tomorrow, and by ten o'clock I'm hoping I'll be on my way to Leone. I remember when Richie was born. I can almost smell his sweet, milky breath and feel the weight of him wrapped up and tucked in the corner of my arm. I'd planned to be a good mother. When did I stop trying? Was it after the divorce? Before? When my mother came to live with me, I guess it was just easier to let her take over. Little by little I turned the raising of my son over to her while I took up with people like Tucker.

A woman enters the church. As I pick up my things and prepare to leave, I watch her as she bends her knee, genuflects and crosses to the statue of Mary. The sound of a coin as it falls into the collection box echoes across the space that separates us.

When I step out of the church's shadow, I am again momentarily blinded and put my hand up to shield my eyes. The sun is white-hot and the heat nearly takes my breath away. There is no one else in sight except two small boys. They run up to me. One elbows the other who says, "You Norte Americano?" I say yes and they both laugh and run off.

I look at my watch. There is just time to reach the cantina and Mr. Lopez.

Critique of Revision

Toni,

You've done some very good work in this revision. First, the elimination of Kay has given us much more focus on Virginia, Tucker, and Jack. Kay may have her own story in the future. Sometimes we have peripheral characters in a story who have stories of their own and it will be up to us to write them.

I have some small concerns throughout the story such as more embodiment of dialogue—see page two, for example—but most of these concerns are relatively minor. As you focused on the elimination of Kay and a new ending in this draft, there are still some concerns that I mentioned in my last critique—moving the cantina into the hotel, for example—that you may want to consider addressing in your subsequent drafts.

What I would like to focus on here is Virginia's character and the ending.

You have given Virginia a clearer sense of character here by mentioning the divorce and how she has given up being a mother. I think you will have to go a couple of steps more to really draw her out, however. I wonder why she got divorced. Divorces were certainly rarer then, so I wonder what happened. That might bring some bearing on her present circumstances. Still, you have done a better job with her in this draft.

The ending is much better in this draft, but I don't think it is quite there. I think you are right in leaving out the market scene—that was a distraction. I don't know what we gain by having her exit the church to be addressed by a couple of boys, however. (I suppose it is possible that having one boy address her could remind her of her own son and her own maternal obligation, but that is not evident in this draft.) The boy asking if she is North American does not carry any weight. I think the weight we are looking for in the ending will be found back in the church. The title of the story is "Benedictions" after all. As you know, a benediction is a prayer for protection. What is it she needs protection *from*? Herself, it seems. But why?

Your last two sentences read: *I look at my watch. There is just time to reach the cantina and Mr. Lopez.* I am curious about your choice of having her appear to be almost late. I understand why you have made the decision—that time is running out for her, for all of us, and we better get on the straight and narrow and make some good decisions. But in the story, it doesn't work because she has no idea how long Mr. Lopez will stay at the cantina. He arrives at 2 P.M. He could stay until three. Or four. And the reader does not know what time it is when she looks at her watch.

I think a preferable ending would be inside the church, where you could illustrate the same thematic concern by having Virginia reflecting in the quiet solitude only to be interrupted by a woman who comes in and kneels beneath the crucifix—make it the crucifix—and begins to pray. That may be enough. The reader will see Virginia watching this woman pray for protection, and maybe the reader will wonder why Virginia doesn't pray as well. She sure does need the help.

O.K. Enough. You have greatly improved the story in this draft. I think you are just a few drafts away from finishing this. Then you might go find Kay and write a story about her.

—*Tim*

WORKSHOPPING A STORY IN THE THIRD PERSON

As you read the first draft of Jim Manuel's story "Jacob Boscoe," consider the following:

1. The setting: Do you feel as if you are there? Why or why not? Where do you think the setting is most clearly drawn? How does he achieve that? To what senses does he appeal? Where is the setting undeveloped?
2. The characters: How well do you come to know them? Which do you feel you know best? Whose story is it? What do the characters want?
3. The plot: What is at stake for whom?
4. The dialogue: Is it a close approximation of how these people would speak? Is it sufficiently embodied?
5. The point of view: How would the story be different in another point of view? What is the narrative distance? How does that affect the story?
6. Voice: What is the narrator's voice? Is it affected by the time in which the story takes place?

Books must be read as deliberately and reservedly as they were written.

Henry David Thoreau

Jacob Boscoe

by Jim Manuel

Jacob Boscoe stood at the kitchen sink watching a chick-a-dee in the azalea bush outside the window. The bird had carried a black sunflower seed from the feeder, and now had pinned it against a limb by wrapping his toes around it. He was opening the seed by hammering the wide end of the seed, the flower end, with his beak. Jacob was suddenly aware that his eyes had been open much too wide, too long, and he had the curious feeling his brain was flowing out his eyes. A shimmering heat rose in his head. For a moment he thought he glimpsed the heat that he felt rising in his head in front of his eyes. He shut his eyes and bent over, making a puffing noise. He clapped his right hand over his eyes with such force he caused a sharp pain in the bridge of his nose. He continued to make puffing sounds. He opened the refrigerator door. There was nothing there but three kinds of diet pop. His wife, Elizabeth, had removed even the box of baking soda she usually kept in the refrigerator for a deodorizer five days ago.

He straightened himself and nearly balanced. He spread his feet and leaned against the refrigerator trying to pull open a can of diet pop. His head felt like someone was randomly filling it with helium and suddenly releasing the gas. As the gas pressurized his head, his neck elongated like a piece of bubble gum pulled out of a clown's mouth, and his head floated up. When it released he felt like his neck was shortened as if by the release of a powerful elastic band, and his chin did in fact land hard enough on his chest that he bit his tongue. He managed to hold himself with one hand against the refrigerator, and tilt his head back far enough to swallow a few drops of the pop. He felt a progressing nausea rising from his stomach, and the room began to circle, tilting the floor at sudden, uneven angles.

At the kitchen sink he vomited. There was almost nothing to the vomit, but his whole body wretched, and his stomach flowed in various directions. He wobbled out the door of the house where he had lived for the last few days—Jacob and his wife Elizabeth had just moved to Clarion. He had every intention of robbing the seed out of the bird feeder, but his strength failed and he was forced to sit down on a brick planter that went along the outside edge of the back sidewalk. He sat with his stomach hanging down between his knees. His eyes watered. In a moment of absolute lucidity, in a moment where his mind could have followed the most complex accounting procedure, he hoped he would not fall into an uncontrollable fit of weeping.

* * *

Jacob had been weeping, out of control for half an hour. And even though his mind was occupied with an event very much like a violent rain storm, a storm that seemed to be falling through his head rather than originating there, a bit of his faculties remained intact.

Jacob realized his wife Elizabeth was approaching when he smelled cheeseburger on her breath and clothing. The smell of cheeseburger was followed in rapid succession by the smells of French fries, a strawberry milkshake, and a Butterfinger candy bar. It took him a moment to sort out the candy bar. Elizabeth must have stopped at a 7-Eleven on her way home from Burgertown and bought the candy bar. Although Jacob was weeping so violently he did not want food, he made a mental note to see if Elizabeth might have left the candy wrapper in her car.

She led Jacob into the bedroom and helped him sit down on the edge of the bed. When she knelt down on the floor to remove the shoes and socks she had put on for him that morning, Jacob caught a smell of the French fries again.

He remembered how he liked to eat French fries. First sorting out five or six of the nicest, longest, most symmetrical fries, he liked the ones with some extra brown best, he put them into his mouth one after another, all the while chewing. Then he'd use the tongue to roll them into the back of his mouth and pack them there. The process was repeated four or five times depending on the size of the fries—any little bits and pieces were included at the end.

When the mouth is carefully packed, one swallows, extending the esophagus and widening it. The pleasure swallowing this carefully arranged bite was almost more than he could stand. Elizabeth asked was he choking when she saw tears appear in his eyes on these occasions, and he may have in fact been choking, but the tears were tears of joy, tears of pure pleasure. On occasion Jacob ate as many as six large orders of fries, carefully arranging the bites to stretch and elongate the esophagus.

"Come on Jakie, let's get your shirt and shorts off." His wife's voice focused his attention. He opened his shorts and undid his suspenders, all the while sobbing and puffing in such a way that whistles rose from his throat.

Elizabeth, with Jacob's help, succeeded in getting him undressed and he lay on the bedding sobbing as a powerful fatigue closed his mind. Waves of self-pity passed through him.

"There, there, Jakie." She brought a cool wash cloth from the bathroom across the hall and bathed his face. An observer might have been surprised by the deep concern and compassion in her voice. They might have been surprised by the fact that she was a better than average looking woman, the almost glistening brightness of her brown eyes, the striking beauty of her ash blonde hair which she kept cut in a bob.

Elizabeth's reassurances, the cool cloth on his face, the smell of

French fries that lingered on her breath mixed with the fragment of a dream of six girls dancing to a sprightly show tune, carrying a hero sandwich across their shoulders, danced in his mind. He knew he was dreaming when he realized that he couldn't smell the sandwich. When the girls did a three step forward, one hop backwards routine, shaking their asses at him and exposing their bikini underwear, he was overcome with sadness.

Jacob went to sleep around ten P.M. that night. He was asleep about half an hour when Elizabeth returned to his bedroom and put one of the nasal strips athletes use on his nose. Jacob snored so loudly that he awakened himself in the night, and particularly when he wasn't eating, it was very difficult for him to go back to sleep. Also, he thought the extra air he got helped him sleep.

When he awakened around ten the next morning he got up. He was wandering around the house looking for Elizabeth before he thought of food. He remembered the dancing girls with their huge hero sandwich and their very cute behinds.

When Jacob entered the kitchen where Elizabeth was reading *The Clarion Herald,* she got up and left without saying a word. In a few moments she returned with Jacob's shoes and some clean gym socks. Jacob sat down where Elizabeth had been seated and extended his feet, one at a time, and she put on his shoes and socks.

"Thank you, Elizabeth, darling."

She handed him the morning paper and picked up the video camera. She moved close to the paper and photographed the front page to establish the day with Jacob holding the paper. Then she had Jacob stand against a profile of himself the day he had gone to the doctor and got the examination and the official weight. When she had him carefully aligned, she photographed Jacob again.

"There is clear progress visible," Elizabeth said.

"Yes. I'd say I've lost twenty pound since we started." He lifted his stomach as much as he could—he could not reach the underside of it to lift from the bottom up—and let it drop. "Yes. I think I may have lost a little more than twenty pounds."

Elizabeth ran the tape for a good while from several angles. Even more than Jacob, she was conscious of the need to create believability. They had both believed in the herbal tea they sold, but they both lived in a kind of intellectual, obsessive dread of being sued for false advertising, or making false claims.

Going to the doctor was Jacob's first step in a new round of weight loss. This time he had selected a Doctor Rawlingson because an acquaintance had told him Rawlingson had treated his venereal disease and hadn't shown any sign of moralizing.

When he first saw Jacob it was clear he had to restrain himself from laughing. Jacob thought about walking out, but he had already expended too much energy making the appointment and getting himself there to quit. Jacob explained that he needed to lose some weight, and the doctor composed himself. He checked Jacob's heart and blood pressure. Neither was too bad considering Jacob's condition. He sent Jacob to a lab area where a technician collected a urine sample and drew blood.

Then came the moment Jacob had been waiting for. The doctor and his nurse both accompanied Jacob to the scale down the hall. He was acutely aware that one person was plenty to weigh him, and he was very aware that he was the object of spectator interest among technicians and patients waiting in the lab area. When they weighed him he weighed four hundred forty-two pounds. Neither remarked about breaking the scale. Jacob extended his neck over the nurse's shoulder to see for sure she had written down his correct weight. There it was in large numbers followed by an exclamation point. 442!

Having seen his weight recorded, Jacob liked to think of it as an official weigh-in, he assumed a humble posture as he listened to the doctor's advice. The fellow, Jacob would have to ask Elizabeth what his name was before returning for his next visit, kept it short. Eat less and I'll prescribe some pills that will help you curb your appetite. He also asked Jacob if he wanted to explore surgical options, but Jacob did not for the time being.

Jacob was pleased that the doctor didn't prescribe walking. In an earlier incident Jacob had taken a gung-ho doctor's advice, a doctor who fully believed he was going to rescue Jacob from obesity and put him on the straight and narrow path of healthful living, and gone for a walk. He made it less than two blocks from the house he was renting before the pain in his feet became so excruciating he was forced to sit down on the concrete street curb. He had sat there nearly an hour being called "fatty," "fat man," "fat boy," "lard," "lardo," and "tub-of-guts"—this last by a very attractive little blonde girl of eleven or twelve years—when Elizabeth found him. When Elizabeth helped him to his feet he experienced horrible pain in his feet and ass, as well as numbness in both areas.

Elizabeth wasn't as familiar as she became later, and she tried to help Jacob walk back to the house until Jacob said, "Elizabeth, would you mind going to get the car?" He sat back down on the concrete curb again, and sweated in the afternoon sun until Elizabeth arrived with the car and returned him to their air conditioned, rented house.

It had been seven days since Jacob visited the doctor and began his fast. He drank a little water from time to time, and in the course of the day he sometimes managed to get down a diet soda. He was now at the stage where putting anything in his mouth nauseated him. He found chewing on a toothpick to be a useful distraction, but he had to be very careful because the saliva produced by chewing was capable of nauseating him and bringing on fits of vomiting that were difficult on occasion to stop.

In this period he slept as much as he could, and for two hours every afternoon he packaged the herbal tea that he sold to make his living. He had bought six hundred pounds of the tea already packaged in tea bags.

Jacob liked to sell the stuff in quantities that would last a month, so he packaged the tea thirty bags per box. The boxes he used were shiny, red with the name "Boscoe's Herbal Tea" printed on the box in large yellow letters. He had ordered a run of ten thousand boxes to get a lower price on the printing, but it had been a mistake because it was just too much work to move. At any rate, Jacob packed his herbal tea in boxes of thirty tea bags for two hours, from one to three most afternoons. This kept him occupied and insured that he would be ready when he had lost enough weight to create another surge of business.

By the time he got in his two hours of packing tea, he was ready for a nap. It was during this period that sleep was a blessing.

Jacob arrived at the offices of *The Clarion Herald* ten minutes before his eleven o'clock appointment to see Mitchell Brewster, a reporter who covered the local scene. Jacob had talked to Brewster on the phone, and told him he had a human-interest story about a man who had lost 142 pounds in the last three months.

Brewster came to the front desk and Jacob introduced himself. Then turning to present himself in profile he said, "Would you believe I've lost 142 pounds in the last three months?" He paused allowing Brewster to look him over. "Well, it's true, and I can prove it." He produced a sheaf of eight-by-six inch colored pictures that Elizabeth had taken along the way. He went through the photos which he and Elizabeth had carefully arranged in chronological order. He had weighed once a week during his crash, and the weights were printed on the photographs for the week in a medium pointed, purple, marking pen.

Brewster, who was probably forty-five pounds overweight with a wide protruding stomach and an ample ass, took an immediate interest in Jacob's story. Jacob guessed the interest was as much private as professional.

"How on earth did you manage to lose 142 pounds?" He was shuffling through the stack of photographs, arranging them in chronological order, turning them at angles to the light.

"I want to show these to a colleague," he said. He went to the rear of the office without waiting for Jacob to recount the story of his weight loss. Jacob had been through this before, and he understood that things were going well. Brewster returned to the front without the photographs and invited Jacob to accompany him to an open office area in the rear. There he introduced Jacob to Derek Jones, a man with a stomach as large as Brewster's and an ass to match.

"Mr. Boscoe," Jacob knew he was making progress when they started calling him mister, "has lost one hundred forty-two pounds," Brewster told Jones who was sitting at his desk shuffling through the photographs, stopping to stare at Jacob from time to time. His bottom jaw opened, leaving his lower teeth and tongue exposed. A line of perspiration was visible on his upper lip, and when Jacob looked closely, he could see tiny, flat puddles of perspiration on the man's cheek and neck.

"Do you have any other proof than these photographs?" asked Jones.

"I lost the weight under doctor's supervision. You probably know him, Dr. Rawlingson; he practices at the clinic here in Clarion." Jacob stopped talking and drew up a chair without being invited. He experienced a lightness of head and wobbliness of legs that didn't leave him much choice.

Both Brewster and Jones were apologetic for not offering Jacob a seat, but as far as Jacob could tell, both had been too distracted by the photographs to notice his condition.

"Did Dr. Rawlingson give you some diet pills or something?" Jones inquired.

"No. He offered to help me in that way, but all I needed from him was to monitor my health, you know my heart, my blood pressure, as I went along." Jacob paused trying to decide if this was the right moment to mention Boscoe's Herbal Tea.

"You didn't lose that much weight without help of some kind, did you?"

"I'm happy to say I had help. I've discovered a product, I'm thinking of calling it Boscoe's Herbal Tea, that makes it easy to lose weight." He stood up and whirled around on one foot, raising his other foot to a new level behind him. "I'm living proof that it works, and that it works better than any other product on earth."

Here Jacob laid it on thicker than he normally would have. The truth was the unrelenting fast Jacob had undertaken was so all consuming that he had trouble keeping water down. When he had actually tried to use the herbal tea in a previous round of weight loss, he had felt a vast shimmering that moved from its origin in his head through his entire body, and he had fallen into violent fits of uncontrolled vomiting that required a trip to the emergency room.

His real belief in the tea came from his observation that the tea was extremely helpful in keeping weight off after he quit the fast. He had also received some positive feedback from his customers, but the fact that he did not actually use the tea in the fast section of his weight loss still bothered him, although it bothered him less than it had in the past, less than it bothered Elizabeth.

"If you men know someone who might benefit from my product, I'd be glad to provide them with a complimentary one month supply," Jacob offered.

Jones thought his wife might like to try it. Brewster said he needed to lose a few pounds himself and would be glad to give Boscoe's product a try.

Jacob wrote down their addresses and told them he would deliver the tea. "I'm thinking of buying some advertising for my product in *The Clarion Herald*. If you men are thinking of printing something about my weight loss it would be very nice if my ad could appear the first time the story appears." Jacob was promptly escorted to another desk behind another screen where he bought eight weeks of advertising for his tea.

When Elizabeth returned home that afternoon, Jacob had just finished his packing session for the day. "How did the interview with *The Herald* go, Jacob?" Elizabeth asked.

"Fine. Fine. It couldn't have been better. I'm delivering samples to the two reporters who interviewed me this evening. They were impressed. I think this is going to be our best effort yet," Jacob replied.

"I'm really glad, Jacob. I know how much you believe in the product, and how good it makes you feel when you hear people are getting results with our product."

"Yes, it does. It really does. In the mail this morning there was a letter from Mrs. Alvarez, you remember, the little grandmother I met just when we were leaving Canyon City? She has lost twenty-five pounds and kept it off for three months. She sent a check for thirty dollars for another month's supply." Jacob was beaming as he sat straddling a kitchen chair, his arms resting on the back, his chin resting atop his arms.

"How much did we get in today, Jacob?" Her tone became serious.

"It was actually pretty bad for a Tuesday," Jacob responded. "Besides Mrs. Alvarez, there was an inquiry from someone who heard about us from a friend."

"Thirty dollars, then," Elizabeth inquired, looking hard into Jacob's face.

"Yes. Thirty dollars. The results from Canyon City are definitely running down. There just doesn't seem to be a better way to get folk's attention than to lose 140 pounds. The excitement from the articles in the paper and the ads last about . . ."

"Yes, Jacob, I know. I don't know why you have to turn your life into a living freak show just to earn a living." Her tone was hard, a tone he had not heard her use since she argued with the doctors at Sunrise hospital when their son Jacob was dying seven years ago. "I'm not going to stand around and watch you starve yourself anymore. You were a decent accountant when Jakie died. I don't see why we need to travel around with you making a public spectacle of yourself."

This was new to Jacob. He had fasted two full months to lose the 142 pounds that he had just reported losing at *The Clarion Herald*. And the fast by its very nature enclosed Jacob and he wondered if he had become unaware of Elizabeth. For a moment Jacob reacted as if he were stunned in a fog.

"You don't mean you want to quit right now. I just went through a two-month fast."

"When you gained the weight that year after Jakie died, and you lost the weight using the tea that was fine. But to quit your job, a job that had provided us a good living for eight years, to promote the tea, was absurd.

"I saw it wouldn't work and after the first four weeks it didn't. As soon as people get used to the fact that you lost the weight, they quit buying the tea."

"But, Elizabeth, I found a way to spark their interest, to keep them buying. Don't forget Elizabeth, I've given a lot of people hope. Fat people have a right to hope too, Elizabeth, and I led them to hope."

"I wish that weren't true," Elizabeth responded. "I wish it weren't true."

"What do you mean?" Jacob seemed confused.

"Anyone I know, even the Jacob Boscoe who was a good accountant, would take you for a snake oil salesman if they knew you didn't use the tea in your fasts."

"I believe in the tea. Even though I don't use it in my fasts, I believe in the tea. My fasting is just a way of giving people hope, of leading them to where they can use the tea."

"If the tea worked, we would get reorders Jacob, lots and lots of reorders. The truth is we were a pair of vagabonds, going from town to town, scamming people, conning people by one of the most desperate stratagems in history."

"I do what I do to bring fat people hope. When I gained the weight after Jakie died, I felt awful. When I lost the weight, I felt really good, and as soon as I started selling the tea I saw that I was bringing people hope and the same good feeling I had experienced."

A week passed and the article about Jacob losing 142 pounds appeared in *The Clarion Herald* along with his ad for "Boscoe's Herbal Tea." Orders came in. He had two phone lines into his house and they were both often busy with customers anxious to find out about the salutary effects of Boscoe's Herbal Tea. Jacob talked to numerous desperate people, and the money flowed.

Elizabeth was her usual efficient self in processing the incoming money and double-checking with Jacob to make sure every order got delivered. They sold almost five thousand dollars worth of the tea in the first three weeks after the article and the ads came out. Jacob felt wonderful about his life as he delivered the tea personally to each of the people ordering. He gave encouragement to everyone he talked to, and he felt very good about himself as he told people his story. In short, Clarion was even more of a success than Falls City.

Jacob was now drinking the herbal tea twice a day, and he was able to lose a few pounds doing it. But the money, Jacob's glowing account of his talks with discouraged people, didn't rekindle Elizabeth's enthusiasm for the project. She did the accounting, made deposits, but it would have been clear to anyone besides Jacob that she was discontent and becoming more so every day.

The fourth ad came out on Thursday, and there was a good response again Friday, but by Sunday and Monday sales had trailed off to one hundred dollars a day. They were at home Monday afternoon, hanging around because Jacob didn't want to miss any calls. Elizabeth came into the den where Jacob was waiting at the phone, looking for her purse.

"I'm going over to Shari's. They still have the fresh strawberries on the menu there, and I'm going to have a strawberry waffle."

"What am I going to do if we get a flurry of orders?" He sounded hurt.

"We haven't had a flurry of orders in a week. This promotion is over. I know it, and you soon will." Her voice was cold and sharp edged, a tone with which Jacob was unfamiliar.

"I certainly don't think this promotion is over. There are still a lot of good people right here in Clarion who need our help. God. If there was just another way to get the word out."

"Cut the crap, Jacob. You know as well as I do that the tea is nothing but a laxative. You like the way you feel when you tell people how the tea works for you, but the truth is both you and the tea are a fraud."

"What do you mean a fraud? You know I lost the weight the first time using the tea."

"I don't know how you lost the weight the first time, and I frankly don't care." Elizabeth was angry now, and Jacob sat with his jaw slack, his mouth and eyes open. "I do know this is the fourth fast you have gone through, and you don't use the tea in the fasts. You go prancing up to people's door like the pied piper of fat people, selling them a box of tea for thirty dollars that cost you eighty-seven cents including the cost of the package."

"You tell them how the tea works for you which is a serious lie in the beginning. But to go around selling hope because you can make money doing it and because you feel like some hero of the people doing it, is an awful fraud."

"Elizabeth, you know I just want to help people. You should hear. . . ."

"No, Jacob. I've already heard much, much too much. You go around acting like the patron saint of fat people, but hell, you're still at least eighty pounds overweight. You are a one-man medicine and snake oil show, and I regret to say, I've been your assistant."

"Elizabeth, sweetie." He came to her and put his arms around her. "You're just upset because the sales have dropped off a little. We'll be rolling in the money again tomorrow."

She ducked and pushed out of his arms. "If we get a bunch of orders tomorrow you are going to be the saddest man in Clarion."

He started to inquire why, but Elizabeth cut him off.

"Because you are not selling any more tea, period. You can tell people whatever you want, but if you sell another box of that damn stuff . . ."

"Elizabeth. Shut the fuck up. How are we going to live?" It was hard to tell if he were afraid or angry.

"Listen, fat boy!" Jacob was shocked, and he dropped back onto the green couch where he had been sitting like a man struck with a small caliber bullet. "If you ever talk to me like that again, this fucking freak show of a marriage is over. If I catch you selling so much as one box of the tea, if I hear of you giving anyone false hopes about losing weight using Boscoe's Herbal Tea, I'm going straight to the paper and tell them that I know for a fact that when you are fasting you puke if you swallow too much saliva, that a half cup of the tea would leave you in one of those uncontrolled fits of vomiting."

"Elizabeth, we've taken in over $7,000 on this promotion alone. Think about that for a moment. And you know we don't have to pay any taxes on the cash we take in." He said this with a leer, with an insinuating tone that was rare for him.

"I'm going to town and eat a strawberry waffle. You need to think very carefully about what I've said. Unplug the phone, whatever it takes, but don't be selling another single box of that tea."

She picked up the purse she had come into the den looking for and left.

Two weeks passed during which Jacob had carefully obeyed Elizabeth's instruction on the tea. He told callers he was out of the product, an exotic product of Guatemala, Honduras, or Afghanistan, depending on the day and his mood. The few mail orders that came in, he made a scene of putting the checks in an envelope with a note explaining he regrettably was out of the product and giving the envelopes to Elizabeth to mail. He was sitting on the couch in the den when Elizabeth announced she was going up town to eat and to do some shopping. He had lost some of his energy and good cheer, but he managed a cheerful send off.

When Elizabeth returned, she heard talking in the kitchen. When she entered the kitchen, Jacob introduced her to Mitchell Brewster as "The reporter from *The Clarion* who was so interested in my story."

Elizabeth didn't respond to the introduction. There was huge amount of cash on the table, stacked in two stacks. "What's going on here?"

"Just relax Elizabeth. Just relax and sit down." Mitchell pushed a chair back for her reaching under the table with his foot.

"What's going on here?" Elizabeth looked hard at Jacob, who would have normally wilted under her glare, but did not today.

"You haven't changed your mind about the tea have you, Elizabeth. It's . . ."

"What the hell is going on here?"

"I've told Mitchell all about the tea, about how much money we've made." He nodded toward Mitchell. "Since you've lost interest I've invited Mitch to become my partner. He's greatly interested. He's lost twenty pounds using the tea, and he sees the same great future for it that I see."

Elizabeth sat thinking. "You are mean you are leaving me?" She seemed incredulous.

"You haven't left me many choices Elizabeth. You know how important helping all those people have hope is to me. At least I thought you knew." He was more than a little melodramatic as he made this speech, but he kept a very close eye on Mitchell.

"Mitchell understands my needs. He understands my motivation."

"Where did all this money come from? There's a lot more money here than you or I ever made."

"First, I drew the money out of our account today. That was $5,556." He looked at a note by his right wrist. "Then I've managed to squirrel a little cash away from cash sales; $24,280." He again looked at the note by his right wrist. "That means your half is $15,000." He pushed one of the stacks of money in Elizabeth's direction.

Her hands shook, but she did not reach out and touch the money or try to pull it toward her.

"You son-of-a-bitch. We've actually done without stuff we needed so you could squirrel money away—over twenty thousand. God damn you Jacob, I want it all, or I'm going. . . ." Her fury seemed to consume her voice.

"Elizabeth, Mitch and I are planning on bringing hope to the good people of Anchorage, Alaska. We'll need at least six thousand to get up there and get established."

"Yes. We'll need something. I am completely enthusiastic for the project," he reached over and touched Jacob's hand, "but I don't have much money to help," said Mitch.

Elizabeth raked the money into one stack, then counted out $3,000. "You'll have to bring hope to the good people of Anchorage on three thousand."

"OK, Elizabeth, have it your way." Jacob stood and Mitch followed his lead. "We're both planning to gain weight, then go on a tea diet. We think we may try to lose 300 pounds between us. Just think how it will look in the local paper, 'Roommates lose 300 pounds.' That will bring hope to every fat man, woman, and child in Anchorage and the rest of the state, too. I can just see it now." He was beaming, his face was that of a happy, fat angel.

"I'm staying with Mitch until we can get organized for our move to Alaska; I don't want to keep on disappointing the good folks of Clarion. I'll come by tomorrow to discuss dividing up the rest of the stuff."

"The stuff is mine and that is that. You and your friend Mitch better be getting out of town quick or I'm going to *The Clarion* to expose you." She seemed detached, as if she was an attorney representing someone to whom all this was happening.

"OK. You know that isn't right, Elizabeth, but I don't want trouble. I've moved my personal stuff to Mitchell's place already, and I'm taking the tea and the boxes. I'll get the tea and the boxes tomorrow."

When he came out of the den carrying his briefcase and a handful of envelopes, Elizabeth was standing in the front room, her arms crossed her chest. The door was still open where Mitch had left it when he left.

Jacob came close to Elizabeth as if he had something else to say, but he drew his right arm back, the arm not holding the briefcase, and left, closing the door.

As Jacob came down the stairs on the dark porch, he stumbled. He flung his arms out and upward to balance himself and in a quick movement he dropped the briefcase which sprung open when it hit the concrete walk. Had either Elizabeth or Mitchell seen how much money he rapidly stuffed back into the briefcase, they would have changed considerably their opinions of the deals they had made with Jacob Bosoce.

*   *   *

Before continuing, consider the following questions once again:

1. The setting: Do you feel as if you were there? Why or why not? Where do you think the setting is most clearly drawn? How does he achieve that? To what senses does he appeal? Where is the setting undeveloped?
2. The characters: How well do you come to know them? Which do you feel you know best? Whose story is it? What do the characters want?
3. The plot: What is at stake for whom?
4. The dialogue: Is it a close approximation of how these people would speak? Is it sufficiently embodied?
5. The point of view: How would the story be different in another point of view? What is the narrative distance? How does that affect the story?
6. Voice: What is the narrator's voice? Is it affected by the time in which the story takes place?

When you have finished, look at this same draft with marginalia, and then the critique that follows the draft.

Jacob Boscoe

by Jim Manuel

Jacob Boscoe stood at the kitchen sink watching a chick-a-dee in the azalea bush outside the window. The bird had carried a black sunflower seed from the feeder, and now had pinned it against a limb by wrapping his toes around it. He was opening the seed by hammering the wide end of the seed, the flower end, with his beak. Jacob was suddenly aware that his eyes had been open much too wide, too long, and he had the curious feeling his brain was flowing out his eyes. A shimmering heat rose in his head. For a moment he thought he glimpsed the heat that he felt rising in his head in front of his eyes. He shut his eyes and bent over, making a puffing noise. He clapped his right hand over his eyes with such force he caused a sharp pain in the bridge of his nose. He continued to make puffing sounds. He opened the refrigerator door. There was nothing there but three kinds of diet pop. His wife, Elizabeth, had removed even the box of baking soda five days before.

He straightened himself and nearly balanced. He spread his feet and leaned against the refrigerator trying to pull open a can of diet pop. His head felt like someone was randomly filling it with helium and suddenly releasing the gas. As the gas pressurized his head, his neck elongated like a piece of bubble gum pulled out of a clown's mouth, and his head floated up. When it released he felt like his neck was shortened as if by the release of a powerful elastic band, and his chin did in fact land hard enough on his chest that he bit his tongue. He managed to hold himself with one hand against the refrigerator, and tilt his head back far enough to swallow a few drops of the pop. He felt a progressing nausea rising from his stomach, and the room began to circle, tilting the floor at sudden, uneven angles.

Too many competing images.

At the kitchen sink he vomited. There was almost nothing to the vomit, but his whole body wretched, and his stomach flowed in various directions. He wobbled out the door of the house where he had lived for the last few days—Jacob and his wife Elizabeth had just moved to Clarion. He had every intention of robbing the seed out of the bird feeder, but his strength failed and he was forced to sit down on a brick planter that went along the outside edge of the back sidewalk. He sat with his stomach hanging down between his knees. His eyes watered. In a moment of absolute lucidity, in a moment where his mind could have followed the most complex accounting procedure, he hoped he would not fall into an uncontrollable fit of weeping.

Jacob had been weeping out of control for half an hour. And even though his mind was occupied with an event very much like a violent rain storm, a storm that seemed to be falling through his head rather than originating there, a bit of his faculties remained intact.

Jacob realized his wife Elizabeth was approaching when he smelled cheeseburger on her breath and clothing. The smell of cheeseburger was followed in rapid succession by the smells of French fries, a strawberry milkshake, and a Butterfinger candy bar. It took him a moment to sort out the candy bar. Elizabeth must have stopped at a 7-Eleven on her way home from Burgertown and bought the candy bar. Although Jacob was weeping so violently he did not want food, he made a mental note to see if Elizabeth might have left the candy wrapper in her car.

She led Jacob into the bedroom and helped him sit down on the edge of the bed. When she knelt down on the floor to remove the shoes and socks she had put on for him that morning, Jacob caught a smell of the French fries again.

He remembered how he liked to eat French fries. First sorting out five or six of the nicest, longest, most symmetrical fries, he liked the ones with some extra brown best, he put them into his mouth one after another, all the while chewing. Then he'd use the tongue to roll them into the back of his mouth and pack them there. The process was repeated four or five times depending on the size of the fries—any little bits and pieces were included at the end.

When the mouth is carefully packed, one swallows, extending the esophagus and widening it. The pleasure swallowing this carefully arranged bite was almost more than he could stand. Elizabeth asked was he choking when she saw tears appear in his eyes on these occasions, and he may have in fact been choking, but the tears were tears of joy, tears of pure pleasure. On occasion Jacob ate as many as six large orders of fries, carefully arranging the bites to stretch and elongate the esophagus.

"Come on Jakie, let's get your shirt and shorts off." His wife's voice focused his attention. He opened his shorts and undid his suspenders, all the while sobbing and puffing in such a way that whistles rose from his throat.

Elizabeth, with Jacob's help, succeeded in getting him undressed and he lay on the bedding sobbing as a powerful fatigue closed his mind. Waves of self-pity passed through him.

"There, there, Jakie." She brought a cool wash cloth from the bathroom across the hall and bathed his face. An observer might have been surprised by the deep concern and compassion in her voice. They might have been surprised by the fact that she was a better than average looking woman, the almost glistening brightness of her brown eyes, the striking beauty of her ash blonde hair which she kept cut in a bob.

Agr—pronoun they does not agree in number w/antecedent.

Elizabeth's reassurances, the cool cloth on his face, the smell of French fries that lingered on her breath mixed with the fragment of a dream of six girls dancing to a sprightly show tune, carrying a hero sandwich across their shoulders, danced in his mind. He knew he was dreaming when he realized that he couldn't smell the sandwich. When the girls did a three step forward, one hop backwards routine, shaking their asses at him and exposing their bikini underwear, he was overcome with sadness.

Jacob went to sleep around ten P.M. that night. He was asleep about half an hour when Elizabeth returned to his bedroom and put one of the nasal strips athletes use on his nose. Jacob snored so loudly that he awakened himself in the night, and particularly when he wasn't eating, it was very difficult for him to go back to sleep. Also, he thought the extra air he got helped him sleep.

When he awakened around ten the next morning he got up. He was wandering around the house looking for Elizabeth before he thought of food. He remembered the dancing girls with their huge hero sandwich and their very cute behinds.

When Jacob entered the kitchen where Elizabeth was reading *The Clarion Herald,* she got up and left without saying a word. In a few moments she returned with Jacob's shoes and some clean gym socks. Jacob sat down where Elizabeth had been seated and extended his feet, one at a time, and she put on his shoes and socks.

"Thank you, Elizabeth, darling."

She handed him the morning paper and picked up the video camera. She moved close to the paper and photographed the front page to establish the day with Jacob holding the paper. Then she had Jacob stand against a profile of himself the day he had gone to the doctor and got the examination and the official weight. When she had him carefully aligned, she photographed Jacob again.

"There is clear progress visible," Elizabeth said.

"Yes. I'd say I've lost twenty pounds since we started." He lifted his stomach as much as he could—he could not reach the underside of it to lift from the bottom up—and let it drop. "Yes. I think I may have lost a little more than twenty pounds."

Elizabeth ran the tape for a good while from several angles. Even more than Jacob, she was conscious of the need to create believability. They had both believed in the herbal tea they sold, but they both lived in a kind of intellectual, obsessive dread of being sued for false advertising, or making false claims.

Going to the doctor was Jacob's first step in a new round of weight loss. This time he had selected a doctor Rawlingson because an acquaintance had told him Rawlingson had treated his venereal disease and hadn't shown any sign of moralizing.

When he first saw Jacob it was clear he had to restrain himself from laughing. Jacob thought about walking out, but he had already expended too much energy making the appointment and getting himself there to quit now. Jacob explained that he needed to lose some weight, and the doctor composed himself. He checked Jacob's heart and blood pressure. Neither was too bad considering Jacob's condition. He sent Jacob to a lab area where a technician collected a urine sample and drew blood.

Then came the moment Jacob had been waiting for. The doctor and his nurse both accompanied Jacob to the scale down the hall. He was acutely aware that one person was plenty to weigh him, and he was very aware that he was the object of spectator interest among technicians and patients waiting in the lab area. When they weighed him, he weighed four hundred forty-two pounds. Neither remarked about breaking the scale. Jacob extended his neck over the nurse's shoulder to see for sure she had written down his correct weight. There it was in large numbers followed by an exclamation point. 442!

Having seen his weight recorded, Jacob liked to think of it as an official weigh-in, he assumed a humble posture as he listened to the doctor's advice. The fellow, Jacob would have to ask Elizabeth what his name was before returning for his next visit, kept it short. Eat less and I'll prescribe some pills that will help you curb your appetite. He also asked Jacob if he wanted to explore surgical options, but Jacob did not for the time being.

Jacob was pleased that the doctor didn't prescribe walking. In an earlier incident Jacob had taken a gung-ho doctor's advice, a doctor who fully believed he was going to rescue Jacob from obesity and put him on the straight and narrow path of healthful living, and gone for a walk. He made it less than two blocks from the house he was renting before the pain in his feet became so excruciating he was forced to sit down on the concrete street curb. He had sat there nearly an hour being called "fatty," "fat man," "fat boy," "lard," "lardo," and "tub-of-guts"—this last by a very attractive little blonde girl of eleven or twelve years—when Elizabeth found him. When Elizabeth helped him to his feet he experienced horrible pain in his feet and ass, as well as numbness in both areas.

Elizabeth wasn't as familiar as she became later, and she tried to help Jacob walk back to the house until Jacob said, "Elizabeth, would you mind going to get the car?" He sat back down on the concrete curb again, and sweated in the afternoon sun until Elizabeth arrived with the car and returned him to their air conditioned, rented house.

It had been seven days since Jacob visited the doctor and began his fast. He drank a little water from time to time, and in the course of the day he sometimes managed to get down a diet soda. He was now at the stage where putting anything in his mouth nauseated him. He found chewing on a toothpick to be a useful distraction, but he had to be very careful because the saliva produced by chewing was capable of nauseating him and bringing on fits of vomiting that were difficult on occasion to stop.

In this period, he slept as much as he could, and for two hours every afternoon he packaged the herbal tea that he sold to make his living. He had bought six hundred pounds of the tea already packaged in tea bags.

Use spacebreak to indicate temporal shift.

Jacob liked to sell the stuff in quantities that would last a month, so he packaged the tea thirty bags per box. The boxes he used were shiny, red with the name "Boscoe's Herbal Tea" printed on the box in large yellow letters. He had ordered a run of ten thousand boxes to get a lower price on the printing, but it had been a mistake because it was just too much work to move. At any rate, Jacob packed his herbal tea in boxes of thirty tea bags for two hours, from one to three most afternoons. This kept him occupied and insured that he would be ready when he had lost enough weight to create another surge of business.

By the time he got in his two hours of packing tea, he was ready for a nap. It was during this period that sleep was a blessing.

Jacob arrived at the offices of *The Clarion Herald* ten minutes before his eleven o'clock appointment to see Mitchell Brewster, a reporter who covered the local scene. Jacob had talked to Brewster on the phone, and told him he had a human-interest story about a man who had lost 142 pounds in the last three months.

Clarify the passing of time.

Brewster came to the front desk and Jacob introduced himself. Then turning to present himself in profile he said, "Would you believe I've lost 142 pounds in the last three months?" He paused allowing Brewster to look him over. "Well, it's true, and I can prove it." He produced a sheaf of eight-by-six inch colored pictures that Elizabeth had taken along the way. He went through the photos which he and Elizabeth had carefully arranged in chronological order. He had weighed once a week during his crash, and the weights were printed on the photographs for the week in a medium pointed, purple, marking pen.

Why such detail describing a pen? Will it be important? Probably not.

Brewster, who was probably forty-five pounds overweight with a wide protruding stomach and an ample ass, took an immediate interest in Jacob's story. Jacob guessed the interest was as much private as professional.

"How on earth did you manage to lose 142 pounds?" He was shuffling through the stack of photographs, arranging them in chronological order, turning them at angles to the light.

"I want to show these to a colleague," he said. He went to the rear of the office without waiting for Jacob to recount the story of his weight loss. Jacob had been through this before, and he understood that things were going well. Brewster returned to the front without the photographs and invited Jacob to accompany him to an open office area in the rear. There he introduced Jacob to Derek Jones, a man with a stomach as large as Brewster's and an ass to match.

"Mr. Boscoe," Jacob knew he was making progress when they started calling him mister, "has lost one hundred forty-two pounds," Brewster told Jones who was sitting at his desk shuffling through the photographs, stopping to stare at Jacob from time to time. His bottom jaw opened, leaving his lower teeth and tongue exposed. A line of perspiration was visible on his upper lip, and when Jacob looked closely, he could see tiny, flat puddles of perspiration on the man's cheek and neck.

"Do you have any other proof than these photographs?" asked Jones.

"I lost the weight under doctor's supervision. You probably know him, Dr. Rawlingson; he practices at the clinic here in Clarion." Jacob stopped talking and drew up a chair without being invited. He experienced a lightness of head and wobbliness of legs that didn't leave him much choice.

Both Brewster and Jones were apologetic for not offering Jacob a seat, but as far as Jacob could tell, both had been too distracted by the photographs to notice his condition.

"Did Dr. Rawlingson give you some diet pills or something?" Jones inquired.

"No. He offered to help me in that way, but all I needed from him was to monitor my health, you know my heart, my blood pressure, as I went along." Jacob paused trying to decide if this was the right moment to mention Boscoe's Herbal Tea.

"You didn't lose that much weight without help of some kind, did you?"

"I'm happy to say I had help. I've discovered a product, I'm thinking of calling it Boscoe's Herbal Tea, that makes it easy to lose weight." He stood up and whirled around on one foot, raising his other foot to a new level behind him. "I'm living proof that it works, and that it works better than any other product on earth."

Here Jacob laid it on thicker than he normally would have. The truth was the unrelenting fast Jacob had undertaken was so all consuming that he had trouble keeping water down. When he had actually tried to use the herbal tea in a previous round of weight loss, he had felt a vast shimmering that moved from its origin in his head through his entire body, and he had fallen into violent fits of uncontrolled vomiting that required a trip to the emergency room.

His real belief in the tea came from his observation that the tea was extremely helpful in keeping weight off after he quit the fast. He had also received some positive feed back from his customers, but the fact that he did not actually use the tea in the fast section of his weight loss still bothered him, although it bothered him less than it had in the past, less than it bothered Elizabeth.

"If you men know someone who might benefit from my product, I'd be glad to provide them with a complimentary one month supply," Jacob offered.

Jones thought his wife might like to try it. Brewster said he needed to lose a few pounds himself and would be glad to give Boscoe's product a try.

Jacob wrote down their addresses and told them he would deliver the tea. "I'm thinking of buying some advertising for my product in *The Clarion Herald*. If you men are thinking of printing something about my weight loss it would be very nice if my ad could appear the first time the story appears." Jacob was promptly escorted to

Heighten the tension throughout by indicating possible health risks such as diabetes.

Too much detail slows down the pacing.

another desk behind another screen where he bought eight weeks of advertising for his tea.

When Elizabeth returned home that afternoon, Jacob had just finished his packing session for the day. "How did the interview with *The Herald* go, Jacob?" Elizabeth asked.

"Fine. Fine. It couldn't have been better. I'm delivering samples to the two reporters who interviewed me this evening. They were impressed. I think this is going to be our best effort yet," Jacob replied.

"I'm really glad, Jacob. I know how much you believe in the product, and how good it makes you feel when you hear people are getting results with our product."

"Yes, it does. It really does. In the mail this morning there was a letter from Mrs. Alvarez, you remember, the little grandmother I met just when we were leaving Canyon City? She has lost twenty-five pounds and kept it off for three months. She sent a check for thirty dollars for another month's supply." Jacob was beaming as he sat straddling a kitchen chair, his arms resting on the back, his chin resting atop his arms.

"How much did we get in today, Jacob?" Her tone became serious.

"It was actually pretty bad for a Tuesday," Jacob responded. "Besides Mrs. Alvarez, there was an inquiry from someone who heard about us from a friend."

"Thirty dollars, then," Elizabeth inquired, looking hard into Jacob's face.

"Yes. Thirty dollars. The results from Canyon City are definitely running down. There just doesn't seem to be a better way to get folk's attention than to lose 140 pounds. The excitement from the articles in the paper and the ads last about . . ."

"Yes, Jacob, I know. I don't know why you have to turn your life into a living freak show just to earn a living." Her tone was hard, a tone he had not heard her use since she argued with the doctors at Sunrise hospital when their son Jacob

Using 'ago' takes the readers out of the story and puts them into their own time frame was dying seven years ago. "I'm not going to stand around and watch you starve yourself anymore. You were a decent accountant when Jakie died. I don't see why we need to travel around with you making a public spectacle of yourself."

This was new to Jacob. He had fasted two full months to lose the 142 pounds that he had just reported losing at *The Clarion Herald*. And the fast by its very nature enclosed Jacob and he wondered if he had become unaware of Elizabeth. For a moment Jacob reacted as if he were stunned in a fog.

"You don't mean you want to quit right now. I just went through a two-month fast."

"When you gained the weight that year after Jakie died, and you lost the weight using the tea that was fine. But to quit your job, a job that had provided us a good living for eight years, to promote the tea, was absurd.

"I saw it wouldn't work and after the first four weeks it didn't. As soon as people get used to the fact that you lost the weight, they quit buying the tea."

"But, Elizabeth, I found a way to spark their interest, to keep them buying. Don't forget Elizabeth, I've given a lot of people hope. Fat people have a right to hope too, Elizabeth, and I led them to hope."

Embody this dialogue.

"I wish that weren't true," Elizabeth responded. "I wish it weren't true."

"What do you mean?" Jacob seemed confused.

"Anyone I know, even the Jacob Boscoe who was a good accountant, would take you for a snake oil salesman if they knew you didn't use the tea in your fasts."

"I believe in the tea. Even though I don't use it in my fasts, I believe in the tea. My fasting is just a way of giving people hope, of leading them to where they can use the tea."

"If the tea worked, we would get reorders Jacob, lots and lots of reorders. The truth is we were a pair of vagabonds, going from town to

town, scamming people, conning people by one
of the most desperate stratagems in history."

"I do what I do to bring fat people hope.
When I gained the weight after Jakie died, I felt
awful. When I lost the weight, I felt really good,
and as soon as I started selling the tea I saw that I
was bringing people hope and the same good
feeling I had experienced."

A week passed and the article about Jacob
losing 142 pounds appeared in *The Clarion Times*
along with his ad for "Boscoe's Herbal Tea."
Orders came in. He had two phone lines into his
house and they were both often busy with customers anxious to find out about the salutary
effects of Boscoe's Herbal Tea. Jacob talked to
numerous desperate people, and the money
flowed.

Elizabeth was her usual efficient self in processing the incoming money and double-checking with Jacob to make sure every order got
delivered. They sold almost five thousand dollars
worth of the tea in the first three weeks after the
article and the ads came out. Jacob felt wonderful
about his life as he delivered the tea personally to
each of the people ordering. He gave encouragement to everyone he talked to, and he felt very
good about himself as he told people his story. In
short, Clarion was even more of a success than
Falls City.

Jacob was now drinking the herbal tea twice
a day, and he was able to lose a few pounds doing it. But the money, Jacob's glowing account
of his talks with discouraged people, didn't rekindle Elizabeth's enthusiasm for the project.
She did the accounting, made deposits, but it
would have been clear to anyone besides Jacob
that she was discontent and becoming more so
every day.

The fourth ad came out on Thursday, and
there was a good response again Friday, but by
Sunday and Monday sales had trailed off to one
hundred dollars a day. They were at home Monday afternoon, hanging around because Jacob
didn't want to miss any calls. Elizabeth came into

the den where Jacob was waiting at the phone, looking for her purse.

"I'm going over to Shari's. They still have the fresh strawberries on the menu there, and I'm going to have a strawberry waffle."

"What am I going to do if we get a flurry of orders?" He sounded hurt.

"We haven't had a flurry of orders in a week. This promotion is over. I know it, and you soon will." Her voice was cold and sharp edged, a tone with which Jacob was unfamiliar.

"I certainly don't think this promotion is over. There are still a lot of good people right here in Clarion who need our help. God. If there was just another way to get the word out."

"Cut the crap, Jacob. You know as well as I do that the tea is nothing but a laxative. You like the way you feel when you tell people how the tea works for you, but the truth is both you and the tea are a fraud."

"What do you mean a fraud? You know I lost the weight the first time using the tea."

"I don't know how you lost the weight the first time, and I frankly don't care." Elizabeth was angry now, and Jacob sat with his jaw slack, his mouth and eyes open. "I do know this is the fourth fast you have gone through, and you don't use the tea in the fasts. You go prancing up to people's door like the pied piper of fat people, selling them a box of tea for thirty dollars that cost you eighty-seven cents including the cost of the package."

"You tell them how the tea works for you which is a serious lie in the beginning. But to go around selling hope because you can make money doing it and because you feel like some hero of the people doing it, is an awful fraud."

"Elizabeth, you know I just want to help people. You should hear. . . ."

"No, Jacob. I've already heard much, much too much. You go around acting like the patron saint of fat people, but hell, you're still at least eighty pounds over weight. You are a one-man medicine and snake oil show, and I regret to say, I've been your assistant."

"Elizabeth, sweetie." He came to her and put his arms around her. "You're just upset because the sales have dropped off a little. We'll be rolling in the money again tomorrow."

She ducked and pushed out of his arms. "If we get a bunch of orders tomorrow you are going to be the saddest man in Clarion."

He started to inquire why, but Elizabeth cut him off.

"Because you are not selling any more tea, period. You can tell people whatever you want, but if you sell another box of that damn stuff . . ." Embody

"Elizabeth. Shut the fuck up. How are we going to live?" It was hard to tell if he were afraid or angry.

"Listen, fat boy!" Jacob was shocked, and he dropped back onto the green couch where he had been sitting like a man struck with a small caliber bullet. "If you ever talk to me like that again, this fucking freak show of a marriage is over. If I catch you selling so much as one box of the tea, if I hear of you giving anyone false hopes about losing weight using Boscoe's Herbal Tea, I'm going straight to the paper and tell them that I know for a fact that when you are fasting you puke if you swallow too much saliva, that a half cup of the tea would leave you in one of those uncontrolled fits of vomiting."

"Elizabeth, we've taken in over $7,000 on this promotion alone. Think about that for a moment. And you know we don't have to pay any taxes on the cash we take in." He said this with a leer, with an insinuating tone that was rare for him.

"I'm going to town and eat a strawberry waffle. You need to think very carefully about what I've said. Unplug the phone, whatever it takes, but don't be selling another single box of that tea."

She picked up the purse she had come into the den looking for and left.

Two weeks passed during which Jacob had carefully obeyed Elizabeth's instruction on the tea.

He told callers he was out of the product, an exotic product of Guatemala, Honduras, or Afghanistan, depending on the day and his mood. The few mail orders that came in, he made a scene of putting the checks in an envelope with a note explaining he regrettably was out of the product and giving the envelopes to Elizabeth to mail. He was sitting on the couch in the den when Elizabeth announced she was going up town to eat and to do some shopping. He had lost some of his energy and good cheer, but he managed a cheerful send off.

When Elizabeth returned, she heard talking in the kitchen. When she entered the kitchen, Jacob introduced her to Mitchell Brewster as "The reporter from *The Clarion* who was so interested in my story."

Elizabeth didn't respond to the introduction. There was huge amount of cash on the table, stacked in two stacks. "What's going on here?"

"Just relax Elizabeth. Just relax and sit down." Mitchell pushed a chair back for her reaching under the table with his foot.

"What's going on here?" Elizabeth looked hard at Jacob, who would have normally wilted under her glare, but did not today.

"You haven't changed your mind about the tea have you, Elizabeth. It's . . ."

"What the hell is going on here?"

"I've told Mitchell all about the tea, about how much money we've made." He nodded toward Mitchell. "Since you've lost interest I've invited Mitch to become my partner. He's greatly interested. He's lost twenty pounds using the tea, and he sees the same great future for it that I see."

Elizabeth sat thinking. "You are mean. You are leaving me?" She seemed incredulous.

"You haven't left me many choices Elizabeth. You know how important helping all those people have hope is to me. At least I thought you knew." He was more than a little melodramatic as he made this speech, but he kept a very close eye on Mitchell.

He would not acquiesce like this after all that fasting.

Time?

"Mitchell understands my needs. He under-stands my motivation."

"Where did all this money come from? There's a lot more money here than you or I ever made."

"First, I drew the money out of our account today. That was $5,556." He looked at a note by his right wrist. "Then I've managed to squirrel a little cash away from cash sales; $24,280." He again looked at the note by his right wrist. "That means your half is $15,000." He pushed one of the stacks of money in Elizabeth's direction.

Her hands shook, but she did not reach out and touch the money or try to pull it toward her.

"You son-of-a-bitch. We've actually done without stuff we needed so you could squirrel money away—over twenty thousand. God damn you Jacob, I want it all, or I'm going. . . ." Her fury seemed to consume her voice.

"Elizabeth, Mitch and I are planning on bringing hope to the good people of Anchorage, Alaska. We'll need at least six thousand to get up there and get established."

"Yes. We'll need something. I am completely enthusiastic for the project," he reached over and touched Jacob's hand, "but I don't have much money to help," said Mitch.

Elizabeth raked the money into one stack, then counted out $3,000. "You'll have to bring hope to the good people of Anchorage on three thousand."

"OK, Elizabeth, have it your way." Jacob stood and Mitch followed his lead. "We're both planning to gain weight, then go on a tea diet. We think we may try to lose 300 pounds between us. Just think how it will look in the local paper, 'Roommates lose 300 pounds.' That will bring hope to every fat man, woman, and child in Anchorage and the rest of the state, too. I can just see it now." He was beaming, his face was that of a happy, fat angel.

"I'm staying with Mitch until we can get organized for our move to Alaska; I don't want to keep on disappointing the good folks of Clarion.

I'll come by tomorrow to discuss dividing up the rest of the stuff."

"The stuff is mine and that is that. You and your friend Mitch better be getting out of town quick or I'm going to *The Clarion* to expose you." She seemed detached, as if she was an attorney representing someone to whom all this was happening.

"OK. You know that isn't right, Elizabeth, but I don't want trouble. I've moved my personal stuff to Mitchell's place already, and I'm taking the tea and the boxes. I'll get the tea and the boxes tomorrow."

When he came out of the den carrying his briefcase and a handful of envelopes, Elizabeth was standing in the front room, her arms crossed her chest. The door was still open where Mitch had left it when he left.

Jacob came close to Elizabeth as if he had something else to say, but he drew his right arm back, the arm not holding the brief case, and left, closing the door.

As Jacob came down the stairs on the dark porch, he stumbled. He flung his arms out and upward to balance himself and in a quick movement he dropped the briefcase which sprung open when it hit the concrete walk. Had either Elizabeth or Mitchell seen how much money he rapidly stuffed back into the briefcase, they would have changed considerably their opinions of the deals they had made with Jacob Bosoce.

Critique

Jim,

A very interesting story here, Jim. The title works well—you seemed to have found the fattest letters in the alphabet. What I'll do here is go through this page by page before addressing some bigger concerns.

I think you might want to try a new beginning showing him gaining weight—you know, have him eating lots and lots. He cannot have a dramatic weight loss if he's not huge, and the contrast of gorging himself would enhance the fasting.

You have too many images in that second paragraph, and they end up competing for the reader's attention. Just as I begin to get used to the helium image I am asked to see the image of gum being pulled out of a clown's mouth and then the head floating. Too much. Stay with one concrete image there.

I love the dream of the dancing girls and the hero sandwich, by the way. I actually started laughing. But do you want that of your reader? It might turn out to be a distraction. Jacob is really suffering here and you want your reader to suffer with him; the humor might not be what you want. Still, it is funny.

From page eight to page nine when Jacob goes to the newspaper office, you need to clarify the passing of time. The first eight pages of the story move very slowly, and then, all of a sudden it seems he has lost all this weight. You need to indicate time passing with both verbal indicators and a space break to indicate that temporal shift. You might write, "Five weeks later, Jacob went to the offices of *The Clarion Herald*. . . . Something like that.

In class, we've talked about the need for the specific detail, and you do well in that area in this draft, but there are times when we get bogged down with too many details here as on page nine when you write: *He had weighed once a week during his crash, and the weights were printed on the photographs for the week in a medium pointed, purple marking pen.* What happens here is that because you describe the pen so carefully, the reader's attention is drawn to the pen and not the photos. I suppose the type of pen one uses can reflect some aspect of one's personality, but it might take a psychoanalyst to determine what apsect. The word *pen* would suffice in this case, I think.

This brings us to the concern of pacing. By page eleven, we are somewhat bogged down in how slow the story is moving. I suppose this is intentional in that you are using the pace of the story to reflect how slow and lethargic Jacob is in his obesity, but it can be tedious for the reader to move so slowly. Increasing the tension—raising the stakes—will keep us turning the pages, and one way you can do that is to give Jacob some very real health risks such as diabetes. Sumo wrestlers in Japan often become diabetics because the fat surrounds the cells, preventing the insulin from transporting sugars into the cells.

Thus, Jacob might become temporarily diabetic until he loses his weight. There are other health risks as well. But the key here is Jacob's greed. Thus, if he is willing to risk his own health in his pursuit of money, then that adds more weight (sorry) to this pursuit and it increases the tension. One of the first questions we ask of our characters is what do they want. You have established that here. But the next question is, how badly do they want it, and we answer that when we see Jacob risk his health.

Another example of too much detail affecting the pace of the story occurs on page twelve when you write *Jacob wrote down their addresses and told them he would deliver the tea.* I don't think we need the sentence at all in that we already know the men are going to try the tea and the reader can infer that it will be, somehow, delivered.

On page thirteen, you write that their son died *seven years ago*. I think it is almost always a mistake to use *ago* because the word reminds the reader of both story time and real time and we want the reader to stay in story time.

In other words, the reader may think of seven years ago from the time in his life when he is reading the story. Instead, use the word *before*. It will keep us in the story and out of our own lives. This is a small point, Jim.

On this same page, you indicate he had a job as an accountant, and that would be a pretty good job to give up to go out and pursue this diet business, one where he is not making much money, it seems. Thus, I think you need to clarify and make credible why he would have given up his former job to get into something like this.

On page fourteen, you have a large section of naked dialogue. I would go back and embody it. Let us see what they are doing and where they are doing it as they talk.

On page fifteen, use a space break before *A week passed* to indicate a temporal shift.

On page nineteen, Jacob acquiesces to his wife's demands that he quit selling the tea, and frankly I do not believe he would give in so easily, not after all that agonizing and tough, tough work of fasting and losing all that weight. This is, of course, the chief conflict in the story and it is a big one. Maybe he will tell her he will quit selling the tea, and maybe he even thinks he will, but when she leaves, the phone rings and he gets an order and thinks, just one more, and then the phone rings again, and he thinks, just one more—this would parallel a person trying to diet with a bag of cookies before him.

The ending: I don't think we have it yet. First, Mitchell has become Jacob's partner in business, but it also seems that he has become his partner sexually as well (page twenty, that gesture of Mitchell touching Jacob's hand makes me think that).

Now, it is possible that you did not intend this, or that you did.

Either way, it is a distraction from the story for there really were no sexual undercurrents earlier. I am not even sure we need Mitchell. If we are going to have the ending of Elizabeth confronting Jacob and Jacob preparing to leave, then what does Mitchell's presence add to this? Not much, I think (unless you are thinking of adding him in as a partner in more ways than one, and this, as I stated, would be an unearned distraction—unearned because there was no evidence earlier in the story that would make this plausible).

My last area of concern is one of setting. I never really get a feeling for what physical world I am supposed to be in, and putting these characters in the physical world would help your story tremendously. Let me see their house, their neighborhood, the town of Clarion. And you might clarify the time of year as well. Make it a hot, humid summer that Jacob has to walk through. That would add even more weight (again, sorry) to his suffering his way to riches.

O.K., enough. Quite an interesting idea at work here. I look forward to a revision.

Revision

Jacob Boscoe

by Jim Manuel

Jacob Boscoe began breakfast with two stacks of strawberry pancakes with double whipped cream topping, two sides of ham, two sides of sausage, and three sides of pepper bacon. He broke the meat in pieces and ate it with bites of pancake, a system he employed because he liked the spicy taste of the meat penetrating the taste of the syrup-sweetened strawberry pancakes. He also liked the crunch of the meat, which he ordered "crisp," among the smooth textured bites. Even though Boscoe was a voracious eater, he paused many of the bites beneath his nose to enjoy, with little quick sniffs, what he called the "bouquet."

He no more than swallowed the last bite than he called out to the Burger Town server working the counter. "Cheryl. Is it too early for some fries?"

Without responding to Boscoe she turned and asked the cook, "Can we do fries now, or are we still tied up with breakfast hash browns?" The cook said something Boscoe couldn't understand.

"O.K.," Cheryl said, turning to Boscoe with a bright smile. "We can do fries." She talked as if she knew him.

"Give me four large orders, and, Cheryl, will you please give me lots of nice long ones? It's O.K.," he turned the palm of his right hand toward her, "to charge me extra." He pushed his curled brown hair off his per-spiring forehead and mopped his face with a wad of paper napkins. "Oh, yes. If it isn't too much trouble, cook them a few seconds longer." He requested his fries extra brown as if it were a spontaneous inspiration, even though he had made the same request almost every day that month. This morning Boscoe wanted four orders rather than the usual three because he was eating what he called "his last meal." He was starting a diet and had a doctor's appointment at eleven.

Dr. Rawlings and his nurse accompanied Jacob from the lab, where Jacob gave blood and urine samples, down a short hall to the scale. Jacob had experienced the doctor's anger and the crushing humiliation of breaking the scale at another clinic, and he reminded himself that he had checked to make sure this clinic had a five hundred pound scale. Jacob knew that weighing him required one person, that either the doctor or the nurse was a spectator. He weighed four hundred forty-two pounds, and was relieved when no fat jokes materialized. Jacob stretched his neck across the nurse's shoulder and looked to see that she had written down his weight. Large black numbers followed by an exclamation point recorded the number: 442!

Satisfied, Jacob considered this event an official weigh-in, he assumed a humble posture and listened to the doctor's advice. He slumped his shoulders downward and extended his huge stomach by pulling his wide shoulders back and pushing his hips forward. The doctor kept it short. "Eat less and I'll prescribe some pills that will help you curb your appetite. We'll give you a call when we get the lab work back. There are often serious complications accompanying obesity like blood sugar imbalance." The nurse opened the door, and Rawlings put his hand on Jacob's back and steered him out.

Jacob stood watching a chick-a-dee in the azalea bush outside the kitchen window. The bird had carried a black sunflower seed from the feeder and pinned it against a moss-covered limb by wrapping his toes around it. He was opening the seed using his beak as a hammer. Jacob became aware that his eyes had stayed open much too wide, much too long, and he felt his brain had liquefied and was flowing out his eyes. A furious, shimmering, desert-like dry heat took over the vacated space in his head.

He shut his eyes and bent over, making puffing noises that rasped in his throat. He clapped his right hand over his eyes hard enough to cause a sharp pain in the bridge of his nose. He continued to make rapid puffing sounds as he opened the refrigerator door. There was nothing but diet pop. A week ago Elizabeth had removed even the deodorizing baking soda when she followed Jacob's request and cleaned all food out of the house.

He straightened himself a moment, then lost his balance. He spread his feet as far as he could, which was not far enough to separate his thighs, and leaned against the refrigerator trying to force a fingernail past the fat end of his finger and under the diet pop pull tab. His head felt as if some prankster had pumped it full of helium, and it was floating upward. His neck seemed to elongate and he experienced a great distance between his body and his head.

He managed to hold himself with one hand and his stomach against the refrigerator and tilt his head far enough back to swallow a few drops of the pop. Nausea rose through his stomach, and the room rotated, tilting the floor at sudden, odd angles. At the kitchen sink he vomited a small amount of a burning, yellowish fluid; his whole body retched, and his stomach flowed upward in waves. He wobbled out the back door of the house where he had lived for the last month. He intended to eat the seed in the bird feeder, but his strength failed, and he was forced to sit on the red brick planter that bordered the back sidewalk.

He sat with his stomach hanging between his knees. His eyes watered. He used the tail of his green tank top to mop the sweat off his hot face. His intestines writhed inside him like snakes. Hunger had become a horrifying nightmare, dominating his life. He hoped he would not again lose complete control.

Jacob realized his wife Elizabeth was approaching when he smelled cheeseburger on her breath and clothing. The cheeseburger smell was followed in rapid succession by the smells of French fries, strawberry milkshake, and a Butterfinger candy bar. The candy bar took him a moment. Elizabeth must have stopped at 7-Eleven coming home from Burger Town and bought the candy bar. Jacob was so miserable he wept, yet he took a small pleasure in the absolute clarity with which his sense of smell identified the foods Elizabeth had eaten.

Taking Jacob's arm she led him through the house and helped him sit on his bed. When she knelt and removed the shoes and socks she had put on for him that morning, Jacob smelled the French fries again and remembered Cheryl bringing the large orders of fries at Burger Town last week.

"Come on, Jacob, let's get your clothes off." His wife's voice ended a vision of long, floating French fries and refocused his attention. He opened his Bermuda shorts and undid his suspenders, all the while sobbing and puffing so that thin whistles rose from different places in his throat.

Undressed, he lay sobbing as a powerful fatigue closed his mind. Self-pity engulfed him. "Come on, Jacob. Relax, try to sleep"—there was compassion in her voice. She brought a wash cloth and bathed his face.

Elizabeth's reassurances, the cool wash cloth on his face, the faint smell of French fries, mixed with dream fragments as he lingered just outside the gates of sleep. In one fragment five girls danced though his head to a show tune carrying a long hero sandwich across their shoulders. When the girls did a three-step-forward, one hop-backward routine, shaking their asses and exposing their red bikini underwear, sadness overcame him. He knew he was dreaming when he realized he couldn't smell the sandwich.

The next morning he was wandering the house in his robe before he remembered the dancing girls' very cute behinds and their long hero sandwich. When Jacob entered the kitchen where Elizabeth was reading the *Clarion Times*, she got up and left after giving his hand a squeeze. She returned soon bringing fresh clothes and his sneakers. She dressed him with a grace and integrity that Jacob noticed even though he had for some time taken Elizabeth's kindness for granted.

"Thank you, Elizabeth, dear."

She took pictures of him holding the paper with both a video and a Polaroid camera. Jacob then posed against a profile of himself drawn on a white wall the day he visited the doctor. When Elizabeth was satisfied with the alignment, she photographed him again with both cameras.

"You can see the progress," he said. Even though the fast left him miserable, he enjoyed successful progress reports. Each week, weigh-in-day was his best day.

"Yes. I can see the progress," Elizabeth said.

"I'd say I've lost twenty pounds since we started—not a bad weigh-in the first week." He lifted his stomach as much as he could, he could not reach the underside to lift from the bottom, and let it drop. "Yes. I think I may have lost a little more than twenty pounds." Jacob then mounted the balance beam scale and adjusted the weights; Elizabeth photographed him again. On the Polaroid photograph's white back, she wrote the weight—423 pounds.

As the fast wore on, Jacob drifted from soporific fogs to sleep and back. He hallucinated, often about food, but sometimes about sexual encounters involving beautiful women. When he was not in one of these states, time dragged and wild hunger dogs, huge and lean, ravaged him.

Late one afternoon the dogs were on him with all their fury. A taste of water didn't help, sucking a toothpick didn't help. Out of sheer desperation he decided to go for a walk. When he stepped outside, the blazing afternoon sun blasted his already-excited nervous system and he experienced terrible chills and shivers. Flash floods of anger followed, and he became so dizzy he had to bend over and put his hands on his knees.

He managed two blocks before the heat and terrible pain in his feet collapsed him on the concrete street curb. Soon he attracted the neighborhood children. In the hour-and-a-half he sat there sweating and wheezing, he was called "fatty," "fat man," "fat-so," "fat boy," "fats," "lard," "lard ass," "lardo," and "tub-of-guts,"—this last by an attractive little blonde girl of eleven or twelve years who poked him several times with a long stick. When Elizabeth found him and helped him stand, he experienced a combination of horrible pain and numbness in his feet and his ass. He was nodding toward unconsciousness when Elizabeth got him into her air-conditioned car.

Jacob reached his goal of losing 140 pounds eleven weeks after he began the fast. He lost three pounds the last day and so, when he called the local paper to report a human interest story, he reported that he knew of a man who had lost 142 pounds.

After the final weigh-in he began eating again; it took a week's adjustment so he could eat and be sure he wouldn't vomit or become nauseous. The dizziness and hot flashes that had plagued him during the fast diminished as did the food hallucinations. He stayed awake more now, doubling the two hours a day he had worked packaging his herbal tea during the fast. Although he now ate, he was very careful not to gain weight. He drank the herbal tea he promoted and proclaimed it a great benefit.

Jacob arrived at the offices of the *Clarion Times*, the local weekly paper, ten minutes before his eleven o'clock appointment with Mitchell Brewster, a reporter who covered the local beat. He stood leaning his stomach against the counter as he waited.

Brewster came to the front desk where Jacob introduced himself. Stepping back from the counter and presenting himself in profile he asked, "Would you believe I've lost 142 pounds?" He paused, allowing Brewster to look him over. "Well, it's true, and I can prove it." He produced the colored weigh-in photographs and handed them to Brewster. Jacob's weight and the weigh-in dates were printed on the backs in purple marking pen.

Brewster, who had a wide protruding stomach and an ample ass, took an immediate interest. Jacob guessed the interest was as much personal as professional.

"How on earth did you manage to lose 142 pounds?" Brewster shuffled through the photographs, watching their chronology, turning them at angles to the light. "I want a colleague to see these," he said, and hurried off. Experience told Jacob that this was a good start. Brewster didn't have the photographs when he returned and invited Jacob to a rear office area. There he introduced Jacob to Delbert Jones, a man who had a stomach as large as Brewster's and a matching caboose.

"Mr. Boscoe has lost 142 pounds," said Brewster. Jones, who was sitting at an old wooden teacher's desk, stared up at Jacob, then continued examining the pictures. His jaw dropped, leaving his lower teeth and tongue exposed. A perspiration line was visible below his chin cleft, and when Jacob looked close enough to count his four gold capped molars, he also saw tiny, flat perspiration puddles on the man's cheeks and neck.

"Do you have proof other than these photographs?" asked Jones.

"Besides the weigh-in session photographs, we did a videotape. I also lost the weight under a doctor's supervision. You must know Dr. Rawlings"—Jacob was feeling expansive—"he practices here at the clinic." Jacob stopped talking and drew up a chair without being invited. He had experienced a light headedness and wobbliness that didn't leave him much choice. When he saw his shaking legs didn't show through his maroon sweats, he relaxed.

Brewster and Jones apologized for not offering a seat.

"Did Dr. Rawlings prescribe something?" Jones inquired.

"Oh, no. He offered, but all I needed was someone monitoring my health, you know, my heart, my blood pressure, as I went along." Jacob was troubled saying this because he had not gone back to the clinic. Nor had he returned the call after the clinic's nurse left a message asking him to drop by and go over his lab work. He feared Rawlings might not back the claim that he supervised the weight loss, if Jones should call. Jacob became aware of another fear connected to this situation; it was the fear Elizabeth had heard the neglected message, that her fears about his health would grow.

"You didn't lose that much weight alone, did you?" Jones asked.

"I'm happy to say I had help." Jacob exuded good will as he found the opening he sought. "I've discovered a wonderful product, I call it Boscoe's Herbal Tea, that makes losing weight easy. It's one hundred per-cent natural." He stood and whirled his wide six foot frame around on one foot, raising his other foot knee-high behind. "I'm living, healthy proof that the tea works, and that it works better than any other product on earth." Again unsteadiness forced him to sit. He closed his mouth tight and breathed through his nose so Brewster and Jones would not hear him wheeze.

Jacob laid it on thick, but the truth was that the fast he had under-taken was so consuming he had trouble keeping down water. He found chewing a toothpick gave some relief from the hunger that stalked him, but he had to be very careful not to swallow the saliva it stimulated. Even his own saliva caused him to vomit. When he had once tried his tea dur-ing a fast, a vast shimmering had risen from his stomach through his entire body; brief, rapid, nervous spasms, and violent uncontrolled fits of vomiting forced him to make a trip to the emergency room.

His belief in the tea originated after the company where he worked downsized and Jacob lost his job. He gained 120 pounds following the layoffs. A friend told him about the herbal tea, and when Jacob lost the weight he had gained, he credited the tea. A reporter writing about downsizing and its community-wide impact interviewed Jacob. The original article became a series; one article covered Jacob's situation and the weight he gained and lost. The interest the story aroused amazed Jacob. Calls requesting information besieged him the next week. He enjoyed the attention, and he became a local folk hero, albeit a small one. He also perceived what he took to be an excellent business opportunity and began selling the tea; when the original weight loss interest petered out, he spawned the promotional scheme that still drove his life.

"If you boys know someone who my product might benefit, I'd be glad to provide complimentary supplies," Jacob offered. Jones thought his wife might like to try it. Brewster said he needed to lose "a few pounds himself," and would be glad to give Boscoe's product a try.

Jacob wrote their addresses, the notation "free samples," and said he would deliver the tea. "I'm thinking of buying product advertising in the *Clarion Times*. If you print something about my weight loss, it would be wonderful if my first ad could appear when the story runs." Jones escorted Jacob to another office, where he bought eight weeks of advertising.

Jacob and Elizabeth celebrated launching another promotion. They still weren't keeping food, so they brought home Chinese and half a case of tall Budweisers. They sat at the kitchen table eating and drinking the beer they iced in a champagne bucket. Neither was a drinker, and the beer buzzed their heads; they enjoyed it amid laughter. Elizabeth asked Jacob how the *Times* interview went.

"Fine. Fine. It was great. I'm delivering the two reporters who interviewed me samples. They were impressed. This is going to be our greatest effort yet," Jacob replied.

"I'm glad, Jacob. You believe in the product, and I know how good you feel when people tell you they've lost weight." She gave him an unenthusiastic smile.

"Yes, I do. I really do. This morning there was a letter from a grandmother I met just when we were leaving Canyon City who has lost twenty-five pounds and kept if off for three months. She sent a check for thirty dollars for another month's supply." Boscoe was beaming as he sat straddling a kitchen chair, his hairy arms stacked on the back, his chin resting atop his arms.

Elizabeth opened a second beer. "What was the take today, Jacob?" Her serious tone did not reflect Jacob's optimism.

"It was pretty bad for a Tuesday," Jacob responded, trying to remember if he hadn't told her what they had taken that morning. "Besides the check I mentioned, there was an inquiry from a woman who heard about us from a friend."

"Thirty dollars, then," Elizabeth said, studying Jacob's hands as he finished his beer.

"Yes. Thirty dollars. The Canyon City results are running down. There just doesn't seem to be a better way to get folks' attention than losing 140 pounds. The excitement from the newspaper articles, the before-and-after photographs, and the ads. . . ."

"Yes, Jacob, I know." She interrupted him raising her voice and stamping her foot. "How much longer do you plan to be the star fat man in a circus side show just to earn a living?" Her tone hardened; he had not heard her use this tone since she dealt with the bill collectors who called in the months after he lost his job.

"You starve yourself months on end. I'm sick of it, and for that matter, I'm sick of your gluttony, too. You were a decent accountant; there is no need to travel around making yourself a public spectacle when you could get another good job. Besides, you've never made as much promoting the tea as you did as an accountant, and we didn't have to move all the time."

Jacob was shocked. He had fasted two plus months to lose the 142 pounds that he had reported losing at the *Clarion Times*. Jacob felt disoriented; he wondered if the beer was too much for Elizabeth. Even though Rawlings had assured him all medical information was confidential, the thought crossed his mind that the clinic had called again. Elizabeth had expressed concern about his health before, and he understood that any suggestion of a medical problem would cost him her support with the promotions.

"You don't mean you want to quit right now? I've just been on a strict diet two months. You know we are getting ready to make a lot of money." He was tentative, and he couldn't tell whether Elizabeth had detected it or not.

"When you gained the weight after the layoffs, and then you lost the weight using the tea, that was OK. Giving up your career to promote the tea was a big mistake. I saw it wouldn't work and told you so, and, after the first four weeks, it didn't. It's been the same ever since. As soon as people got used to the fact that you lost the weight, they quit buying the tea."

"But Elizabeth, I found a way to spark their interest, to keep them buying. Don't forget, I've given a lot of people hope. Fat people have a right to hope, too, Elizabeth, and I lead them to hope." He paused to catch his breath.

"Listen, Elizabeth," Jacob was half-way through his sixth beer. "I've got this incredible idea for the promotion to end all promotions. When we finish here and move on, when I start to eat to gain weight again, you could join me. Maybe you could gain, say, sixty pounds, then we could advertise husband and wife lose. . . ."

"Have you lost your mind?" Her brown eyes glistened, her fists clenched. Her fair round face flamed red. "Haven't you heard a damn word I've said? You know very well I don't let myself gain even a pound. I've been following you around now four years, waiting for you to come to your senses. Anyone I know, even the Jacob Boscoe who was a decent accountant, would call you a snake oil salesman if he knew you didn't use the tea on your diets. How the hell can you suggest I gain weight like you?"

"Even though I don't use it on my diets, I believe in my tea." He cut her off, trying to escape the consequences of his blunder. "My dieting is just a way of giving people hope, of leading them to where they can use the tea. I am the artist who leads the way." He seemed very pleased with this last remark.

"If the tea worked, we would get re-orders, Jacob: lots and lots of re-orders." She lost some of her fire, and she said this as if she regretted something, as if she had discovered losing something precious, and her tone softened. "The truth is we are a pair of vagabonds, going from town to town, scamming people, conning people by one of the most desperate stratagems in history."

"I do what I do to bring fat people hope." He hurried, guessing Elizabeth was feeling guilt for helping him. "When I gained the weight after the layoff, I felt awful. When I lost the weight, I felt good again, and as soon as I started selling the tea I saw that I was bringing people hope and the same good feeling I had experienced."

The Clarion Times printed an article about Jacob losing 142 pounds along with the first of eight half-column ads for "Boscoe's Herbal Tea." The article and the ad included before-and-after photographs. Orders arrived. Jacob had a second phone line installed, and customers often occupied both lines with anxious inquires regarding Boscoe's Herbal Tea. Jacob talked to dozens of desperate people and handed out hundreds of before-and-after photographs. Money flowed, and Jacob pushed the conversation with Elizabeth and the neglected test results out of his mind.

They sold ten thousand dollars worth of tea during the three weeks after the article and the ads came out. Jacob felt wonderful about his life as he delivered his customers their tea. He encouraged everyone he met. When Cheryl, the server from Burger Town, recognized him from his ads and called, he even took her a sample. Arriving at Burger Town with Cheryl's tea, he ran into Mitchell Brewster, who was also having wonderful success. Cheryl took a break and the three discussed the tea. When the little group broke up and he left, Jacob felt great about himself and his product.

Jacob continued drinking the herbal tea, and he lost a few more pounds. But the new weight loss, the money, Jacob's glowing account of his talks with discouraged people, did nothing to rebuild Elizabeth's confidence. She still helped processing money and checking deliveries, but anyone except Jacob would have known that she was a woman who had seen something from which she could not look away.

The ad for the last week's promotion came out Thursday, and there was a good response Friday, but by Sunday and Monday sales dwindled to sixty dollars a day. They were home because Jacob, who suffered when business declined, didn't want to miss calls. Elizabeth came into the den where he waited by the phone.

"I'm going over to Shari's. They have the cheesecake special this week; it'll be awhile because I'm going to read the paper."

"What am I going to do if we get a flurry of orders?" He sounded hurt.

"It has been three weeks since we had a flurry of orders. This promotion is dead. I know it, and you should." Her voice was acid edged and contrasted with her warm good looks and the short, yellow-and-brown cotton summer dress she was wearing.

"I don't think this promotion is over." He stood and profiled himself to remind her how much weight he had lost. "There are still a lot of good people here who need help. God. If there was just another way to get out the word."

"Cut the crap, Jacob. You know as well as I do that the tea is just a laxative and a diuretic. You feel good when people tell you how the tea helps them, but the truth is, both you and the tea are a fraud."

"How can you say such a thing? You know very well," he was shaking his right index finger at her, "I lost the weight the first time using the tea." He sat down on the couch.

"I don't know how you lost the weight the first time and neither do you." Storms of rising and falling anger consumed Elizabeth, and Jacob sat with his jaw slack, his mouth and pale blue eyes open. "I do know this is the fifth diet you have completed, and you didn't use the tea once. You go prancing up to doors like the Pied Piper of fat people, selling a box of tea for thirty dollars that cost you eighty-seven cents including advertising and the cost of the package."

Jacob saw he had taken the wrong tack, but she started again before he could control the conversation.

"It is a serious lie to tell people that the tea works for you. But to sell hope because you can make money doing it and because it makes you feel like some working class hero, is an out-and-out fraud."

Jacob stood up and raised his hands as if to surrender.

"Not to mention," Elizabeth continued, jabbing at the couch with her finger, "I'm worn out following you from town to town, from one rented house to another. And I am fed up with having a husband who is two hundred pounds overweight. Even our sex life depends on how fat you are. It may come as a shock to you, but I don't enjoy having my sex life determined by how far your guts hang down. You get so damn fat you can't get ahold of yourself to masturbate. Hell, you go on as if you aren't ruining your health and our marriage."

This was the first double-barreled blast Elizabeth had ever leveled at Jacob. He had on occasion wondered what Elizabeth thought about his huge stomach covering his genitals, but he had never imagined she was capable of a blast like this. He also guessed he was right about her intercepting one of the messages from the clinic.

"Elizabeth, you know I just want to help people. You should hear. . . ."

"No, no, Jacob. I've already heard much, much too much. You act like the patron saint of fat people, but hell, you're still at least eighty pounds overweight right now. And why haven't you gone back to the clinic like they asked? You're afraid, aren't you? You're nothing more than a one-man medicine and snake oil show, and, I regret to say, in the name of making this marriage work, I've been your assistant." She seemed unsatisfied explaining her behavior this way.

"Elizabeth, sweetie." He came to her and put his arms around her, guessing as he had before that she was feeling guilt. "You're just upset because the sales have dropped off a little. We'll be rolling in the money again tomorrow."

She ducked and pushed away. "If we get any orders tomorrow you are going to be one sad character." Her voice dripped, her brown eyes flamed.

He started to inquire why, but Elizabeth cut him off.

"Because you are not selling any more tea, period." She slashed a "v" in the air with her hands. "You can tell people whatever you want, but if you sell another box of that damn stuff. . . ."

"Shut the fuck up, Elizabeth. How are we going to live?" He stood up. It was hard to tell if he was afraid or angry.

"Listen, fat boy!"

Jacob crossed his hands over his stomach and stumbled back onto the green couch, like a man shot in the stomach with a small-caliber pistol at close range. His face turned gray-green. His whole body shook.

"If you ever talk to me like that again, this side show marriage is ended. If you sell one box of the tea or I hear of you giving anyone false hopes, I'm going straight to the paper. I'm going to tell them that I'm certain that when you are dieting you puke if you swallow too much saliva, that the one time you tried the tea on a diet it brought on uncontrolled vomiting. I drove you to the emergency room myself."

"Elizabeth, we've made $18,000 on this promotion alone. Think about it. And you know we don't have to pay taxes on the cash." He made this last remark in a whisper, as if something important was left unsaid that Elizabeth ought to understand.

"I'm going to town. You think about it. Unplug the phone, whatever it takes, but don't sell any more tea." She stubbed off this last sentence as if ending something larger than a conversation.

She picked up her engraved brown leather purse, slung the strap over her shoulder, and marched out. Jacob sat on the couch pitying himself.

Jacob followed Elizabeth's instructions. He told callers he was out of the tea, an exotic product of Guatemala, Honduras, or Afghanistan, depending on the day and his mood. He made a little scene giving Elizabeth the few mail orders and checks that arrived and asking her to return them. He did not respond to her repeated suggestion that he return to the clinic for his test results.

He was sitting on the couch in the den when Elizabeth reminded him she had a late appointment to get her already short blonde hair cut. He had lost his energy and good cheer, but he walked her to her car and waved as she drove away. Evening was easing into the streets.

When Elizabeth entered the kitchen, Jacob stood. "Elizabeth, I'd like to introduce you to Mitchell Brewster, the reporter from the *Times* who was so taken by my story."

Elizabeth didn't acknowledge either man. Two large stacks of cash dominated the table. Jacob couldn't tell if she intended rudeness or if she was shocked to see so much money. "What's going on here?" She banged her heel on the floor.

"Relax, Elizabeth. Just sit down and relax," Jacob said. Mitchell pushed a chair back by reaching his foot under the table.

"What's going on here?" Elizabeth asked again. She sat down and looked hard at Jacob.

"You haven't changed your mind have you, Elizabeth? It's. . . ."

"What the hell is going on here?" She was almost shouting. She took her purse from her lap and hung it over the back of the chair.

"I've told Mitchell about the tea, about the money we've made." He nodded toward Mitchell. "Since you've lost interest, I've invited Mitch to become my partner. He's greatly interested. He's lost twenty pounds using the tea, and he sees the same great future for it that I see."

Elizabeth sat blinking her reddening eyes; her hands were white with red streaks from the pressure she exerted making fists and pressing her knuckles against the table. "You mean you are leaving me, after the stinking shit I've put up with to keep this marriage together for the last four years?" She jerked her head back and brushed her nose with the back of her hand.

"You haven't left me much choice, Elizabeth. You know how important keeping hope alive in all those people is to me. At least I thought you knew." He appeared to believe himself.

"Mitchell understands my needs. He understands my motivation."

"Where did all this money come from? There's a lot more money here than we ever made."

"First, I drew the money out of our account today. That was $5,556"—he looked at a note by his right wrist. "Then I've managed to squirrel away a little from cash sales: $24,280. That means your half is $15,000." He pushed one of the two stacks of money in Elizabeth's direction.

Her hands opened and closed, but she did not reach for the money.

"You cock-sucker. We've done without things we needed so you could rathole money—over twenty thousand. You bastard; I've put on your shoes and socks for you, I've helped you change your shorts when they were soaked with sweat and full of shit, when you stunk so bad. . . ." Fury seemed to choke her voice.

"Elizabeth, Mitch and I are planning to take the tea and its message of hope to the good people of Anchorage, Alaska. I'll need my half traveling and getting established."

"Yes," said Mitch. "We'll need something. I am optimistic, but I can't help much." He was leaned back in his chair, tapping one foot under the table and twisting his hands together on his chest.

Elizabeth reached her arms around both stacks of money, interlocked her fingers, and jerked the money into one pile. She counted out $3,000. "You boys can bring hope to all those good people on a mere three thousand. Did you tell your new partner you don't drink the tea on your diets?" She studied Mitch's face.

Mitch, who had shaken when Elizabeth raked in the money, appeared to have a response to her query, but Jacob cut him off.

"Have it your way, Elizabeth. Mitch understands the entire project and my motivation. We'll make do with the three thousand." He stood up and stuffed the money into his pants pocket; he appeared calm. Mitch stood also and kept trying not to look at all the cash disappearing into Elizabeth's purse.

"We're both planning to gain weight, then go on the tea diet. The two of us want to try losing 300 pounds. Just think how it would look in the local paper: 'Roommates lose 300 pounds.' That will bring hope to every fat man, woman, and child in Anchorage, and the whole state, too. I can see it now." Jacob's face was turned upward, beaming, radiating good will. For a moment he appeared oblivious of Mitch or Elizabeth.

"I'm staying with Mitch until we can organize our move; disappointing the good folks here is breaking my heart. We can discuss dividing the rest of the stuff tomorrow." He was matter-of-fact, an odd contrast with the radiant good will he had just projected.

"What you call 'the rest of the stuff' is my stuff. You and your friend Mitch better follow your plan to leave town. I'm sure Delbert Jones would listen to what I know about you and your new partner and your famous tea."

"That isn't right, Elizabeth, and you know it, but I don't want trouble. Most of my personal stuff is at Mitchell's place already, and I'm taking my car, the tea, and the boxes. I'll pickup the tea boxes tomorrow."

When he came out of the den carrying his briefcase, Elizabeth was standing in the front room, her arms folded on her waist as if she might be cold or frightened. The door stood half open, the way Mitch left it.

"I'm sorry it ended this way, Elizabeth. If only you could see the possibilities." He sounded convinced that Elizabeth had committed some great wrong.

"The only possibility I can see is filing for a divorce tomorrow and trying to find my way back to a normal life," she said.

Jacob either didn't hear her or didn't respond to this parting shot, and he left slump-shouldered with his head hung as if in utter defeat and closed the door. Descending the dark porch stairs, Jacob stumbled. He flung his arms out and upward to balance himself, and in the quick movement he dropped his briefcase which hit the concrete walk and sprang open. Bundles of wrapped hundred dollar bills scattered along the walk. Jacob looked around ensuring that he was unobserved. With an alacrity that might have surprised either Elizabeth or Mitchell, he returned the bills to his briefcase. He took a key from his pocket and locked both briefcase locks. He thought he would buy a new briefcase, one with reliable locks, before his Alaskan trip. Maybe he would buy it tomorrow, when he returned to Canyon City to get the cash he had left in a safety deposit box there.

Critique

Jim,

The revision is greatly improved. The new beginning with him eating breakfast and then French fries is just wonderful. You do a great job there with the specific inventory of food he consumes—and the amount as well. This beginning pulls us right into the story because we are immediately curious about what kind of man would eat all this food, and eat it in the way he does.

And you have eliminated most of the problems that were in the earlier draft. A few remain, of course, but not many. On page four, there is a problem with that first sentence after the space break for he would surely know she was approaching when he smelled her breath. I'll buy his extrasensory awareness to the degree of smelling the cheeseburger on her clothing from a short distance, but smelling her breath at such a distance is going too far.

On page six, they would greet each other good morning before she leaves the room to fetch his clothing. You could always use indirect dialogue there.

Page seven: you do a good job of making time pass with that first sentence after the space break.

On page nine and later, you have increased the tension by alluding to health concerns. I think, however, we could make these allusions even clearer. I would go ahead and have Elizabeth confront him saying she got the doctor's message about high blood sugars revealed in the tests as well as high blood pressure that should be addressed. He'll ignore the threat and then, at the end of the story, he will be going off to Alaska as a potential time-bomb. That would help your ending which still needs some fine-tuning. (Make some covert reference to his health problem in the ending.)

On page ten where they celebrate the launching of another promotion by eating and drinking, you need to show his reaction to having food and drink for the first time in so long. As it is, there is no reaction at all.

On page eleven, "stamping her foot" seems a strange gesture.

Embody the dialogue on pages twelve and thirteen, and on page twelve, you may want to rethink the amount of time she has been following Jacob. Four years seems too long for her to have been patient with his dieting enterprise.

My other two concerns besides the ending are closely related. You'll notice that I wrote "embody" in the margins during most of the dialogue. You really need to embody that dialogue, and the reason you haven't, I think, is because the setting is never really clear. In other words, there is no *place* for them to do anything as they talk. I think that you may not be *seeing* your own setting at this point and you probably need to create one to envision as you do another draft. You could always use your own living room to describe, or a friend's, but there must be a concrete world for Jacob and Elizabeth to have their disagreements in. Believe me, it will help ground the reader in the story.

Finally, the ending. I'm still not convinced that Mitchell would leave a good job and go off with Jacob. I think it would be better if Jacob were to go off by himself, especially if you have clarified the health dangers he is ignoring. The health problems may be the key to the story and the key to the ending. You would have to go back and highlight them as I have already mentioned in this critique, and then, when he stumbles down those stairs and drops his briefcase, you could give him a physical description that would be reflective of high blood pressure or high blood sugar. You would have to make it clear to the reader that what you are describing in the end is tied with the doctor's warning that Elizabeth confronts him with. Then his unmitigated greed, along with his confused sense of altruism, would come to light in the end.

Good work here, Jim. I'll look forward to seeing another draft.

—*TIM*

Glossary

Alliteration: the repetition of consonant sounds, usually occurring at the beginnings of words, which produces an echo effect and links words through their sounds.

Ambiguity: open to more than one meaning.

Antagonist: character who opposes or rivals the protagonist.

Arc: the curved shape of a story—as opposed to the straight line of an anecdote—with its establishment of initial conflict followed by its rise in complication, its climax and its denouement.

Assonance: the repetition of vowel sounds in the final syllables of words; it produces an effect similar to alliteration.

Backstory: the history of the story prior to page one of the written text.

Cacophony: the blending of sounds to produce a noisy or unpleasant effect on the ear—it has the opposite effect of **euphony**.

Caesura: a pause within a line that usually occurs because of punctuation—maybe a comma. A caesura may also happen because of the way two words fall next to each other rhythmically.

Character: the person or people of the story; greater than or equal to plot in importance.

Clichés: phrases or images which are, and have been, so commonly used that they are not original at all.

Connotation: the cultural and contextual definition of a word.

Denotation: standard, or dictionary, definition.

Dénouement: final resolution of the plot; follows the climax.

Dialogue: verbal exchange between characters; **direct dialogue**—two or more people are speaking in a scene; **indirect dialogue**—speech that is reported, as in *John told him he could come*.

Diction: word choice.

Enjambment: (also known as the "run-on line") the line's grammatical sense and meaning carry over into the next. Hence, the line "runs on."

Euphony: the blending of sounds to produce a pleasurable effect on the ear.

Exposition: "telling" or "explaining," as differentiated from *scene,* which is "live" action.

Extended or **controlling metaphor:** a metaphor which extends itself throughout an entire poem. It may control the entire poem, being the dominant image that drives the poem's meaning.

Falling meter: stressed to unstressed syllables.

First Person Point of View: one of the characters narrates the story using the pronoun *I.*

Flashback: narrator goes back in time to narrate some backstory. Sometimes a space-break is used to indicate this temporal and spatial shift.

Flashforward: narrator goes forward in time to narrate some future story; rarer than a flashback.

Foil: a character who, through contrast, heightens the distinctive characteristics of other characters.

Foot: one measure of stressed and unstressed syllables.

Futurestory: the future of the story after the last page of the written text.

Image: picture created by words.

Implied metaphor: implies rather than states, what main object is being compared to, usually through action or by ascribing attributes.

In medias res: in the middle of things; meant to instruct a writer to begin his story in the middle where the conflict exists.

Irony: the use of events or conditions that produce unexpected outcomes or contradiction. Some event we (or a character) may think to be true but turns out otherwise may be ironic. Irony may be conveyed by an underlying voice or tone.

Line: a line of text in a poem.

Metadiscourse: The narrator announces his presence and enters the story by commenting on the story itself, as in *I am having trouble with the plot, but bear with me.* This can occur with an omniscient narrator.

Metaphor: a comparison that says one thing *is* another.

Meter: the arrangement of measured rhythm in poetry (*measured* is a key word here; think of how music is measured); based on the positions of the stressed and unstressed syllables in words.

Mood: author's emotional and intellectual attitude toward a story as well as character's emotional and intellectual attitude in a story.

Narrative Distance: temporal (and spatial) distance from which a story is told. If a narrator is thirty-six years old and he is telling the story of an event that took place when he was twelve, the narrative distance is twenty-four years.

Onomatopoeia: the sound or rhythm of a word mimicking the object or phenomenon to which it refers.

Pacing: the speed in which events take place. Good pacing requires the writer to know what to leave in in exposition or scene, and what to leave out.

Persona: the speaker of the poem (or story) and the one who takes on the point of view.

Personification: giving a nonhuman object some human characteristic.

Plot: the series of events in a story, no matter how those events are organized.

Point of view: the stance taken by the persona—the attitude and the view of the world he imparts to the reader. Along with stance and attitude comes tone.

Protagonist: literally "the first actor" but generally considered to be the chief character.

Real subject, or generated subject: what the poem comes to say, ultimately the most powerful of the subjects in the poem. This is the subject that may be referred to as the core, the heart, or the kernel of the poem.

Red herring: a false clue in a story wherein the reader has been duped to believe some object or action has an importance that it does not. This is something to avoid.

Resonance: the emotional reverberation that a character in a story has caused the reader to feel, often occurring at the climax and/or the denouement of a story.

Rhyme: an echoing produced by close placement of two or more words with similarly sounding final syllables. Types of rhyme: **masculine rhyme**, in which two words end with the same vowel consonant combination (hand/band); **feminine rhyme**, in which two syllables rhyme (shiver/liver); **end-rhyme**, in which the rhyme comes at the ends of the lines (this is probably the most commonly used rhyme); **internal rhyme**, in which a word within a line rhymes with another word in that line, or rhymes with a word of similar placement in the following line; **slant rhyme**, in which the sounds nearly rhyme but do not form a "true rhyme" (land/lend).

Rising meter: unstressed syllables to stressed syllables.

Scene: "live action," in which the reader views events as they unfold. There is often dialogue in a scene.

Sestina: a poem that comprises six stanzas, each with six lines, and a three-line stanza called an envoy. Hence there are always thirty-nine lines in a sestina. The last words of the first six lines of the poem are repeated as the end words of the following five stanzas, and all the words must be included in the envoy. It is a traditional French form that was used in writing love poetry in the thirteenth century.

Shift in point of view: usually the error of leaving third person limited point of view for third person multiple, but may be the more egregious error of shifting from third person to first or second.

Simile: a comparison using the words *like* or *as.*

Stanza: a group of lines in a poem separated from another group of lines by a space break. In free verse, these groups of lines do not need to be the same in number, but a stanza usually signifies that there is some type of organizational structure to the poem. A writer often organizes lines into stanzas based on some conceptual coherence.

Style: a writer's rhetorical strategy which includes her use of diction.

Syntax: word order.

Theme: the central meaning of the story derived from the characters' actions and reactions in relation to the plot.

Third Person Limited: the point of view of "he" or "she," limited to one character in a story. In other words, if you limit the point of view to the character Susan, you cannot narrate a scene unless Susan is present.

Third Person Multiple: the point of view of "he" or "she," not limited to one character. In other words, you may narrate a scene when Susan is present and then another scene when Susan is absent and other characters occupy the scene.

Third Person Omniscient: the point of view which the narrator is all-knowing and that narrator may narrate any character's thoughts. The narrator may even interject thoughts that are not those of any of the characters; however, such interjection is rarely done and is often viewed as somewhat archaic.

Tone: the emotional sense behind the voice of the persona sometimes communicated through the use of irony, hyperbole, and understatement.

Triggering subject: the subject that causes the poem to come up in the first place, to be written. It's the subject that the reader first attaches to and that often guides them further into the poem.

Voice: the expressive force and tone of the words spoken by the author and the **persona** in the poem; in the story, it is the combination of style and tone.

Contributors' Biographies

Diana Abu-Jaber is Writer-in-Residence at Portland State University and also writes for *The Oregonian* newspaper. Her first novel, *Arabian Jazz,* won the Oregon Book Award.

Diane Averill teaches creative writing at Clackamas Community College. She is the author of two collections of poetry, *Branches Doubled Over With Fruit* (University of Central Florida Press) and *Beautiful Obstacles* (Blue Light Press).

H. Lee Barnes teaches creative writing at the Community College of Southern Nevada. His fiction has appeared in numerous literary journals and *Gunning for Ho,* a collection of short stories, was published in 1999 (University of Nevada Press).

Ron Carlson is a professor of creative writing at Arizona State University. His most recent book is *The Hotel Eden* (Norton), a collection of short stories.

Tracy Daugherty is an associate professor of English at Oregon State University. His most recent book is the novel *The Boy Orator* (SMU Press).

Debra Magpie Earling is an assistant professor of creative writing at the University of Montana. Her fiction has appeared in numerous literary journals and anthologies.

Beckian Fritz Goldberg teaches creative writing at Arizona State University. Her latest collection of poems is *Never Be the Horse* (University of Akron Press, 1999).

James Hoggard teaches literature and creative writing at Midwestern State University in Witchita Falls, Texas. His most recent collection of poems, *Medea in Taos* (Pecan Grove Press).

Lynn Hoggard is professor of French and English at Midwestern State University in Texas. She has translated collections of poetry by Paul Valery and Henri Michaux. She was a featured poet in *A Certain Attitude: Poems by Seven Texas Women* (Pecan Grove Press).

Craig Lesley is the Ford Chair at Willamette University. His most recent novel is *Storm Riders* (Picador).

Valerie Miner teaches in the MFA program at the University of Minnesota. Her most recent book is the novel *Range of Light* (Zoland Press).

Alberto Ríos is Regents' Professor of English at Arizona State University. He is the author of numerous books of poetry and stories. His latest, *Capirotada,* is a collection of personal essays (University of New Mexico Press).

Kevin Stein is professor of literature and creative writing at Bradley University. His latest collection of poems is *Chance Ransom* (University of Illinois Press).

Virgil Suarez teaches creative writing, and Latino/a and Caribbean Literature at Florida State University in Tallahassee. His most recent collections of poems are *You Come Singing* and *In The Republic of Longing*.

Gary Thompson has taught in the Creative Writing Program at California State University, Chico for twenty-five years. His poems have been published in many magazines and anthologies; his most recent collection is *On John Muir's Trail* (Bear Star Press).

Amy Sage Webb is an assistant professor of creative writing at Emporia State University. Her fiction has appeared in numerous literary journals.

INDEX